The Journal of Contemporary Heathen Thought

The Journal of Contemporary Heathen Thought

Edited by

Christopher A. Plaisance
Vincent Rex Soden
Ben McGarr

Volume II

2011–2012

The Journal of Contemporary Heathen Thought
Volume 2, 2011-2012
Editors: Christopher A. Plaisance, Ben McGarr and Vincent Rex Soden

© 2012, Heiðinn Publications. Copyrights for individual articles, poems and images rest with their respective creators. All rights reserved. No part of this book, either in part or in whole, may be reproduced, modified, stored in a retrieval system, transmitted or utilized in any form or by any means, electronic, mechanical, or otherwise, without prior written permission from the publisher and/or authors, except for brief quotations embodied in literary articles and reviews, or those works designated by their author as being in the common domain.

Note: The ideas expressed herein belong to the individual contributors and are not necessarily representative of the contributors as a whole nor the editorial staff.

Contributors: Stephen M. Borthwick, John Michael Greer, Zacrey Monte Hansen, Helsson, Joshua Hughes, Henry Lauer, Ed LeBouthillier, Þorbert Línleáh, Guido von List, Friedrich Bernhard Marby, Stephen Pollington, Christopher A. Plaisance, Jennifer Roberge-Toll, Vincent Rex Soden, Kris Stevenson, Bron Taylor, and Stefn Thorsman.

Cover art by Arrowyn Craban-Lauer.
Cover design by Christopher A. Plaisance.

ISBN: 146794842X
EAN-13: 978-1467948425

The Journal of Contemporary Heathen Thought may be reached at
Email: heathen.editor@gmail.com
Web: http://www.heathenjournal.com

Table of Contents

Editorial Preface	vii
Dedication	xi

Germanic Revivalism

On the German Priesthood of Wuotan *Guido von List*	1
The Origins of Matter *Friedrich Bernhard Marby*	33

Essays and Poems

Huuetstêneslioth: Lay of the Whetstone *Þorbert Línleáh*	57
The Natural Order and the Ensouled Folk *Stephen M. Borthwick*	59
The Emergent Hierarchy: An Evolutionary Recasting of Neoplatonic Polytheism *Christopher A. Plaisance*	73
Hero, Anti-Hero, Villain *Kris Stevenson*	155
Entropy Personified *Zacrey Monte Hansen*	169
The Horned Man *Stephen Pollington*	177
Against the Primitivists *Stephen M. Borthwick*	187

Interviews and Book Reviews

On Heathen Clergy:
An Interview With Stefn Thorsman and Ed LeBouthillier   207

Green Heathenry:
An Interview With Bron Taylor   219

Polytheism in the Modern World:
A Conversation with John Michael Greer   227

The Uses of Wodan
Henry Lauer   247

Staðagaldr
Christopher A. Plaisance   258

Wyrd Words
Christopher A. Plaisance   260

The Folk
Helsson   262

Deep Ancestors
Christopher A. Plaisance   264

Summoning the Gods
Christopher A. Plaisance   266

Editorial Staff   271

Contributors   273

Editorial Preface

We must now conceive of this whole universe as one commonwealth of which both gods and humans are members.
—Cicero[1]

The year's wheel has turned once again, and with its turning comes the second volume of *The Journal of Contemporary Heathen Thought* (hereafter referred to as *JOCHT*). We hope to have returned from our absence with renewed vigor and tenacity. It has, admittedly, been more than a year since volume one first saw print, but we believe the wait has been worth it. This volume of *JOCHT* stays, we think, even truer to the ideals set forth in volume one's preface. In our quest to actualize these principles, the material present in this volume is far more academic and directly related to our mission statement than those of the first volume. And, given the largely positive reviews that our first offering received, we hope that this present work will exceed our readers' expectations. To begin, let us start with a restatement of our mission:

1. To provide a medium through which those involved in the advancement of Heathen thought may promulgate their ideas.
2. To encourage the expansion and development of the burgeoning strains of thought which seek to analyze Heathenry by means of the methodologies of academic philosophy, theology and religious studies.
3. To bring together those thinkers involved in the *writing* of such and those members of the greater Heathen community interested in the *reading* of such so as to better facilitate the development of the academic field of Heathen studies.

Though we have stayed true to our mission, this volume brings some changes in format—changes that, we believe, will aid in the actualization of these goals. The most notable among these is that the first section of the journal is a new addition. Beginning with this volume, it is our intention for each subsequent work to host a special feature section. In the present volume, the special feature is a selection of original renditions of previously untranslated material from two notable personalities of the late 19th and early 20th century Heathen revivalist movements in Austria and Germany: Guido von List and Friedrich Bernhard Marby. Von List's essay, "On the German Priesthood of Wuotan," makes an attempt at reconstructing what the priestly caste of the ancient Germanic peoples would have been like. Marby's piece, "The Origins of Matter," presents the author's at-

---
1 Marcus Tillius Cicero, *De Legibus* I, 7, 22.

tempt to reconcile the theoretical physics of his day with von List's Armanic runosophy. Our hope is that the translation and publication of these two pieces will take steps towards furthering our understanding of the motivations and beliefs of the men who first began reviving Heathenry. While their Theosophically influenced philosophies are unlikely to regain currency in modern Heathenry, a full understanding of our religious movement's origins is an absolutely necessary step in our move towards understanding our faith on an academic level.

The second section, which contains essays and poems, is structurally similar to that of the last volume, but content-wise is strikingly different, with the essays being far more academically oriented. The section opens with the poem "Huuet-stêneslioth," by Þorbert Línleáh, which is presented side-by-side in Old Saxon and Modern English. The first two papers—Stephen Borthwick's "The Natural Order and the Ensouled Folk" and Christopher A. Plaisance's "The Emergent Hierarchy"—present something of a dialogue between hermeneutics of Heathen theology as informed by orthodox Platonism and evolutionary Neoplatonism respectively. Following this exchange is another pair of essays, both of which analyze themes present both in Heathen myth and modern fiction. In the first paper, "Hero, Anti-Hero, Villain," Kris Stevenson returns to *JOCHT* with an interpretative comparison between the Eddic Loki and Milton's Lucifer. The companion essay, Zacrey Monte Hansen's "Entropy Personified," similarly analyzes the dragon Níðhögg's thematic relationship to two modern literary figures: the Man in the Yellow Suit from Natalie Babbitt's *Tuck Everlasting*, and Hastur from Robert W. Chambers' *The King in Yellow*. Stephen Pollington follows this with his essay, "The Horned Man," which explores various representations of horned male figures in early North European art. The section concludes with another piece from Borthwick, "Against the Primitivists," which argues against a primitivist movement that the author sees taking root in Heathenry today.

While the third section's book reviews are largely unchanged, this volume's interviews are more in-depth and have been conducted with individuals whose work is more pertinent to the journal's mission statement than was volume one's single piece. The first interview is with Stefn Thorsman and Ed LeBouthillier, the directors of the Ásatrú Folk Assembly's clergy program, on the function of Heathen clergy in today's society. The second queries Bron Taylor, a professor of philosophy at the University of Florida, on the relevance of his book, *Dark Green Religion*, and its religious brand of deep ecology to the Heathen revival. The section concludes with a lengthy interview with John Michael Greer, author of (among many books) *A World Full of Gods*, on the epistemology of polytheistic religious experience.

As this preface is being written, preparations are already being undertaken to en-

Editorial Preface

sure that the forthcoming third volume, again, not only lives up to our mission statement, but exceeds past efforts. What we are seeking to do is to take the necessary steps towards rectifying the vast gap that currently separates the depth and sophistication of contemporary Heathen thought from that of the world's major religions. What Heathenry currently lacks is the kind of systematic, multi-disciplinary, academic treatment that comprises theology, philosophy and religious studies. In other words, what is absent is a distinct discipline that could be called Heathen studies. We cannot, however, do this ourselves. *JOCHT* cannot exist without contributions from *you*, our readers. What we need from our readership is the same kind of scholarly analyses of Heathen doxa and praxes that have been presented in the journal thus far. This is not only to say that we are in the market for completely original theses. As mentioned in volume one's preface, we hope that some of the journal's pieces will elicit formal response essays of comparable depth and quality to the original work.

It is also worth repeating that the journal itself is not intended to be a partisan publication. We do not intentionally advocate nor give preference to any particular interpretation of Heathenry. This is to say that *JOCHT* is not specifically a folkish *or* universalist serial, and it is not our intent to exclusively foster submissions solely from one side of the spectrum. Additionally, we are completely and entirely *apolitical*. We do not advocate *any* political position or agenda and do not accept submissions which are overtly political in nature. With all of this in mind, if you are a thinker, poet, or artist who would like to join us and submit material for consideration, please contact the staff. We are accepting essays, dissertations, poems, artwork, book reviews and interviews on a continual basis. Inquiries regarding the suitability of a topic can be addressed via email[2] or our internet discussion forum.[3] If our work resonates with you, please, join us. *Wæs þu hæl!*

—The Editors
Winter, 2011

---

2 Submissions can be sent to: heathen.editor@gmail.com
3 The forum is accessible with registration at: http://www.heathenjournal.com/forum/

Dedication

This journal is dedicated to Friedrich Bernhard Marby (1882-1966), a man devoted body and soul to the Heathen revival. At a time when opposing the reigning authorities often led to death or imprisonment, Marby stood firm in his opposition to the "Irmin-Kristianity" advocated by the Third Reich's chief runologist, Karl Maria Wiligut, and as a result was censured by Heinrich Himmler and eventually imprisoned in a concentration camp for eight years and three months. A true martyr, Marby's sacrifice ought never be forgotten, and to this end we are proud both to host an original translation of one of Marby's essays and to dedicate this present volume to his memory.

Hail to Thee!

Germanic Revivalism

You will see one according law and assertion in all the earth, that there is one God, the king and father of all things, and many Gods, sons of God, ruling together with him. This the Greek says, and the Barbarian says, the inhabitant of the continent, and he who dwells near the sea, the wise and the unwise. And if you proceed as far as to the utmost shores of the ocean, there also there are Gods, rising very near to some, and setting very near to others.

—Maximus Tyrius

On the German Priesthood of Wuotan[1]

Guido von List

Those who can closely trace the development of the Germanic *ethos* and know how to rid themselves of the Christian bias and narrow-mindedness which cloud our view of German prehistory can see immediately that the pre-Christian Germanic peoples were in the fullest sense a cultured Folk. They achieved a high level of development though the exact opposite has, as a general rule, been accepted of them today when their developmental level is compared to that of the Indians of the far West.

The key to such knowledge lies in breaking free from the immense defamation which is still repeated uncritically to this day wherein the pre-Christian Germans have become "blind Heathens" and idolaters. This is easily proven as a great untruth. Or did Tacitus not speak clearly enough in Chapter 9 of his *Germania* when he says:

> For the rest, from the grandeur and majesty of beings celestial, they judge it altogether unsuitable to hold the Gods enclosed within walls, or to represent them under any human likeness. They consecrate whole woods and groves, and by the names of the Gods they call these recesses; divinities these, which only in contemplation and mental reverence they behold.[2]

And, in fact, the esoteric portion of the German cult of Wuotan provides such noble ideas of deepest wisdom that it is understandable how Christianity found relatively easy entrance when it was not only prepared for in its esoteric portion, but was even in many ways influenced by this German faith.

This explains the state-building power of the Germans, which is acknowledged by historians of both ancient and modern times. After the fall of Rome, the Germanic states not only covered nearly all of Europe but had penetrated deep into Africa, even as far as the Canary Islands. Indeed, to this day all the thrones of Europe, with the sole exceptions of the Sultanate of Istanbul and the royal throne

---

1 Translated from the original German *Von der Deutschen Wuotanspriesterschaft* (1893) by Vincent Rex Soden. All footnotes are those of the translator.
2 *Tacitus: Germania*, trans. Thomas Gordon, (New York: P.F. Collier & Son Company, 1910), http://www.fordham.edu/halsall/basis/tacitus-germanygord.asp (accessed August 12, 2011).

of Sweden (House of Bernadotte), are in the possession of Germanic families, which likely share a common pre-Christian origin in a single ancient ruling house.

If the state-founding power of the Germanic peoples is nowadays commonly acknowledged, and if the great wisdom of their theology can be proven, then there must be an education of the Folk as to their impact. Their significance goes far beyond any stage of half-savagery, which is commonly assumed and supported by the pens of biased and spiteful Roman, Greek and Frankish writers.

If in pre-Christian times this religion and its philosophy were the effluence of a powerful folk-spirit, and if this religion deified the ideals of the German Folk which live on to this day, then it must necessarily have been the case that its guardians, or—to employ a not altogether fitting but nonetheless understandable word—their priests, were the leaders of the Folk. And, indeed, they not only *were* the leaders then but *are* to this very day. The deified ideals of the Germans and the Germanic concepts of virtue are living even now. The German poet is their priest and should the German Folk ever prove untrue to their ideals then the terrible *Zeit der Götterdämmerung*[3] shall begin, and along with the downfall of the Gods—that of the German Folk itself.

Therefore, the Roman clergy, as much as it tried, was never able to be a leader of the Folk for any duration and every attempt at such leadership was accompanied by disastrous consequences.

Is the preeminent position of power—a position of power which the Christian priest in Germany was never capable of reaching—of the pre-Christian priest of Wuotan understood? It is only logical that he who functioned as the visible representative and pinnacle of all ideals should have reigned as a divinity and been vested with all the highest dignities of the state. A pre-Christian German king unified in his person the trinity of divine power: Becoming, Being and Waning. As a priest he solemnly commemorated the ancient age and essence, as a king he ruled the present and as a judge he sought to lessen the consequences of debt. Hence, the fabled divine origins of the royal families of which legends tell. This also explains the three names of the Norns: Urda, Verdandi and Skuld. These names were incorrectly interpreted as meaning Past, Present and Future. More correctly, they would be understood as Origin, Becoming and Debt. Debt is simply the self-caused future fate that the judge sought to mitigate, through

---

[3] *Zeit der Götterdämmerung*: age of the twilight of the Gods. The word comes from a misconstructed translation of *ragnarök* ("fate of the Gods") as *ragnarökkr* ("twilight of the Gods").

Figure 1: Guido von List

atonement and penance, and without resorting to vengeance or administering punishment. The German knew only a benevolent, and not a vengeful or wrathful, God.

But it is only understandable that a state had to have servants to assist it. One priest alone could not be entrusted and even less so would a single judge have sufficed. There were priests, judges and government officials which, as representatives of the highest position, shared in the accomplishment of the ongoing tasks and, of course, were divided into positions of rank.

These representatives of the king, who had now become active priests, statesmen and judges, comprised the actual intelligence of the Folk. They were the ones who faithfully preserved and taught the old traditions and, consequently, education was in their care.

Therefore, hardly any more hints are necessary that that part of the Folk which was called upon to be the guardian of its spiritual treasures and formed the ruling class comprised also the nobility of the Folk. They established their power not merely by sword and shield as a widespread falsity would have us believe. The pre-Christian Germanic nobility was truly the shelter of the national sanctuaries of every kind and they fully earned their privileged position. The reasons for their later excesses at the end of the *Minnesang*[4] period shall be covered in greater depth in the course of this study.

The priesthood of the Wuotan cult was not less privileged than the nobility. They also had possession of estates and other rich manors and they were free to look after their most important office: education in the *Halgadome*.[5]

These *Halgadome* were the temple sites of the pre-Christian Germans and, as with the later Christian monasteries which developed from them, the living spaces of the priests of Wuotan were located within. The priesthood that lived in these monastic communities situated in such deep, peaceful forests devoted themselves not only to religious studies, but also to astronomy, natural history and medicine, as well as history, music and everything that men would later call "high culture."

---

4 *Minnesang* was the tradition of lyric and song writing which flourished in 12th century Germany. Similar to the troubadours of Provençal and the trouvères of Northern France, *Minnesänger* wrote courtly romances in the Middle High German language.

5 On page 57 of his book, *The Occult Roots of Nazism: Secret Aryan Cults and Their Influence on Nazi Ideology* (NewYork: New York University Press, 2004), Nicholas Goodrick-Clarke writes: "the Armanist centres or 'high places' (Halgadome) were the seat of government, the school and the lawcourt."

Of course, historians tell nothing of these *Halgadome* in German lands, but the sagas know and tell of them. A body of pre-Christian German literature, which fell victim to monkish fanaticism along with the salvaged runic alphabets, also brings forth documentation for their necessary existence. Not only these and related reasoned conclusions alone, but also parallel appearances in Gaul, Scotland and Ireland where such schools are historically proven urge us to conclude that very similar institutions must have existed in Germany. Priesthoods appeared in those lands which are of the same phenomena and are fundamentally of the same religious ideas. Germany was left out as a link in this chain. Since no historian ever mentions them and simply keeps silent on the matter, the possession of schools by the German priesthood of Wuotan has been made to become questionable.

We are reminded that the Druidic schools must certainly have had a great similarity with the priesthood of Wuotan here in Julius Caesar's *Gallic War* (*Commentarii de Bello Gallico* VI, 13), in which he describes them in detail.

He writes:

> But of these two orders, one is that of the Druids, the other that of the knights. The former are engaged in things sacred, conduct the public and the private sacrifices, and interpret all matters of religion. To these a large number of the young men resort for the purpose of instruction, and they [the Druids] are in great honor among them. For they determine respecting almost all controversies, public and private; and if any crime has been perpetrated, if murder has been committed, if there be any dispute about an inheritance, if any about boundaries, these same persons decide it; they decree rewards and punishments; if any one, either in a private or public capacity, has not submitted to their decision, they interdict him from the sacrifices. This among them is the most heavy punishment. Those who have been thus interdicted are esteemed in the number of the impious and the criminal: all shun them, and avoid their society and conversation, lest they receive some evil from their contact; nor is justice administered to them when seeking it, nor is any dignity bestowed on them. Over all these Druids one presides, who possesses supreme authority among them. Upon his death, if any individual among the rest is pre-eminent in dignity, he succeeds; but, if there are many equal, the election is made by the suffrages of the Druids; sometimes they even contend for the presidency with

arms. These assemble at a fixed period of the year in a consecrated place in the territories of the Carnutes, which is reckoned the central region of the whole of Gaul. Hither all, who have disputes, assemble from every part, and submit to their decrees and determinations. This institution is supposed to have been devised in Britain, and to have been brought over from it into Gaul; and now those who desire to gain a more accurate knowledge of that system generally proceed thither for the purpose of studying it.

The Druids do not go to war, nor pay tribute together with the rest; they have an exemption from military service and a dispensation in all matters. Induced by such great advantages, many embrace this profession of their own accord, and [many] are sent to it by their parents and relations. They are said there to learn by heart a great number of verses; accordingly some remain in the course of training twenty years. Nor do they regard it lawful to commit these to writing, though in almost all other matters, in their public and private transactions, they use Greek characters. That practice they seem to me to have adopted for two reasons; because they neither desire their doctrines to be divulged among the mass of the people, nor those who learn, to devote themselves the less to the efforts of memory, relying on writing; since it generally occurs to most men, that, in their dependence on writing, they relax their diligence in learning thoroughly, and their employment of the memory. They wish to inculcate this as one of their leading tenets, that souls do not become extinct, but pass after death from one body to another, and they think that men by this tenet are in a great degree excited to valor, the fear of death being disregarded. They likewise discuss and impart to the youth many things respecting the stars and their motion, respecting the extent of the world and of our earth, respecting the nature of things, respecting the power and the majesty of the immortal gods.[6]

From these reports on Druidry by Caesar we can draw some fairly certain conclusions about the features of the German priestly order, although it should nevertheless be remembered that the German priesthood did not stand as independent

---

[6] W.A. McDevitte and W.S. Bohn, trans., *Caesar's Gallic War*, (New York: Harper and Brothers, 1869), http://www.perseus.tufts.edu/hopper/text?doc=Perseus%3Atext%3A1999.02.0001%3Abook%3D6%3Achapter%3D13 (accessed August 13, 2011).

as the Gallic and did not provide a counter-balance in the kingdom as the second power in the state, but rather was inseparably bound with it. This also explains why Christianity found an easier entrance in Gaul than in Germany, where the kings recognized a limitation to their authority whereas the Gallic kings were less apt to do so.

In Caesar's report, we see what the schools themselves were involved with, that there must have been many of them and that he expressly mentions a great school in Britannia, which at that time correlated with what would later be called a university.

There must have also been similar academies in the German lands, for the priesthood of Wuotan possessed advanced astronomical and medicinal knowledge from a remote period which, along with the other sciences they practiced, could have only been obtained through regular schooling and a systematic education of the Folk.

It is known that the Goths of the ancient age knew well the twelve signs of the Zodiac, the course of the planets, the phases of the moon and the course of the stars. Jordanes testified to this specifically of the Goths that lived beyond Scandinavia. Are Frode,[7] the oldest Nordic recorder of the sagas, said the following:

> It was also at that time, when the wisest men in this country had reckoned 364 days in the two seasons of the year (which makes 52 weeks, or twelve months of thirty days each and four days left over), that they noticed from the course of the sun that summer was moving backwards into spring; but no one could tell them that there was one day more in two seasons than was equal to the number of full weeks, and that was what was causing it.[8]

What Are Frode is saying is that the mistake lies in the fact that the year is divided in two equal halves of 26 weeks each. Furthermore, Are Frode mentions that the Icelander Thorster Surt[9] had suggested to the assembly that after every seventh summer the days added to the year should amount to seven. As a result, it was decided that every year would have 365 days, but that the leap year would add one day more.

---

7 Ari Þorgilsson (1067–1148 AD), often referred to as Ari the Wise (*Ari hinn fróði*).
8 Anthony Faulkes and Alison Finlay, ed., Sian Grønlie, trans., *Íslendingabók, Kristni Saga – The Book of the Icelanders, The Story of the Conversion* (Exeter: Short Run Press Limited, 2006), 55, http://www.vsnrweb-publications.org.uk/Text%20Series/IslKr.pdf (accessed November 1, 2011).
9 Þorsteinn Surtr.

This note about the calendar reform clearly indicates advanced knowledge of astronomy at an early time, as well as that this knowledge was common and by no means newly introduced. The *Ynglinga Saga* also speaks of the existence of schools, and particularly points out schools for the priesthood, in the following: "Through runes and singing Odin taught his arts; through these he taught the sacrificial priests, from these many others learned, and so the magical arts spread."

It is no wonder then that knowledge of the runes was widespread and that the layman, making use of a runic calendar,[10] could calculate the seasons himself. The Roman clergy of the time, however, despised these "Heathen" runic calendars and predetermined the seasons at the yearly synods in order to inhibit their use. The Catholic prelate Claus Magnus reported that the Swedish country folk "knew how to find all the necessary times on their runic calendars from the knowledge passed down from their ancestors; they had known the festive days and the phases of the moon ten, six hundred, even a thousand years previous."

This fact speaks strongly in favor of the existence of a common schooling system, one so prevalent that the Christian age in Germany has only been able to demonstrate something similar in the most recent of times.

Just how common runic writing was is shown by the fact that the runes were used for a considerable time alongside the Latin script and, indeed, that there were many who could read and write only with runes. Even to this day, farmer's almanacs with rune-like symbols are printed, which are designed for illiterates.

Until now the title of that order has been the Wuotan "cult," a foreign word brought by the priests who did not understand the order, but from here on the correct term will be applied since it approaches something closer to its meaning. Namely, the priests of Wuotan were the well known, though misinterpreted, skalds and bards.

It has already been stated above that in the "Druid schools" the main focus was

---

10 Runic calendars indicate a perpetual calendar based on the nineteen year long Metonic cycle of the moon. In astronomy and calendar studies, the Metonic cycle or Enneadaccaeteris is a period of close to nineteen years, which is remarkable for being very nearly a common multiplier of the tropical year and synodic month. In early calendars, each of the nineteen years in the cycle was represented by a rune; the first 16 were the 16 runes of the Younger Futhark, plus special runes for the remaining three years: Arlaug, Tvimadur, and Belgthor ("Rune Calendar," *Absolute Astronomy*, http://www.absoluteastronomy.com/topics/Runic_calendar [accessed August 15, 2011]).

on the highest development of the power of memory, so that the mystery of the scholarly sciences did not have to be committed to writing. Therefore, for mnemonic reasons, the lessons were presented in the form of didactic poems and alliterative verses. The only aid for the memory was the runic staff (which later became the notorious wand with "magic characters") on which was carved the row of runes from which the carrier built alliterative verses. These didactic poems were spoken, and others sung. The priests who were aided by this poetry were poet-singers, or in the old terminology: skalds and bards.

Before this study is developed further, evidence should be provided that both of these words, which denote the same concept, belong to the German language. A superficial account could show that the word "bard" stems from the Celtic language and actually meant a Druid, whereas "skald" belongs to the Scandinavians.

"Bard" comes from "*baren,*" "*barlan,*" "*bairen,*" that is, to make a great or powerful noise. Corrupted in the vernacular as "*blärren,*" "*Geblärr,*" for *lärmen.*[11] "*Bar*" = sound (*Skall*), noise. "*Bard,*" "*Barde,*" "*Bardur,*" "*Bardel*" = shouter, singer. In Thuringia, singers are still called "*Bardel,*" and the word is even used as a part of surnames. The examples using "*Bar*" are the following: Bardamann (singer); Bardagemadur (poet); Bardaleodi; Barlyo (bard or hero song); Barditus (from Tacitus, actually corrupted from Barit-Bardaleodi or Barlyd); Siegebard (victory singer); Brisbard (Breisbard); Barnveld (shouting field, singing field); and so on. Particularly important is the fact that in the law-book of the Nuremberg Meistersingers[12] their songs were simply called "*Bar.*" Konrad von Würzburg, the famous Meistersinger and fiddler, explicitly called his song for King Otto a "bard song."

Just like "bard," "skald" is also able to be attested as a German word. Nowadays, it is still in common use as "*Schall*"[13] and "*schallen.*"[14] It comes from "*Skal*" = sound; "*Skald*" = song; "*Skala*" = poetry; "*Skaldscap*" = the art or science of songwriting; "*skald*" = singer; "*skaltan*" = to sing; "*Skaldasangar*" = song singer, master of song; "*Skalvingi*" = poetic rapture. "Strubiloskaller" is a female German name from a Roman gravestone which was found in Wiener-Neustadt. The name means "wild-haired singer." (*strubilo*: ragged, fuzzy, compare to: *Strubelliese.*) The name Gottschalk could also perhaps have come from "*Kot-Skalde,*"

---

11 *Lärmen*: to make noise.
12 Meistersingers (German: *Meistersänger,* or simply *Meistersinger*) were members of German guilds for lyrical poetry and composition from the 14th to 16th century. Von List is here making a reference to their law-books, called *Tabulatur,* which set down the rules for their art.
13 *Schall*: sound.
14 *Schallen*: to ring out, to resound.

which then would mean "singer of God," instead of "servant of God."

After this necessary demonstration of the German origins of both words, the evidence for which could still be easily increased, we can now pick up where we had left off.

These poet-singers, then, were the true priesthood of the Wuotan cult and they formed the order of bards or skalds. While they were at the *Halgadomen* in the bardic schools, they cultivated and propagated their secret teachings, the esoteric portion of the cult of Wuotan. There they also celebrated mysteries[15] (of which more will be said later) and appeared as singers and speakers at various occasions before the Folk where they recited their teachings under the guise of myths and fairy tales, which have come down to our own day. That was the exoteric portion of their teachings, whose counterpart in Christianity is called "legend."

The Folk needed a tangible form of religion at all times. They wanted a personal, anthropomorphic God to venerate which could easily captivate their naïve senses. They wanted minor auxiliary Gods with which they could communicate intimately, just as they also preferred to speak to the chamberlain rather than the king himself. This need was satisfied then with the trilogy, the *dodecalogy*, of the Æsir and with the numerous manifestations of secondary beings, of both the male and female gender. It was the skalds who poetically developed the mythology of the Gods because they were ever guided by the systems of nature myth and knew to veil the moral philosophical core.

The Christian indoctrinators wanted to adopt this system through the creation of a *Heiligenhimmel*,[16] but they were less fortunate in doing so because they drew not from the soul of the Folk nor from nature, but were compelled to proceed abstractly, and therefore got on the wrong track through a labyrinth of erroneous paths.

Here, just as everywhere else, the esoteric was present side by side with the exoteric, and the skald also had a dual figure. As a sage or philosopher, he was at work in the quiet hermitage of his *Halgadom* or in front of his audience which he gathered around him under the sacred enclosure of the old lindens, which stood

---

15 A mystery is a religious cult whose rites and doctrines are closed to the uninitiated.

16 Original: *"Heiligenhimmels,"* or "Heaven of the Saints." The word refers to the Virgin Mary, saints, angels, prophets and other Biblical figures and their stories and symbols which often appear in elaborately decorated frescoes of European churches and cathedrals. Von List is here suggesting that the combined legends of these Christian figures and the church imagery teeming with saints and angels is meant to imitate the many Gods and sagas of Heathenry.

near every *Halgadom*. But, as a poet-singer, he came before the Folk as a "*Mime*"[17] (from Mimir) in the mystery plays and worked on the imagination and emotions of the Folk. As a sage, he gave universal truths. As a poet-singer, he employed imagination and emotion to reach the same goals by evoking enthusiasm and, if necessary, fanaticism by which the audience was inflamed and carried away by his passion. For this purpose, he accompanied his songs with music, be it the harp, the lyre, the fiddle or flute, and the ever present drum or cymbal. Yes, even the name of the "*Geige*,"[18] derived from Gygas, means "magic."

The songs sung by the skalds were divided into many varieties; there were the songs in praise of Gods, and those of heroes, songs of disgrace and defiance, songs of joy and sadness, love songs, songs of marriage and many others.

Thus, the bards were the organs of speech—in a similar sense as the modern press—by which the Folk were extremely affected. They not only offered the famous deeds of heroes and kings, the history of antiquity, or cheerful fairy tales to the Folk, but they also prepared them for heroic actions and decisions through enthusiastic songs. Through their art they guided the decisions of the Folk.

But at the court of the king, they again preserved the ancestral customs and traditions; they acted as the master of ceremonies in the modern sense. Therefore, it will no longer appear strange if we see "minstrels" and "fiddlers" acting as envoys to the king; it was not the warrior heroes, but rather the most learned and skilled of their Folk who acted as messengers. With fiddle in hand, we see them —even in the 12th century—riding from the country as heralds; carrying out peace negotiations, bridal announcements and other difficult tasks for their kings.

> There come to us new tidings, which I will confess to you
> Lord Etzel's fiddlers, I have seen here!
> They have sent your sister to the Rhine
> It is King Etzel's will, that we welcome them.
>
> They have ridden already, the messengers to the palace;
> Never has a prince's minstrel come so gloriously…
> —
> There came the noble Volker, the bold minstrel
> Towards the court with reverence
> …
> As everyone thronged around the guests,

---

17 *Mime*: thespian.
18 *Geige*: fiddle, violin.

> The bold Volker spoke to those gathered round the Huns:
> How dare you not let the warriors pass?
> Shall you not let us, terrible suffering will come upon you!
>
> I will club you with such a heavy strike from my fiddle,
> Were you to take one, you may well weep for it!
> What keeps us warriors from passing through? Methinks it well;
> All swords have been called upon, though not all are of equal courage![19]

From history as well as from poetry the evidence may suffice, but it may also show, contrary to the customs of the Gallic Druids, the German bards and skalds were also brave warriors. A comparison could be made such as that between the knightly orders of the early Middle Ages and the monks in their monastery.

A precious piece of evidence is the legend of the monk, Ilsan. It tells of how he is discontented in the monastery, how he prepares himself to leave, but finds that the abbot and convent object, so he frees himself by force. That is an old hero, an old skald, who was too confined by the monastery walls to which he could not grow accustomed. This was no Gallic Druid, but rather a German bard.

By the sixth century an ill-fated resistance by the German faith was becoming more and more apparent as Christianity pressed forward slowly but surely through force and guile. Through concessions of the most diverse kinds and by admitting native customs into their liturgy, the Christians sought to knock the worshipers of Wuotan out of competition. But one of the most perilous events for the German faith was the introduction of church hymns by Pope Gregory the Great,[20] because in place of German songs the Folk were provided chants. This shrewdly calculated action would have damaged the bards even more had these Christian spiritual songs been in the German language, but they were not because the Church proved to be inconsistent in their efforts towards denationalization. Luckily, the Christian song remained a meaningless chant. Many of the monks who sang these songs could not understand them, but the songs remained completely incomprehensible to the Folk and they did not succeed in suppressing or transmogrifying, as in the case of the Romance-speaking peoples, the language in Germania at all.

And yet, the bards were pushed back. The epics that had long been sung in the

---

19 This segment is taken from *Das Nibelungenlied*.
20 The widespread belief that Pope Gregory the Great had developed the chanting used in Rome, which was later spread throughout Christian Europe, led to this musical form being called "Gregorian chant." The fact is that the style probably did not appear until 800, roughly 200 years after the Pope's death.

German provinces to the glory of Arminius the Cheruscan, those of Siegfried and Brunhild, of the vengeance of Kriemhild, of Dietrich von Bern, of the Nibelungs, as well as of the Amelungs[21] originated in these German skaldic *Halgadome*, from out of which a small portion were saved in Scandinavia where we find a record of them in the Eddas, albeit in altered form. To this accident we owe their preservation. It is these, the lays of Sigurd, which prove to be clear parallels of the lays of Helgi and reveal their German origin from small local features (such as the mention of the Black Forest and the like). And it is these songs which form the basis of the later Nibelung epic, the Lay of Gudrun and others.

As is known, Carolus Magnus[22] gathered these songs which were even then pursued with blind rage by the fanaticism of the monks and expediently destroyed and eliminated. He collected them, let them be written down and learned them himself. But after his death, they, along with other writings and invaluable monuments of Germanic antiquity—alas!—were lost.

The old German bard songs are forgotten and lost. Some bards ventured forth once again under Emperor Otto I in the ancestral styles and, although Christianized, they were carrying on the tradition of their predecessors. The Holy Father invited them to Pavia because of this heresy, and they were suppressed. Yes, the persecution against the old German literature even went so far that Pope Gregory charged Bishop Desiderius of Vienne[23] with the greatest crime: that he read Heathen books with his friends. He himself, in his presumed spiritual omnipotence, allowed for many old manuscripts to be cast into the fire. So it seems that by the end of the tenth, or at latest the beginning of the eleventh, century the last remnants of bardic literature were destroyed, and so thoroughly was this done that, apparently, it even disappeared from memory. Pope Sylvester, known in German as "*Waldteufel*,"[24] even made it compulsory for the monks to search out all bardic and skaldic writings everywhere and burn them as spell-books. They were written in runes—the "magic symbols"—and were probably the books of which the sagas occasionally tell. The monks cleaned up so thoroughly that, excepting the runic alphabets and the Merseburg Incantations,[25] everything was destroyed—*ad*

---

21 The followers of Dietrich von Bern are referred to as *Amelungen* in the *Niebelungenlied*. They are also called Amelungs, Amalings, or Amali.
22 Charlemagne.
23 Desiderius was Bishop of Vienne from 595-606.
24 *Waldteufel*: forest devil.
25 The Merseburg Incantations are two Medieval spells written in Old High German, and, along with the *Muspilli*, are the only known examples of Germanic Heathen belief written in that language. Each begins by telling the story of a mythological event and follows with a spell. One is an incantation to break bonds and the other is to cure injured horses. "Uuôdan" (Odin), "Frîia," (Freya) "Balder," (Baldr) "Sunna" (Sól)

majorem dei gloriam.[26]

Of course, it is no wonder that with such thorough persecutions of the skalds and their works by the Roman Church that the *Halgadome* also roused the holy wrath of the monks for two very important reasons. Firstly, the *Halgadome* were "castles of the Antichrist, of the devil," they were the dissemination points of blind Heathendom. Secondly, they were immensely rich, most being located in prime locations, which made the opportunity to found monasteries there extremely alluring since all the provisions had already been made. This also explains the springing up of monasteries, which cost their founders very little. Something similar happened again some thousand years later during the Reformation when the confiscation of Church lands was not an irrelevant motivation.

The *Halgadome* were, of course, closed immediately, but they were not replaced by any new Christian schools, and so Germany was ridden of schooling. A period of incredible brutality and stupidity entered our history under the blessings of the bishop's crook. Ever so gradually, and sparsely, the monastery schools grew, which taught only in the Latin language. They educated new priests to further and, when possible, complete their denationalization project. There is even the legend of the Devil's school on the Venusberg[27] (*Halgadom*), at which the Devil taught the black arts, and the traveling students of the Middle Ages claimed that they had learned magic there.

The round towers of *Halgadome* were replaced by Christian churches. A strange phenomenon can be observed in Germany in which the oldest Christian churches are rotundas. The Folk still remembers them from pre-Christian times, calling them downright Heathen temples or attributing them to the Knights Templar; for no other reason other than that they associate temples with the Templars. In this way, all of the interpretations of the decorative and enigmatic imagery of these buildings are lacking because they are always interpreted as either coming from the Bible or the simple fancy of the masons (!?) instead of as from the symbols of the Wuotan mythos for which they were ordained. (For further details on this see my essay "*Deutsche-Mythologische Bildwerke an der Stephanskirche zu Wien*," Laufer's General Art History, 1889, Issues 9, 10 and 11).

But, what does a German think about this curious heritage from his ancestors!? These buildings must be Roman or (allegedly) come from the building projects of

---

and Sinthgunt are among the deities mentioned. They were first discovered in a theological manuscript from Fulda in the cathedral chapter library at Merseburg in 1841.
26 "For the greater glory of God."
27 The Venusberg is a mythical mountain situated in Thuringia, Germany where Venus had a court. The legendary knight Tannhäuser spent a year there worshiping her.

medieval monks; no German scholar has dared to say that such buildings could have been built by our pre-Christian ancestors, "barbarians" to which the monks had to first bring the "light of Christianity." It is far too dangerous. A man could easily be denounced as a heretic.

Banished and on the run, the skalds and bards left the country retaining their old treasures in their memories thanks to their mnemonic training, even if they denied the existence of this knowledge. They were banished "to the wolves (of Wuotan, the Wild One) on the heath" and formed the basis of the "humble folk of the heath."[28] All who were declared "unfaithful" in the Middle Ages were considered complicit with the priesthood of Wuotan.

Once the keepers and guardians of the German ideals had been dispossessed and the Folk had become fully dumbed down and brutish, then from Rome, God's Vicegerent reigned absolutely over the minds of peoples and kings, fortified by artificially created mass stupidity on the cliffs named Canossa.[29] Atop Canossa he built a nearly impenetrable fortress from which a self-serving Popery controlled an ignorant and stubborn nobility and a shamefully humiliated and nearly denationalized Folk. Rome, which could not master Germania with sword in hand, this same Rome bound the Mighty in chains as he, wearing a cilice and carrying a censer, submissively walked barefoot over the Alps.[30]

And yet! One of the best sang:

> Disloyal are both court and neighbor,
> And violence stalks its prey,
> Peace and justice have mortal wounds.[31]
> —Walther von der Vogelweide[32]

The *Minnesänger* were the resurrected bards and skalds who had preserved the old songs and brought them back as new. It was precisely in the *Minnesinger* period that the great epics, faithfully preserved from the sagas, like the *Nibelun-*

---

28 Original: "*Völkleins auf der Heide.*"
29 The castle at Canossa in Northern Italy is most well known for the penance Holy Roman Emperor Henry IV performed around the month of January 1077 by standing three days outside in the snow in hope that Pope Gregory VII would reverse his excommunication from the Church, which he eventually did. The castle itself was built around 940.
30 A reference to Holy Roman Emperor Henry IV's walk to Canossa.
31 From the poem *Ich saz ûf eime steine.*
32 Walther von der Vogelweide (c. 1170-c. 1230) was one of the most celebrated of the German *Minnesänger.*

genlied, the lays of Gudrun and the smaller poems were created, and they were largely within the same tradition. How could such a thing have been possible without a direct connection through secret propagation of the order's rules and teachings in the form of a secret society, under whose framework the Christianizing order of skalds gradually developed into the Christian society of "*Minnesänger*"? The name "*Minne-Sänger*" says this clearly enough. The concept of "*Minne*" means not love, but rather memory, and this became their name of identification and honor. Yes, it must have developed in this way! The ancient bards must have found in the *Minnesänger* their direct reproduction, whose banner, the sacred symbol of their unrelinquished heritage, they only unfurled again when they were strong enough to appear on the battlefield and achieve victory for German ideals. Under this proud banner, in this new, great blossoming of German song and literature, the venerable old priesthood of the German faith returned to the German Folk the veneration of women which had been withdrawn by misogynist Christianity; a fact which is still too little appreciated. They raised up the noble Freyja as the Virgin Mary, the Allmother Frouwa as the Mother of God, the radiant Peratha[33] as the Queen of Heaven and the towering Gothic cathedrals which sprouted skywards like flowers, the most fragrant blossoms of the Christian Middle Ages,[34] they considered a Marian devotion. Thus, the temporary amalgamation between Germandom and Christianity was complete.

The Meistersingers were the successors of the *Minnesänger* as priests of the immortal ideals of the German faith and one could still be exiled as one of the dispossessed "*Völklein auf der Haide*,"[35] from this newly resurrected forest of German poets, in which any individual could feel himself called to be a bard or skald, yet the Folk had still not forgotten their poets and thinkers.

But let us return to pre-Christian times.

It has been stated above that the kings came from sons of the Gods, that is to say they were descendants of the Gods as the myths and sagas suggest. This was not apotheosis in the Roman mythological sense, because Germanic "Heathendom" did not know the deification of men, that was reserved by the "Roman Church" for their canonizations. Also, this was not just flattery, nor any self-arrogance on the part of the royal houses, but rather an essential mystical consequence.

---

33 Perchta.
34 Here Von List plays on the German word *Dome* (cathedrals) by positioning "(*Halga-*)" before it, creating *Halgadome* and thus indicates a relation between the two.
35 Here Von List uses the phrase "*Dichterwald der Deutschen*" ("forest of German poets") and contrasts it to the "*Völklein auf der Haide*" ("people of the heath"), which brings to mind the fact that a heath is created by the clearance of forest and woodland.

The God in question, or better put, the physical and psychological embodiment of the One God (Allfather)—the personification of an ideal concept—was thought of as a divine person who was his own priest, and this priesthood would have then been transmitted to other people in a mystery. These people were then thought of as his children and grandchildren if he was declared the progenitor of a royal house, or his priesthood multiplied by adoption through the ceremony of a mystery.

In this way, Wuotan was his own priest and in this capacity (as Hangatyr) offered himself up to himself. Among the Gods was one of the first sacrificers, Brage[36] with the rune-adorned tongue; whose wife, Iduna, possessed and preserved the golden apples of rejuvenation. As Iduna descended the World Ash, Brage guarded her. That is to say, that in times when winter befalls a Folk (just as there are springtimes of the Folk there are also Folk winters) it is precisely their poets who preserve the gold of poetry to return it to the Folk in the recurring spring. Lucky for us, that Brage guarded Iduna. Lucky for us, that unknown poets and singers preserved the gold of the German mythos so that their successors, the *Minnesänger*, could generate it again.

Just as the Gods had their priesthood, the Goddesses had their own as well; and these were composed of the matrones,[37] the *Albrunen*,[38] the witches, the drudes[39] and the *Walen*;[40] Christianity arguably adopted their nuns from the Norns, but their misogynistic tendencies never allowed them to attain an actual female priesthood.

In no other Folk in the world did the feminine priesthood have such prominence as among the Germanic Folk, simply because women did not enjoy such high, near deifying veneration by any other Folk. It is attested that in pre-Christian Germania there had been quite a few women who became renowned for a higher, nearly transcendental wisdom; but this can be easily explained.

---

36 Bragi.
37 Matrones: Lat. "matrons," female deities (almost universally depicted in groups of three) that were commonly venerated by the early Germanics and depicted in their religious art. They have subsequently been identified as being connected to the Medieval Scandinavian cults of the Dísir.
38 Prophetic women.
39 Drudes were a kind of witch in German folklore that were associated with dreams and the Wild Hunt. Importantly, they were virgins or priestesses who, by virtue of a particular type of possession, could separate their spirits from their bodies.
40 *Walen* is the German word used for the *vǫlur* (O.N.), *völvur* (Icel.).

The pure, infallible natural instinct, the intuition to recognize what is natural, was lost by men in the constant struggle for conquest, but it was preserved by the women who carried out their duties in more intimate, but not pettier domains.

Only the recognition and appreciation of this residual feeling of inwardness remained with the men as a last treasure. The women had still preserved this and the great respect that the men had for them led to the exalted veneration of women which only the Germanic Folk knew, and which Tacitus praised so much. This veneration of woman was beautifully deified by the great national epic of the German Wuotan mythos.

Later in time, we see other women, though fewer, that have retained such full purity of their primordial spirit such as that that led to the glory of Aurinia,[41] Gauna (Kunna)[42] or Veleda.[43] The ancients were correct to attribute something divine to these women; it is nothing less than the primordial-divine that shone forth from them which to this day we still love above all else in our women when we find it. This divine quality of the woman is still best called inwardness.

A trinity can also be demonstrated among the priestesses; numerous folk legends say that there are three of them, call them three names and relate specifically that the third is black in color. This corresponds to the trinity of the Norns: The Primal Age, Becoming and Consequences of Debt (Urda, Verdandi and Skuld). Therefore, the third is black, dark; the third is the evil-counseling Norn, the *Unheilsrätin*, which weakens or nullifies the *Heilsrat*[44] of the two good Norns since

---

41 Much like Veleda, Aurinia was a seeress and prophetess. In chapter 8 of *Germania*, Tacitus writes: "They even believe them endowed with something celestial and the spirit of prophecy. Neither do they disdain to consult them, nor neglect the responses which they return. In the reign of the deified Vespasian, we have seen Veleda for a long time, and by many nations, esteemed and adored as a divinity. In times past they likewise worshiped Aurinia and several more, from no complaisance or effort of flattery, nor as Deities of their own creating."

42 In his *Historia Romana*, Cassius Dio says "Masyus, king of the Semnones, and Ganna, a virgin who was priestess in Germany, having succeeded Veleda, came to Domitian and after being honoured by him returned home." *Dio Cassius: Roman History*, trans. Earnest Cary, (Harvard University Press, 1914-1927), http://penelope.uchicago.edu/Thayer/E/Roman/Texts/Cassius_Dio/home.html (accessed August 20, 2011).

43 Veleda was a priestess and prophetess of the Bructeri, who prophesied the initial victories of the rebels against the Roman army in the Batavian Rebellion of the years 69-70 AD.

44 *Heilsrat*: literally "counsel of hail." The word "hail" in this context refers to health, wholeness, well-being and haleness. A *Heilsrätin* would be a female giver of *Heilsrat*. An *Unheilsrätin* would be the opposing negative version of a H*eilsrätin*.

the consequences of debt often destroy luck and prosperity for generations to come. But the black shrouds of the wicked Norn conceal not only the consequences of her own "debt," but also a sinister doom since both man and the Gods are subject to their destined conclusion and not masters of their fate. Therefore, German law knew only atonement and penance, not vengeance and punishment. Even what we today call the death penalty was in pre-Christian times simply called atonement.

Even to this day, the Folk distinguishes between three types of priestesses become "monsters"; they know of witches, drudes and *Walen*, which fully correlates to the concept of a divine trinity, such as the following trilogies; "Wodan, Willi, We," "Wuotan, Donar, Loki," "Freya, Frouwa, Helia," "Urda, Verdandi and —Skuld."

Herein lies the "unity of the sacred three," in the sense of the origin, further development and waning of a new becoming. The entire structure of the Folk was organized in the same manner from the smallest unit to the complete state, in law and religion, in the military and labor, or organized into classes as the "sovereign class," the "military class" and the "productive class." On these three mighty, brazenly forged pillars rest the unanimously recognized state-founding abilities of the Germans.

But how did the male priesthood of bards and skalds form into the *Minnesänger*? The arrival of Christianity forced them onto a different course of development. Through persecution and monkish hatred, noble and holy priestesses were perceived as the practitioners of a terrible witchcraft with all of its gory and demented consequences.

And here we must be reminded of a fact that thus far has been seemingly ignored in this essay: the magic arts of the Germanic priesthood.

In those remote times, man knew only the perceptible manifestations of natural forces and through his emotional sense, which still prevailed over his intellectual sense, came to the hypothesis that these manifestations had to point to the existence of an immeasurably higher being than himself, a being to which he must bow to in fear and trepidation to obtain grace before its eyes. The fog which traveled around the mountain peak cultivated the first naïve idea of Godhood in his sensory world, and formed the idea of hostile pairings which combated each other. He considered it a consolation that the light, warm and good was always victorious over the dark, cold and evil. Our ancestors, in the childhood of a nascent Folk, were in much more direct communication with nature than us, their penned up, city-dependent offspring, so it is easy to understand that by far the largest part of that sense of nature is lost in us, which science can only inadequately replace. Derived from this sense of nature are all mysterious spells and magic phenomena to which belong, for example, sympathetic cures, whose healing power has been proven in many cases and modern science cannot explain. But there are even more profound and mysterious things to mention.

There are obviously forces of human nature in motion here which modern science has yet to decipher, and which heretofore could develop more powerfully but today are unusual and stunted in consequence of their disuse. The latter perhaps only to the extent to which we utilize our intellectual understanding over remembering to return to our emotional senses.

If these dormant powers of man, many of which were unexpected before discovery, had already been investigated, much of the unexplainable would be explained. Instead, many of these powers seem to be ridiculed, quite naturally, as superstition. Man only denies them today because he cannot explain them, yet in his self-arrogance he does not want to admit that he cannot interpret them, which is why he prefers to call the unexplainable simply non-existent, a superstition.

The enormous error of the witch trials, which carried out about nine and a half million witch executions within eleven centuries, was that the Christian Middle Ages persecuted witchcraft as a religious heresy whereas it was purely human and had nothing in common with Christianity nor any other religion. It was merely based on the use of those secret powers, now lost to us, which appear stunted in the human race today, because for centuries their cultivation has been neglected.

Perhaps the witch trials so thoroughly destroyed those natures that they can only be gradually developed again in the human race. But just as the Middle Ages treated witchcraft erroneously, in that they considered it from a religious point of view and persecuted it as heresy, likewise the modern anthropologist is caught in the same error, viewing witchcraft in light of false information and declaring it a superstition.

We cannot exclude the possibility that the science of the twentieth century will recognize the reality of witchcraft.

It follows that witchcraft did not in any way only arise when Pope Innocent VII enacted his infamous Bull in the year 1485, which was the cause of the witch trials. Rather, it existed—like the skalds and bards—since the beginning of the German Folk; it was older than Christianity, because it existed when the highly honored female priesthood of the Wuotan cult manifested, physically and psychologically, countless blessings upon the Folk through counsel and deed.

Inseparably linked with witchcraft are the infamous witches' dances, which also deserve our full attention because the witches' dance is nothing less than a highly sacred mystery quite similar to those of Dionysus or analogous ceremonies of related religious systems.

These highly sacred ceremonies developed from the feminine priesthood of the Wuotan cult, in whose mysteries the *Heilsrätinnen* played the leading part.

However, contemporary indicators are understandably lacking—particularly in regard to reports of German skaldic schools—and so the evidence for these mysteries must be adduced retroactively from medieval witchcraft to find the main thread which seems likely to lead back to primitive times.

There were primarily seven stages of witchcraft in the protocols of the witch trials which were indicated to facilitate verdicts.

The first of these seven stages was the Seduction. This was done by the Devil himself, never in his true form, but rather in the guise of a seducer (incubus) or a seductress (succubus). Most witches fell into the Devil's trap of adultery, whereas warlocks were taken by their own free will, or could likewise be ensnared by his illicit love.

The second stage was reached when the Seduction—whether it be by the incubus or the succubus—was complete. The victorious seducer returned for three, nine or fourteen days and would only then reveal his true nature to the seduced. The fee for the sin, which the Devil had paid in clinking gold, turned into horse dung with the women, but to broken shards for the men. The first moment of recognition always inspired terrible fear in the seduced, because they realized too late how hopelessly entangled in the snares of hell they had become. Thus, they came to the third stage of witchcraft wherein the (alleged) Devil demanded that the seduced deny God and the holy saints or face immediate death. Then followed the fourth stage: the witch's baptism and wedding to the (supposed) Devil, which took place in a proper Christian marriage a few days later where the bride and groom were given different names which would henceforth be used in the witches' dances. Of course, the seduced had to make an unconditional vow of silence, in particular to not make any confession to the spying priest and to not receive the Eucharist, but rather to throw it in the trash or otherwise dishonor it.

At the "witches' wedding" or "witches' baptism," which were regarded as initiation ceremonies into the witch orders, the "witches' mark" was imprinted; it was a bloody service, because this type of wound only healed after several weeks. It is mentioned specifically that the evil one "took blood from her hidden place."

Thus, the newly initiated witch was ready to take part in the "witches' dance" as the fifth stage of development. The way in which these witches' dances proceeded is known to us. The vulgar description of these gatherings in the trial records can certainly seem a little tempting, but they were indeed wild orgies, entirely licentious and devoted to the most savage sensual pleasure. (Mind you, this was taking place by the 15th century.) Besides, it would be a great mistake if one were to take "riding on a broomstick" literally. The witches traveled to the gatherings by foot or rode on horseback and even if certain magic blessings came into use, these witches' sabbaths proceeded in a completely natural manner. The fact that these witches' covens were not inventions, but were actually held, was confirmed by Vogt in his interesting book: *Disputatio de conventu sagarum ad sua sabbatha* (Wittenberg 1667), in which the actual existence of the witches' dances and festivals is proven.

As for the witches' ointment, this consisted of the broth of a sacrificial meal, which in earlier times was always a human sacrifice, either a man or a child. The killing was carried out by hanging, after which the hanging body was torn to pieces. Later, when it became difficult to obtain this kind of offering, they contented themselves with the stolen corpses of thieves from the gallows or with the bodies of children. In the latter group, the bodies of unbaptized children took preference. Witches' powder was taken from the coal of burnt bones.

These witches' dances took place three times a year, on Walpurgis, and a fortnight after Midsummer and Christmas.

The sixth stage was the knowledge of magic, which, of course, always appears in the trial records as a product of wickedness, which originally magic had not been.

The seventh and final stage consisted of the "highly forbidden" art of weather brewing. This was an especially dangerous act which from time to time endangered lives or led to discovery.

The facts were obscured by the furor of the witch hunts and the tendency of the judges to extort statements which were as absurd as imaginable. Divested of these outrageous components, the facts point to nothing less than a secret society; partly in the sense of our modern Spiritist groups and partly in that of a wild, savage orgy, but the whole in a sort of deformity and degeneracy which would still be prosecuted today by the state attorney.

However, it is now evident that witchcraft was at the time of its wildest degeneracy shortly before its expiration; previously, it had conducted itself better.

Witchcraft has now turned out to be primarily a secret society. Furthermore, it is established that the presiding Devil was stamped as the Evil One incarnate only at the time of the witch trials because previously it had been Wuotan, the father of the Gods, himself. This was done symbolically, or by a visible representative who appeared in the guise of the God. The masquerade of the group's leader and the distinguished participants, in representation of the divine court, led to the mystery plays which celebrated the mythos in dramatized form. This is the beginning of the dramatic arts in Germany, which had been sought heretofore in the cloister mysteries of the Middle Ages without considering that, if it were correct, the "actors"[45] would certainly not have been numbered among the "unfaithful people." This was only because they belonged to the old priesthood of Wuotan, just as the bards and the executioner, the old sacrificer. The name "Mine" corresponds precisely to that of the giant "Mime" (Mimur) with whose head Wuotan exchanged words of wisdom and was the personification of memory.

Some of these mystery plays have come down to us. Apart from the dramatized poems in the Edda, we may add the "Dragon-Slaying" in Furth in Bavaria, the "Three Kings Play" in Styria and Carinthia, and other similar plays.

The trial records also mention the masquerades and state that the reason for them was so that people could attend the gatherings unrecognized, and therefore undiscovered and without risk; the true reason had long been forgotten.

Among those mentioned as present at the dances were minstrels and fiddlers, which have already been mentioned above as belonging to the guild of skalds and bards; and they were also regarded as unfaithful throughout the Middle Ages.

The condemnation of this entire profession as unfaithful designated them as complicit with the defeated followers of Wuotan. The Church not only persecuted these dramatic exhibitions but also the dance festivities and especially forbade masked mummeries as Heathen abominations. Indeed, despite their love of mimicry they went so far as to ban the Heathen "flutes and fiddles" and replace it with performances of church music. Even today we have zealots for pure church music, such as the Cecilian Movement,[46] who argue that only organ-accompanied

---

45 The German word for "actors" used in the original text is *Mimen*.
46 The Cecilian Movement was a late 19th century church reform movement based in Italy that called for the revival of Gregorian chant in the Catholic Mass and to do away with the more operatic styles of music being played in churches at the time.

choral music is worthy of the Church. Nevertheless, the Church took the Heathen mystery plays as the model for their passion plays and now claims for them the honor of being the forerunners of modern dramatic poetry. If this were true, then the German thespians would not have been outlawed, but rather they would have been united in some sort of fraternity and revered to some extent.

To turn back to the witch community, it is striking that it increased itself through erotic seduction, which only allowed men the exception to choose by their free will if the erotic temptations proved insufficient.

The female sex, therefore, formed the majority in the "witch orders." They were their main support just as they submit themselves most readily in every religion. This fact has long been recognized to be true. The female sex is more inward than the male; it is more devoted to the emotional than to the intellectual life and therefore easier to win over by sensual tricks to any more or less great idea with good or bad objectives, particularly if it is shrouded in the mystic veils of a "secret" society which is constantly bringing in new members by way of raising children or by its influence on the wider community. For that reason also, the female sex formed the majority in the witch orders. Warlocks numbered only one to every ten to twelve witches. In this case, the sweet fruits of forbidden delights formed the most effective lure for the female sex.

In the phase of corruption in which witchcraft must have found itself at this time, it is understandable that there were the most extravagant vices alongside its primary purpose, as is obvious from the nature of the initiation by the "Seduction." It had been different half a millennium earlier. At that time, witchcraft was the secret order of the last adherents to the German faith, the worshipers of Wuotan, who celebrated "secret, concealed wisdom" in their sacrifices to Wuotan and at the Thing. Out of this "secret outlawry" developed the "holy Vehme,"[47] which strove to preserve both the ancient law as well as the ancient religion and

---

47 The Vehme, or Vehmic courts, were a tribunal system of "free judges" which took jurisdiction over all crimes during the Late Middle Ages in the area of Western Germany, notably Westphalia. The proceedings were occasionally in secret, but those condemned were always executed and left hanging in a tree to advertise the deed and to deter others. The origin of the term is uncertain but appears to come from Middle Low German *vehma*, which means "punishment." If a particular offense was found to be punishable by death a summons to the accused was issued by nailing it to his door. The accused was then given a six weeks and three days grace period in accordance with old Saxon law. The only punishment the court could inflict was death, and if the accused appeared they were immediately hanged. It has been noted that in some cases the accused were released and then hunted down after being given a few hours head start.

whose traces can still be found to this day. For example, the "*Haberfeldtreiben*"[48] of the Bavarian peasants, which degenerated into the orgies of the witches' dances. In passing, it should be pointed out here that the jewel of the human race, the woman, is like a rudderless ship lost in the waves of life if she lacks the leadership of man; the modern emancipation of women is becoming the modern witches' dance of the coming century and will likewise end in horror.

Reports from the eleventh century represent witchcraft in a much more favorable, though already hostile, light than the documents of the witch trials.

Bishop Burchard of Worms, who died in 1024, already mentions the worship of the Devil by groups of women, which was certainly nothing other than what the witch trial records called witches' dances. Such a gathering, which he called a "*consortium*," took women in as members, all of whom, he said, were deceived by the Devil (*a diabolo deceptae*), and they had to travel to the gatherings by his command (*ex praecepto*). Of particular importance is that his report calls each member of the gathering "Holda" in the vernacular language (*vulgaris stultitia*). "Holda" or "Hulda" is but one of the names of the Mother Goddess Frouwa who —a sorceress herself—is the wife of the chief practitioner of magic, Wuotan.

In the vernacular, these witches were called the "*Holden*,"[49] which indicates that they had not yet sunken to "*Unholden*"[50] as they did half a millennium later. Equally noteworthy is that Bishop Burchard further reports that these *Holden* rode on animals, and says nothing of brooms and pitchforks. Incidentally, that he describes the women as calling upon a multitude of Devils demonstrates his understandable, from the ecclesiastical view, hatred for the faith of Wuotan, whose many Gods would have been logically explained as Devils by the Christian clergy. Their praise would surely have included the skalds, who appeared in the guise of the Æsir and were their representatives. Apart from that, the bishop's account is completely silent about what took place at the gathering of *Holden*. Of course, it is bypassed in modern accounts as well. So, the silence was not delib-

---

48 The *Haberfeldtreiben* were a sort of criminal court held in the Bavarian Oberland in which the accused was reproached for crimes in verse. The crimes were often of a moral nature, such as pregnancy before marriage, or involved perceived violations of the people by the authorities or the rich. The name itself literally means "oat field drives" and could refer to the fact that accused women were formerly driven through a field under lashes. The drives nearly always involved multiple people. Those performing the drive were usually masked or had blackened faces so that they would not be recognized. The *Haberfeldtreiben* are often compared to the Vehmic courts, however the two differ greatly in their historical and legal roots and their content.
49 *Holden*: used here as plural of Holda.
50 *Unholden*: monsters.

erate, but rather a sign of the tacit continuance of the cult of Wuotan alongside Christianity as a supplementary belief, which was later transformed into superstition.

And yet, at that time, witchcraft seems to have been more "cult" than "doctrine." This was because the upper classes, the dynastic families and the high nobility had withdrawn from the Wuotan cult in a manner similar to when the so-called better classes held themselves distant from the old folk festivals in the Rococo and *Zopfstil* periods as the age of the Italian operas and the French assemblies begun. The effect was the same; the Wuotan mythos was, in modern terms, simply out of fashion. As the folk festivals became old-fashioned, they were solely upheld by the peasantry, the same way the summer solstice celebrations, the *Wasservogel*[51] and similar festivals are celebrated, but which have been long forgotten by the cities. The exact same relationship existed a millennium earlier between the kings and higher nobility and the old Wuotan mysteries, and then witchcraft, as they distanced themselves from them and left them to the peasants. It was simply that Christianity had come into fashion.

But, if such an ancient folk custom dies off then it has already lost its meaning long ago. So it was in the eleventh century with the gatherings of *Holden*, who had sunken to the state of a "cult without doctrine" and so it went in the eighteenth century with the folk festivals which had lost the mystical-religious essence of the ancient German faith centuries previous.

The class of serfs, the peasants, which always occupies the lowest level of any Folk, were now the sole support of the declining mysteries of Wuotan, and so it is no wonder that witchcraft became bogged down in brutishness. And so it de-

---

51 In a discussion on European rain-spells where a person or an effigy is thrown into a body of water, the book *The Roman Festivals of the Period of the Republic* states the following: "The best known example is that of the Bavarian 'Wasservogel,' which is either a boy or a puppet, as the custom may be in different places; he or it was decorated, carried round the fields at Whitsuntide, and thrown from the bridge into the stream. So constant and inconvenient was this kind of custom in the Middle Ages that a law of 1351, still extant, forbade the ducking of people at Erfurt in the water at Easter or Whitsuntide. In many of these cases the *simulacrum* may have been substituted for a human being, but I find none where the notion of sacrifice survived, or where there was any trace of a popular belief that the object was a substitute for an actual victim. What these curious customs, according to Dr. Mannhardt, do really represent, is the departure of winter and the arrival of the fruitful season, or possibly the exhaustion of the vernal Power of vegetation after its work is done," (William Warde Fowler, *The Roman Festivals of the Period of the Republic: An Introduction to the Study of the Religion of the Romans* [New York: The Macmillan Company, 1899], 118).

clined until it was extinguished during the period of the witch trials some two hundred years ago, no later than the beginning of the eighteenth century.

Hence, it is easy to see why it was the peasantry that provided the majority of witches, while the townsmen and nobility are mentioned only very rarely in the trial records.

Despite all this, witchcraft was not prohibited; only one single act of witchcraft ever drew punishment, and this one severely taboo act was human sacrifice and the eating of children's flesh.

The witch trials only began with the bull of Pope Innocent VIII in the year 1485; only then was witchcraft a crime punishable by death.

During the reign of Emperor Otto the Great in the tenth century, the last flicker of the male priesthood of Wuotan and the ancient order of bards was forcibly suppressed forever, because the meetings of the isolated worshipers of Wuotan could no longer be guided by the theologically learned. The leaders were lacking and their well kept secret doctrine perished with only the "ceremony" and "tradition" remaining. This gradually degenerated into an obscene orgy, a hotbed of vices and crimes, which threatened the Folk with total depravity; the witches' dances had actually become a danger in a different sense than the witch trial judges had supposed.

In Germanic antiquity, however, and even in the early Christian Middle Ages, these meetings were led by the academically trained skalds. Even then, these festivals and dances were not without their excesses, but these erotic ceremonies had deep mythic grounds; they were based on nature religion and were not of the demoralizing sort; simply put, these mysteries were completely analogous to the Dionysian mysteries of the ancients.

These Wuotan mysteries referred to the fertility of nature and had a mystical purpose in this sense, to festively celebrate the awakening of nature to achieve a prosperous year.

But to recognize the parallels between the German witches' dances and the Greek Dionysian mysteries, and logically also between the "witches" and the "Bacchanalians," both mysteries should be placed side by side and compared. One will be amazed by the similarities.

Dionysus (Bacchus) is also called the "Nocturnal," as well as "Blackfoot" or "Goatfoot"; he ruled the Underworld with Demeter, was bearded and horned like a goat, for which he was also called Goat, a goat was sacrificed to him and the well known goat-footed satyrs formed his retinue.

Since the Blocksberg, or more correctly Bocksberg, legends[52] are quite well known, it suffices to only mention the resemblance to the goat-footed Devil, who is often portrayed in the form of a goat.

Also, the fact that the Devil sometimes "seduced" as a man (incubus) and other times as a woman (succubus) is held in common with Dionysus, who changes his sex according to the situation which is why he gathered male as well as female Bacchanalians. The Devil's green color is also Dionysian; the wintergreen, evergreen and the ivy of the jovial wine dispenser's sacred plants.

Also, just like the witches' dances, the maenads[53] formed the majority, and the musicians were not missing from the Bacchanalia either. Dionysian festivals were also celebrated on mountains like the witches' dances and both firmly denied entry to the uninitiated. Like the witches' dances, the Bacchus festivals are repeated three times a year and both mysteries took place in a circle dance, a round dance, with mystical incense—the witches' mist. Masquerades are common to both.

Not only the wanton dancing, but feasting and drinking were also common to both mysteries, not to mention the witches' kitchen. In the Dionysian festivals, it is well known that a man is torn to pieces during the Bacchanalian rage, cooked in a cauldron and eaten by all those present; such gruesome sacrifices are also reported by the records of the witch trials. Only later, when the celebrated mythos was forgotten and lost, when only the soulless ceremony was practiced, when witchcraft had fallen into total decay, they contented themselves with the corpses of thieves stolen from the gallows or the excavated bodies of children.

Human sacrifice should be remembered in the Dionysian festivals, since Dionysus-Zagreus[54] was torn apart by the titans and boiled in a cauldron; a German mythos on this matter is not known, however, or has been lost. But since the witches' dances were often held at high courts, under the gallows—because they

---

52 The Bocksberg in Saxony-Anhalt is the highest peak of the Harz mountain range. The Saxons made animal and human sacrifices on the summit until they were Christianized by Charlemagne. A large portrait of Wuotan was supposedly found there and, in more recent times, it is said to be the gathering place of witches and devils.
53 Maenads (μαινάδες): literally translated as "raving ones." Female cultists of Dionysus, who, in states of ecstatic frenzy, would shout wildly, engage in orgies and hunt down and tear to pieces animals whose raw flesh they then devoured.
54 Zagreus was a name used by the Orphic cults for Dionysus.

had built these on the holy sites of ancient sacrifice—and because the bodies of hanged thieves played a significant role in the witch trials, it is likely that the original witch sacrifices were first killed by hanging.

This assumption, however, is validated by a verse of rune song (*Runatals-thâttr*) in which Wuotan, as self-sacrificing priest, sacrifices himself to himself; the verse reads:

> I know that I hung on a wind-cold tree
> Nine eternal nights
> Wounded with a spear, dedicated to Wuotan
> Myself to myself
> On that tree of which it is hidden to all
> From where the roots run.

It is highly mythically significant that this verse not only forms the introduction to the eighteen runes, which are actually spell songs, but that it also includes the myth of rebirth which appears in the eighteenth rune song, which finds a remarkable confirmation in the mandrake myth.[55]

As a result, the Germanic faith united sacrifice with death in battle, which was also seen as a sort of sacrifice uniting the sacrificed with the divine; the sacrifice, therefore, is actually spiritual rebirth. All mystagogues[56] took part in this spiritual rebirth and earned the same merits as if they had been sacrificed themselves. Since Wuotan sacrificed himself, suicide as self-sacrifice was seen as equally honorable as death in battle.

This mystical philosophy is the secret doctrine of every mystery and formed the essence of the witches' dances in the prime of the ancient faith, and explains the human sacrifice.

Secrecy is common to all mysteries (even the modern ones, such as Freemasonry, nihilism, etc.); that the witch was not allowed to reveal anything, especially in the confessional, is a more than understandable clause of the vow to secrecy. This

---

55 German folk legend tells that the mandrake (*Alraun*) grows as a homunculus (Lat. "little human") beneath gallows where the semen and urine of a hanged man collects in the earth. Likewise, others believed that such homunculi could be created by burying the semen of a young man in the ground and then feeding the developing embryo with more of the same. The belief in palingenesis, the artificial rebirth of living things by chemical means, was common in the seventeenth century.

56 Mystagogue: Grk. μυσταγωγός "person who initiates into mysteries," was an initiatory guide present in the Hellenistic mystery cults.

also provides another parallel with the Bacchanalian mysteries in which the lesser tests lasted ten days, while the witches observed a similar period of time (3, 9 or 14 days); only after this time did the seducer show himself "in his true form," i.e., the neophyte had become an initiate.

The ceremony of the witches' dances is all that remained from the loss of the mystery mythos but that was also neglected because it was ultimately misunderstood itself and mutilated beyond recognition, leaving only the characteristic features. The witches' ritual practiced this mutilation by parodying the Roman-Christian liturgy. In any case, they did this from a very early time.

All that seems to remain of the ancient ritual is the baptism, the witches' mark (as symbolic sacrifice), the dance and the witches' cauldron; perhaps even the green color of the garment worn by the fornicating Devil—the priest parodied. All other customs and symbols only demonstrate the ridiculous peasant mockery of Christian practice.

In terms of Heathen mysteries, the witches' dances may have been maintained until the time of Emperor Otto the Great, sometime in the middle of the tenth century, after which, due to the loss of a strong liturgical leadership, the mythos gradually faded and was finally completely lost. The ritual vegetated for some time but eventually ran wild, so that the once solemn mysteries became undignified, vulgar and blunted. And so the witches' dances became a senseless, foolish parody of church tradition and finally succumbed to a cruel persecution at the close of the seventeenth century.

In the course of time, the original mystery was transformed by similar causes into not only a rampant orgy, but appeared to have also abetted other shady elements, notably vagrants, gypsies, and murderers.

Yet even here an important phenomenon is remembered, which appears to throw an explanatory light on the medieval unfaithfulness of certain persons as well as other unexplainable features of the Middle Ages. This is the Tannhäuser legend of Venus (pronounced *Fenus*). (More about this in my book: *Deutsch-Mythologische Landschaftsbilder*. The Venusberg, page 61, Berlin, Lüstenöder).

It was a serious error to confuse the German *Frau Venus* (Fenus) with the Roman Venus and to claim consequently that our German ancestors had adopted the worship of a Roman Goddess.

The name Venus comes from "*Fene*," which is how Freya was called in southern

Germany and whose name means "*Zeugerin*."⁵⁷ However, her cult bore a great resemblance to the Roman worship of Venus. Her priestesses were, of course, involved in the witches' dances, and the early Medieval *Minneburgen* and *Minnehöfe*⁵⁸ were continuities of her temple in the Christian age. But they also gradually declined, and so it happened that these "whores," as the Middle Ages called them, were declared unfaithful like all other female and male members of the pre-Christian priesthood and the ancient sacrificers, the newly outlawed executioners, who were consigned to careful scrutiny.

It is known that they practiced the now disreputable business of their priesthood outside the cities in the executioner's house.

But just as the laity performed lower church functions beside the priests of the Church (sacristans, beadles, acolytes, etc.), there were also laypersons in the service of the various *Halgadome*. Just as today, fraternities existed in the Middle Ages which often comprised an entire guild. So, every trade in the ancient German faith had its own sacrificial rites. The smiths sacrificed to Wuotan and Frô,⁵⁹ the bakers and millers sacrificed to Donar and the weavers and tailors to the Allmother Frouwa. In the Middle Ages, the bakers had an invocation on every kegel⁶⁰ lane, because kegel was sacred to the thunderer, Donar. Even more examples could be shown. These sacrificers, as already mentioned, did not belong to the learned ordained priesthood nor were they initiates in the highest degrees of the mysteries, but simply laypersons like every diocese still knows today.

Likewise, the priestesses of Venus were not "ordained" let alone "initiates," and therefore should not be confused in any way with the *Heilsrätinnen*. They worshiped as singers and dancers, similar to the lower levels of Indian *bayadère*.⁶¹

The process of amalgamation between the ancient religion of the Germans and Christianity has now been carried out after a full millennium. For this reason, one can declare himself a priest of the ancient faith of German ideals, because they are yet living. The blue *Halgadom* still stands whose vault is just large

---

57 *Zeugerin*: good breeder, teeming woman, mother. From the verb *zeugen*: to engender, beget, procreate, generate, breed.
58 *Minneburgen* and *Minnehöfe* were early Medieval gatherings where questions of proper courtly love were discussed. The events were hosted most commonly by a noblewoman.
59 Freyr.
60 A German lawn game similar to skittles and bowling played with nine pins.
61 *Bayadère*: a term used in Europe for the Hindu *devadasi* ("servant of God") tradition wherein young girls are married and devoted to a deity or temple and which involves dance performance aspects.

enough to serve as the temple of every unfathomable essence that is the embodiment of all German ideals, and it has not yet happened: the saddest age of the Germans, the age of the twilight of their divine ideals!

It is the skalds and bards, the German poets, who exercise this priesthood; but where are the *Heilsrätinnen*?

They are also living and will live on until the *Götterdämmerung*. They give sacrifice to the shining ideals of the noble Lady Frouwa, because Allmother Frouwa is the reflection of the highest German ideal of womanly dignity. Since the German woman, the German wife and the German mother selflessly make sacrifice to her venerable vocation, she has received the highest priestesshood and the worthy *Heilsrätinnen* shine brightly beside the Germanic queen of heaven, the deified German ideal of all womanhood.

Many say that Winter is approaching; but I reckon I hear the call of Spring.

That this may be so, the gracious Norns must grant it.

The Origins of Matter[1]

Friedrich Bernhard Marby

Translator's Introduction

The first half of the twentieth century was a very active time for occultism, esotericism, and various other mystical, holistic, and pseudo-scientific approaches to nature and the body. From the mid-nineteenth century, Central Europe had seen a rise in thinkers and organisations that were specifically aimed at the rejection of empirical science and Enlightenment rationalism, with the intention of "improving health" and purifying the bodies and minds of their followers and, for most writers, thereby improving their "race." Their notion of race, however, was not a biological category as is today endorsed by biologists and forensic anthropologists; rather, they had a mystical and largely philological understanding of race, informed by the writings of Johann Gottfried von Herder and Johann Gottlieb Fichte, who had toward the end of the Enlightenment contributed to the linguistic categorisation of human groups, and laid the foundation for the later discover of the so-called *centum-setum* isogloss between the eastern and western branches of the Indo-European language family. These early writers had suggested that there was a direct relationship between language and cultural groups, a relationship that was embellished over the course of the nineteenth century into the concept of the *Volk*.[2] This notion of *Volk*, tied with the Aryan mythology that was developing at the same time, driven by Enlightenment rejection of Christianity and longstanding anti-Semitic traditions, formed the racial notions of an Indo-European "Aryan race" of which the Anglo-Saxon and German were supposedly the highest exemplars.

With this background, movements like the *Lebensreformbewegung* ("Life-reform movement") arose, promoting a return to nature, water cures, and nudism (the *Nacktkultur*) as a means to improve bodily health during a time of rapid industrialisation and the correctly perceived social decline associated with budding consumerism and industrialised society.[3] In addition to these more benign goals,

---

1 Translated and introduced by Stephen M. Borthwick. The translation was prepared from Marby's "Meine Anschauungen über die Entstehung der Materie, wie ich sie seit 1924 in öffentlichen Vorträgen flarlegte," in *Marby-Runen-Bücherei* 3/4 (1932): 24-40.
2 Dorothy M. Figuiera, *Aryans, Jews, Brahmins* (Albany, NY: SUNY Press, 2002), 63.
3 See: Chad Ross, *Naked Germany: Health, Race, and the Nation* (Oxford: Berg, 2005).

however, the movement also sought specifically to improve the Aryan race through maintaining the physical health of participants, pursuing a programme of nudism and physical exercise that would later be adopted by the National Socialist regime specifically for this very same purpose. Alongside these physical health-clubs and nudist resorts were more spiritual and esoteric movements with the explicit desire to bring people "back to its spiritual roots," in much the same way the *Lebensreformbewegung* sought to bring people back to nature. Writers like Guido von List, Adolf Joseph Lanz (better known as Lanz von Liebenfels), Franz Hartmann, Rudolf Steiner, and others participated in a largely Theosophist-influenced "occult revival" focused on old Germanic mythological texts and runic studies. Much like the *Lebensreformbewegung*, there were more explicitly racist thinkers and more benign thinkers in this movement—the less racist thinkers included chiefly Rudolf Steiner, who was heavily influenced by Buddhism and rejected the racialist leanings of Theosophy to found his own Anthroposophy movement, which is still active among "new age" and occultist circles today. Chief among the racialists were List and Lanz, both specifically concerned with the "spiritual rebirth" of the Aryan race.

Adolf Joseph Lanz was an ex-Cistercian monk who took the name Georg upon entering the monastery and retained it in German form (Jörg) when using his later pseudonym and affected noble title Lanz von Liebenfels. He was the only one of all the esotericists of the period with formal theological training, having taken his monastic vows at Heiligenkreuz Monastery with the community of Cistercian monks in 1897 and teaching novitiates there from 1898 until he was ejected (or left, depending on the account) in April of 1899.[4] He developed an intricate Christian, albeit gnostic and heretical, theological understanding of the world as a conflict between dark-skinned "Sodomite beast-men" and Aryan "electronic God-men" who had been degraded by centuries of miscegenation, bestiality and other forms of fornication.[5] The goal of Christianity, he professed, was to imitate Jesus, one of the pure "God-electrons," in rejecting the practises of the "beast-men" and regaining purity, which would grant the Aryans various god-like, mystical powers. He called this alternatively "Theo-Zoology," "Ario-Christianity," and "Ariosophy," though the last term came to apply to all esoteric strains of thought with a mystical focus on the Aryan race.[6]

Guido von List, born Guido List but, unlike Lanz, having his noble "von" formally cleared with the Austro-Hungarian state, had a similarly Aryan vision of re-

---

4 Wilfried Daim, *Der Mann, der Hitler die Ideen gab* (Munich: Isar Verlag, 1958), 252.
5 See: Jörg Lanz von Liebenfels, *Theo-zoologie* (Vienna: Moderner Verlag, 1905), "*Anthropozoon biblicum*," in *Vierteljahrschrift für Bibelkunde* 1 (1903).
6 Nicholas Goodrick-Clarke, *The Occult Roots of Nazism* (Wellingborough: Aquarian Press, 1985), 227.

ligion, but was far more grounded in Germanic mythology and the Eddas, while Lanz worked primarily with Christian scripture. List's most famous contribution was the invention of the so-called "Armanic *Futharkh*" which he claimed was revealed to him during a period of blindness in 1902. These Armanic runes were largely an adaptation of the younger Futhark, but arranged in such a way that there were more adaptable to the Aryan *völkische* mythology. They would form the basis of Armanism, the official ideology of the *Guido-List-Gesellschaft* and the *Armanenschaft* over the course of the next few decades and have seen several revivals of varying degrees of racism after the fall of Nazi Germany in 1945. He specifically believed that runology was the key to spiritual enlightenment, and that the runes represented a spiritual inheritance from the ancient Aryans.[7]

It is in this continuous trend of runic esotericism and occultism that Friedrich Bernhard Marby began his work in the 1920s. Marby, heavily influenced by both List and Lanz, nevertheless abandoned their focus on racialism and specifically the Aryan mythology; rather, he used the Armanic *Futharkh* as a means to achieve enlightenment and insights into natural and supernatural phenomena that, like most other romanticists and esotericists of the age, he did not believe science capable of providing. His "*Runengymnastik*" exercises, developed in the mid-1920s, consisted of various physical exercises and meditations bearing the indelible mark of both various Theosophical occultism as well as popular *Lebensreform* naturism.

As much as his methods bear the mark of List, with mystical treatment of the Armanic *Futharkh*, Marby is not without influence from Lanz. Specifically, his view of the soul and of the nature of matter, exemplified in this excerpt from the *Marby-Runen-Bücherei*, is heavily marked with the Theo-Zoological understanding of the soul and of the nature of God. Marby proposes that the basis of all existence is in fact some kind of radiated electrical energy, and the soul is a direct reflection of the atom in formation and, subsequently, composition of positive and negative electrical energies. Marby, likewise, makes regular reference to a creator God who is of an electrical nature, further reflecting Lanz's vision of the "*Götterelektron.*" If one did not know that Marby used List's *Futharkh,* one might even think Lanz was his primary influence. However, in contrast to the Christian heretic Lanz, Marby holds that reincarnation is the rule, and that all souls exist for a time in a state of limbo before re-entry into the world. When they re-enter the world, he claims, they are drawn to certain points at which

---

[7] See: Guido Von List, *Die Armanenschaft der Ario-Germanen* (Vienna: Verlag der Guido-von-List Gesellschaft, 1908); *Die Rita der Ario-Germanen* (Vienna: Verlag der Guido-von-List Gesellschaft, 1908); *Das Geheimnis der Runen* (Vienna: Verlag der Guido-von-List Gesellschaft, 1908).

atoms are formed. Lanz did not touch greatly on the afterlife, but it can generally be assumed from his writings that he did not stray too far from a Christian afterlife, if he indeed did not stray into Aristotelian materialism, which is debatable.

In regard to his focus on rebirth and the soul's pre-life, Marby in fact reflects Theosophical influences, which themselves drew heavily on the East, specifically on Hinduism and Buddhism. Rudolf Steiner seems especially exemplary of this tradition, adapting Western figures (like Jesus) to a distinctly Eastern view. Such traditions are influenced by Enlightenment attempts (though they by no means *ended* during the Enlightenment) to "Aryanize" the figure of Christ, the earliest example being Voltaire, who insisted that Christianity could not be of Jewish provenance, and must be descended instead from the "brahmin religions."[8]

While Marby may have been considered unique for his refusal to adopt and pursue a racialist understanding of Armanism, he was far from the only "left-wing" esotericist. Nevertheless, few of the esotericists and occultists from the pre-war and interwar period in Germany escaped the notice, and censure, of the National Socialist state after 1933. Even the *Lebensreformbewegung*, which would later lend many of its beliefs and practises to Nazi public health policies, was initially suppressed. List and Lanz were both silenced, and their organizations forced underground to be resurrected later. Non-racial approaches were met with even harsher measures; in Marby's case, like his contemporary Siegfried Adolf Kummer, the Nazi state went as far as to inter him at Dachau concentration camp during the war. Marby was moved around three different concentration camps and would likely have died in one of them if not for the end of the war in 1945.

The article chosen for translation, "My Viewpoint on the Origin of Matter," is an exemplary work by Marby, including his doctrines regarding the creation of the world, the nature of the soul, the mystical approach to scientific subjects, and the discussion, albeit brief, of his *Runengymnastik* and the benefits of his approach. The article is also typical of Marby's arrogant tone toward the sciences, insisting, as so many esotericists of both his own day and beyond, that he has a deeper and superior method that the sciences can ever hope to achieve and, in the end, they can only hope to arrive at his conclusions later than he will. He is also insistent that science is ignorant of things he knows—not an unusual claim for mysticists, since typically occultists deal with areas science would never venture into, but in Marby's case he is attacking science on its home ground.

---

8 Dorothy M. Figuiera, *Aryans, Jews, Brahmins* (Albany, NY: SUNY Press, 2002), 16-17.

Building on the recent discovery of radiation and the new model of atomic structure developed by Ernest Rutherford, Marby insists that he knew what Rutherford would discover before Rutherford began to research it, specifically using the new (and barely understood) phenomenon of atomic radiation to claim that atoms originated by and large from this radiation, specifically focusing on the phenomenon of spirals in the cosmos to create a worldview in which the atom, the solar system, the galaxy, and indeed all bodies in the cosmos (*Himmelskörper*) are different expressions of the same spiral/spiral-axis structure, which, through their spinning motion, throw off radiation that eventually condenses into new atomic structures.

For all that is wrong with his view (most of both his own and Rutherford's assumptions being disproved later in the twentieth century), Marby did offer remarkably good guesses at phenomena that today are still little understood, such as black-holes and the structure of the universe. Marby does not mention, either because it is unimportant to him or because he did not know, the fact that in space things move in elliptical paths, while in the atom, things are surmised to be more or less round. Of course, Rutherford's atomic model, which Marby uses, has been displaced by several subsequent models, the most recent of which breaks entirely with Rutherford's orbital model in favour of an "electron cloud." Further, Marby makes no account for the neutron (which as of his time was yet undiscovered), therefore envisioning the atomic to purely be the interplay between positive and negative electrical forces.

Marby's fixation on spirals and spiral movements reflects this purely two-fold structure, and in fact is also reflective of the dualism typical of esotericists of the day (indeed, having a long tradition in Western thought as well). Indeed, it was heavily influential on much of the early revival of Heathenry, which is why this article has been translated here: far from being a basis for contemporary Heathen thought, Marby is nevertheless an esoteric giant, and an important interpreter and contributor to the early movement. His work, though heavily flawed, based on a contrived runic alphabet and entirely invented traditions, represents an important piece of Heathen history that has yet remained completely alien in the Anglosphere. In the interest of eliminating any misconceptions about Marby, an exemplary work such as the attached "Viewpoint on the Origin of Matter" had to be chosen to be translated and presented to the public without any attempt to "rehabilitate" Armanism, as has been done by dedicated Armanists like Stephen Flowers (also known by his pseudonym Edred Thorsson, under which he has written several Armanic-influenced works on esoteric runology).

In translating the piece, the greatest care has been taken to preserve the spirit of Marby's often awkward German while nevertheless producing a final product that is readable and smooth in English. Notes accompany the text to clarify certain areas where Marby references things that would be common knowledge to his readers but might not be so obvious to contemporary Heathens as well as to explicitly highlight points where the original presented trouble with translation in the interest of allowing Marby to "speak for himself" as much as possible. It should be noted that Marby himself had no footnotes in the original, so all notes are the translator's in this text. Some typographical oddities appearing in the original text have been preserved as well, to highlight for the reader the often amateurish character of so many esoteric and occultist writings of the period. It is the translator's hope that this work may be followed by other translations slowly bringing to light the works of various early contributors to the so-called "Germanic occult revival" for the contemporary Heathen community in an academic and informed fashion to prevent misinterpretation and error on the part of those who may be misled regarding these authors.

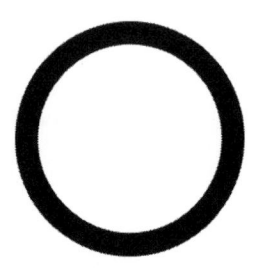

My Viewpoint Regarding the Origins of Matter As I Have Made it Known in Public Lectures Since 1924

The results of the work of Rutherford and his fellow researchers confirm beyond doubt what I had already found through my own methods (although these were and are similar to Rutherford's).[9] Contemporary science remains ignorant as to how an atom comes to be. It knows of free electrons, free out of space and out of earth as from an atom's own radiation, it knows the "material" value of the atom, of the molecule, *et cetera,* but where protons and electrons originate from and why they at once are united and yet act independently of one another are questions that science has of yet been unable to answer. Likewise are these questions

---

9   Ernest Rutherford (1871-1937), was a British physicist and chemist, called "the father of nuclear physics." Recipient of the Nobel Prize in chemistry in 1908 and credited with the first splitting of an atom in 1917, he is responsible for the "Rutherford model" of the atom, which rejected the prevailing model for atomic structure of his day (the plum pudding model). The author here essentially agrees with Rutherford, but his theory also nears Niels Bohr's suggested model.

The Origins of Matter

to which I brought important insights between 1924 and April of this year in public presentations and lectures throughout Germany and Sweden. In these presentations I referred to some self-designed and self-drawn slides, found below, which detail the *becoming* of the atom and of matter in the heavens and therefore as bodies in all space.

Readers who attended my lectures will remember their content well. I now publish some of the slides that give a glimpse into my basic approach—slides that I used in presentations discussing love and marriage, astrology, runes, and the likeness of the becoming of the soul and that of matter in stellar space.

In the images we see:

Figure 1. The *hagal* rune as a sign of the three directions which prevail where there is any space or any matter.[10]

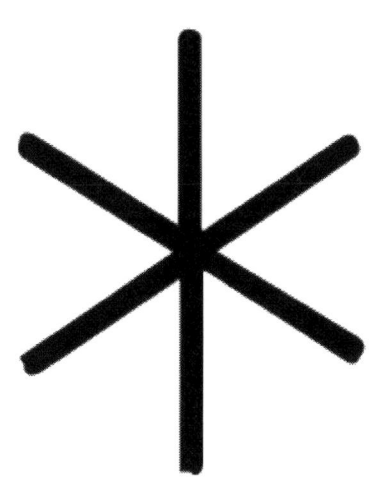

Figure 2. Stellar space shown schematically, using the stars as points and the axes, or mutual influence, of the stars as lines. Where these lines flow and meet (as I stated) something new arises in space: a vortex with its own perception. Materially speaking, this is the birth of an atom, and, spiritually speaking the point to which the human soul (a spiritual force-field) seeking rebirth feels driven. Thus can the spiritual force-field be linked to the nascent atom, that later it

---

10 Remember, Marby is working with the Armanic *Futharkh*, not any actual, historical Futhark.

The Origins of Matter

will be linked by sympathetic (electrical) attraction to the formation of the molecule.

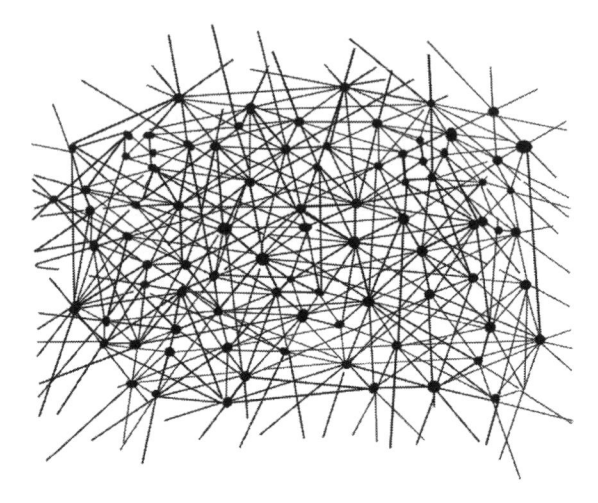

Figure 3. The same as the stellar space in *Figure 2*, but the stars and their radiating axes are shown in white.

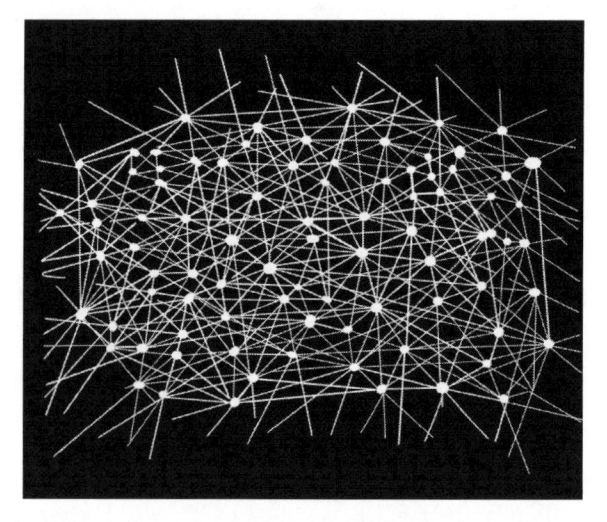

Figure 4. This image, following the schematic diagrams that were explained in my presentations, contains a celestial body (a sphere) with self-perpetuating spiral, evidencing that the theory of radio-waves cannot be applied here. A given electrical value at the surface of a celestial body is constant, and therefore the wavelengths emitted cannot be of the same measurement far from their source as they would near to it. Now, the spiral being pulled very tightly across the surface

The Origins of Matter

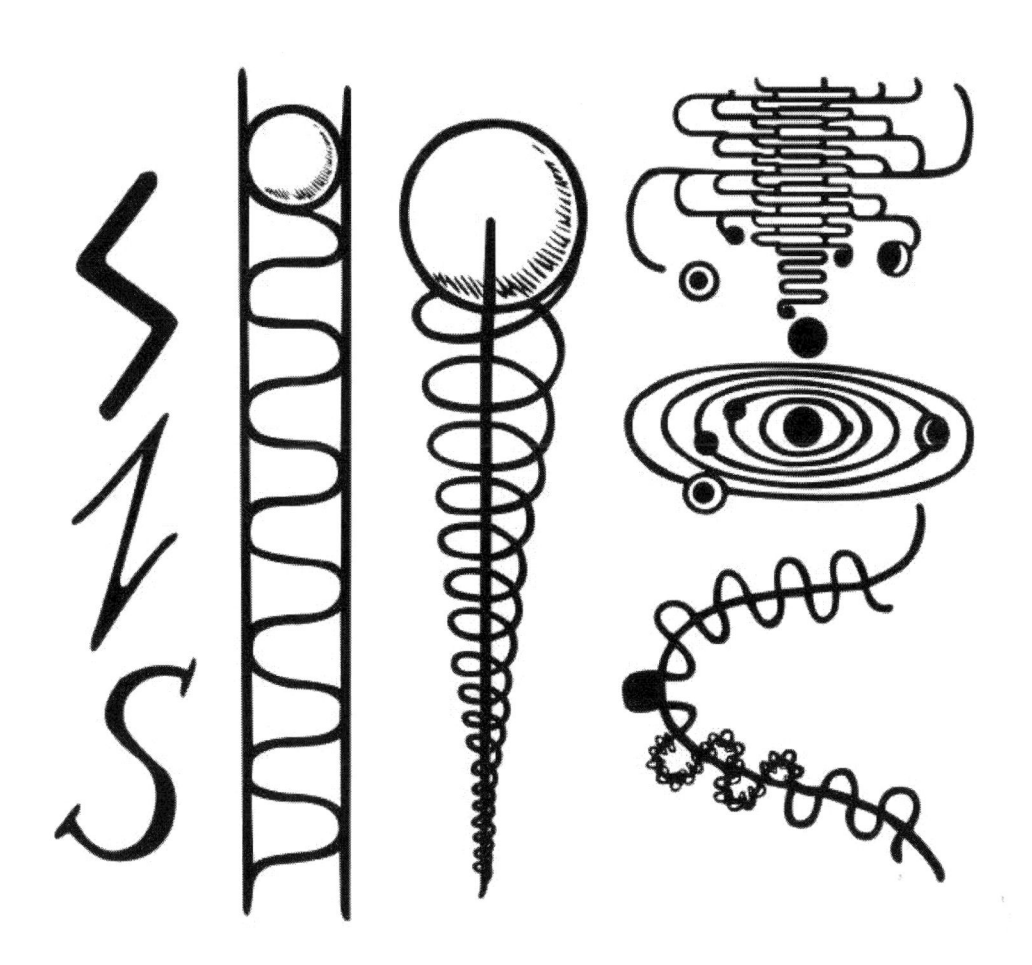

of the sphere, makes the shortening of waves from a given transmitter barely noticeable on Earth.

In addition to this image on the same slide is an illustration of the actual process: from a celestial body the surface energy flows to one side in a spiral wave; the spiral tapers, and its wavelengths are ever-changing. Within this spiral is something unknown to science—the *radiating axis*.[11]

---

11 *Achsenstrahl* is a term borrowed from physics, literally meaning "axis ray" or "axis beam" and referring to the beam of light that passes through the centre of a lens unrefracted, known in English merely as the "axis" of the lens. The German text differentiates between *Spiralachsenstrahl* and *Spiralachsen*; English makes no such differentiation, but to be as specific in translation in possible, where the author uses *Achsen*, it has been rendered "axis" and where he uses "*Achsenstrahl*" it has been rendered "ra-

41

Where this radiating axis and the spiral near one another, a disc- or lens-shaped vortex is created—the atom—which is now free to continue on as its own sensitive entity.[12] Meanwhile, even more atoms are created at this place of atomic formation (where the radiating axis and spiral meet). What occurs here is that, in the atom, the radiating axis forms the atomic nucleus and the spiral becomes the electrons.

On the left of *Figure 4* we see the Germanic *sig* rune (ᛋ), the symbol that our Germanic ancestors, who were aware of all that I have described, used to represent the spiral and expressed linguistically with the "S"-sound. Beneath the rune we see the long-S (ſ) of *Kurrentschrift*, but here the radiating axis is horizontal.[13] Beneath the long-S is the so-called "Latin" S, which itself was also created by the Germans, but is called "Latin" because of its shape, belonging as it does to a rounded script in contrast to the Germanic Runes. (Nevertheless, the "Latin-script" was once the font style used by the Teutonic Order).

On the top right of the same *Figure 4,* we see the movement of the planets around the Sun is, likewise, in spirals. This first image is meant to illustrate the solar system in cross-section. There are only three planetary spirals fully pictured—the large black dot under the tightest spiral is the sun, this first spiral belongs to Mercury, the next tightest spiral is Venus, and the last spiral belongs to Mars. Beneath this is an illustration showing the same, but from above. The bottom right-hand side one sees displayed an illustration of the Sun's movement, the Earth's movement, and the Moon's movement. Here I had to draw the spirals of the Earth and Moon crudely for the sake of the clarity of the overall illustration.

Figure 5 features four individual illustrations. On the top left, many star-axes (spiral-axes) are coming together in space, this being the point of origin of an

---

diating axis." It should further be noted that Marby almost certainly meant to convey the sense of an energy beam.

12 *Empfindungsfeld*, literally "field of sensation," "field of feeling."

13 *Kurrentschrift* was a form of cursive that was taught and used for handwriting in Germany until the 1940s, when the Nazis banned all German black-letter fonts under the influence of Martin Bormann, who erroneously insisted they were "Jewish scripts" (Bormann, however, was notoriously mentally slow, and could well have simply disliked them because he had trouble reading the fonts). Both the old German *Fraktur*, the traditional typeface used in German printing since the 1500s, and *Kurrentschrift* were halted, though an altered form of *Kurrentschrift* known as *Sütterlinschrift* was revived in German schools after the fall of the Nazi regime and taught in German schools until the middle of the 1970s, when it was completely phased out in favour of Latin cursive.

The Origins of Matter

atom with a compound nucleus or of several atoms, as well as, simultaneously, the point which attracts a soul prepared for rebirth (since the soul is a sensing cosmic electrical complex).[14] On the bottom left, we see an atom—specifically the interplay of energies during its formation. On the top right is a soul-atom, be-

ing composed of specific influences from star-axes and star surfaces; proximity and distance of the electrons is determined by the angle at which the spiral-axes meet. On the bottom right we see an atom, with the nucleus at the centre, surrounded by circling electrons, which is likewise an image of the solar system, with the sun at the centre surrounded by orbiting planets. Everything is illustrated here.

---

14 Original: "*die Seele ist ein das All empfindender Spannungskomplex.*"

I am publishing all of this, illustrated in hundreds of lectures since 1924, both to clarify the images in every possible way, as well as to show that I do not need to await the results of experimental science, which can only ever confirm what I have already discovered. This is the great miracle, though! The result will be the same when shown step-by-step as long as science continues to advance, even though the research methodology is different. Science can experiment and calculate and draw its conclusions, and I arrived sooner where they will inevitably come later by a different path.

My own methodology is grounded in the Germanic Runes, the old Germanic "fairy tales," which maintained the old runic expressions, runic customs, and runic traditions among the *Volk*, and clear, objective reflection grounded in the chemistry of my own body and in my soul—and it is clear that all of these several approaches of mine were necessary to yield this singular result.

Now, if science rejects my methodology—as they can—it has been shown in my lectures since 1924 (and by the clear success already experienced by disciples of my methods, advanced in the volumes of the *Marby-Runen-Bücherei*) that my methods do not lack certainty as science does—rather, they are much firmer, and yet I was able to reach these conclusions passively and incidentally, devoting myself to research in the midst of my day-to-day activities.

Now I will present one more illustration, showing how an atom with a double nucleus and two electrons forms, to further clarify what has already been said so far. I feel I must present this illustration here because in my lectures it made it much easier to discuss further observations (ref. *Figure 6.* "The Birth of Matter") in a level of detail not possible here—and now I should like to thoroughly treat this subject and cover all related questions.

The Birth of Matter

In the first decade of this century I was struck, as if by revelation, by the realization that the electrical energy that drives modern technology is actually only a superficial form of electrical energy, and that, further, the nature of electricity is based on the mutual perception of objects and matter and space and the mutual effect of objects upon one another. It further became clear to me that each shape that was somehow different from the spherical form must evidence the consequence of something at least partially destructive, but that a creative/formative effect can come from the surface of a sphere or its interior, as well as from its epicentre. Since the effluence of surface energy of the sphere (the celestial body) had to flow off according to the sphere's own rotation and its own locomotion, the surface energy of the sphere had to migrate in spiral form and, moreover, the result of the size of the sphere and the resultant effluent's wavelength in each spiral segment had to have been in proportion to the length of the spiral-axis itself. However, this spiral-axis extends from the epicentre of the sphere to the point at which the spiral-axis meets with the surface spirals of the sphere—the spiral-axis has its origin in the epicentre of the sphere.

At the meeting point of spiral and spiral-axis the nucleus of the atom is created, specifically consisting of a portion of the radiating axis that has become separated from the radiating axis itself. This tiny particle of the radiating axis "shapes" itself into an atomic nucleus. However, the portion of the spiral that comes so near the radiating axis that it is almost united with it, cannot cease its spinning motion, but must maintain it to continue around the nucleus being formed from the aforementioned segment of the radiating axis. The result is an energy vortex, an electrical entity, an atom in which electrons from the disjointed portion of the spiral particle are formed.[15]

In the atom, therefore, the motion of the electrons, originally from the celestial body's radiated spirals, continues, transformed from the spiral into these electrons. This movement will have to be approximately circular, because the particle of the radiating axis, having become the positively charged nucleus, does not continue its own motion. Where the radiating axis of the spiral and the spiral itself come so close together that the motion of the spiral can refract the radiating axis, this is the point at which the atom can and must form. We call this point the "atomic formation point." Constantly, newly created atoms migrate into this atomic formation point.

The newly formed atoms, since they no longer have a connection to the effluent sensation of their celestial origin, now have a nearly plate-shaped electron vortex as well as a *completely independent sensitivity to the environment.*[16] Thus begins an independent existence in the universe, an independent existence of an electrical entity that dwells in the universe but is exposed to a variety of influences. Each free-standing celestial body has a gigantic sphere surrounding it, in which the atomic formation points are positioned side by side. Since new-born atoms constantly migrate to these atomic formation points, each free-standing celestial

---

15 *Spannungsfeld*: literally "voltage-field," has been translated as "electrical entity" here to avoid awkwardness.
16 Here the author uses a rather awkward word himself, *abflutende*, the participial form of *abfluten*, which is most often used as a biological term meaning "excrete." Since the word itself is related to the verb "to flood" (*fluten*), and *ab* is roughly the German equivalent to the Latin *ex,* it seemed appropriate to translate it as "ex-flowing, out-flowing," thus "effluent."

body is surrounded by a layer of free atoms it has created, hovering at great distance. Radiating axes of the spirals and surface spirals that come together in free space at the atomic formation point typically combine into an atom with one proton and one electron; we know this atom as the Hydrogen atom, which, according

The Birth of Mattter

In figures one and two:

a). The celestial body
b). The celestial body's center point, from which radiates the helical axes.
c, 1–3). The spial axis
d, 1–4). The spiral
e). The atom formation point

In figure two, *e* is the point at which an atom with two protons and several electrons is produced.

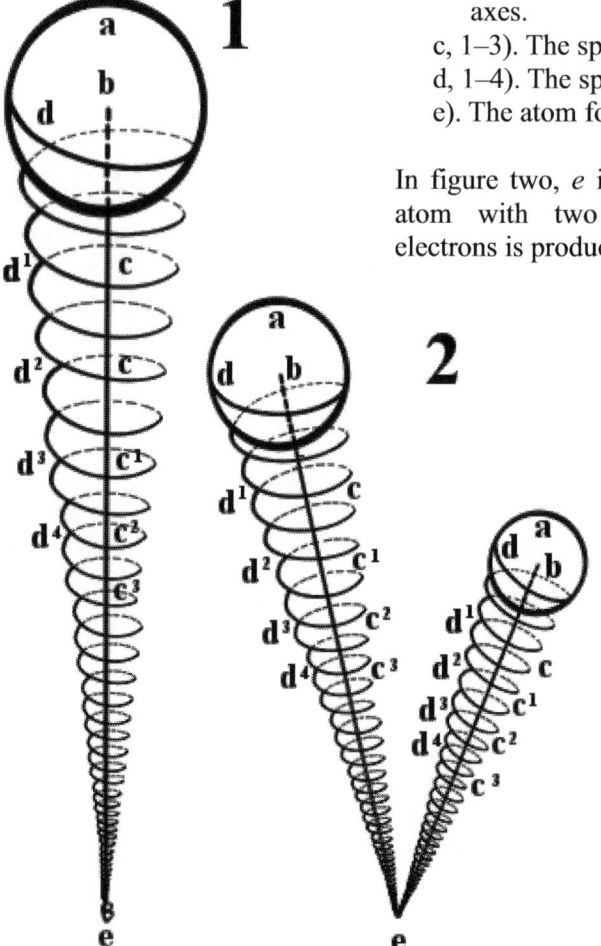

to both ancient and modern science, is the most frequently occurring atom throughout the universe—even in open space.

The physical state of a celestial body, the velocity of its rotation, and its general movement all reflect (apart from the size of the body) the wavelength of the spirals already being expelled. Where two stars are viewed from an atomic formation point such that they overlap, and where the spirals of the further star are so distant that they have no bearing on the nearer body, the waves, etc. are united with the common radiating axis of the two spiral-termini, and the result may be an atom with a single nucleus and two electrons. However, this position is extremely rare, and therefore the formation of such atoms is likewise rare. Thus, where in free space radiating axes and spirals of several celestial bodies meet with their atomic formation points, there the structure of the atom is dependent on the angles at which the radiating axes meet. These angles are standard according to the position of the individual core-particles in relation to one another, and therefore the nuclear grouping; the amount of electrons and the number of core-particles is determined by how many spirals and spiral-axes are involved.

It is firmly and unequivocally established today that hydrogen, oxygen, nitrogen, silicon, and iron can come into being and *do* come into being in open space. Modern science confirms this—what I had already declared in 1926 in a lecture in Stuttgart (specifically in the Civic Museum)—namely that meteors are not "fragments of celestial bodies" but rather merely substance formed from the radiation of the Universe itself, especially iron (in the vicinity of Earth). I concluded this myself because I could see ball-lightning and an especially large number of shooting stars at specific star positions.

The same applies to the formation of hail, snow, and rain—though from different radiating angles. This also means, however, that Hörbiger's "Cosmic Ice Theory" is flawed.[17] The Leonids are thus explained as the earth blundering into

---

17 The "Cosmic Ice Theory" was a pseudo-scientific theory developed by Austrian charlatan and mystic Hans Hörbiger (1860-1931), who held that the universe was made out of ice fragments and that the solar system was in fact formed when a waterlogged star fell into a larger star, creating an explosion that made the milky way (which he held was a grouping of ice blocks). The most significant aspect of the theory was the multiple moon theory, which held that the moon was made of ice, and that it was in fact the sixth of Earth's moons; all of the previous moons had collided with the earth itself and created great catastrophes like the Biblical flood, and this sixth moon was going to do the same. In addition to those he attracted with this doomsday aspect of his theory, Hörbiger also caught the attention of anti-Semites who were looking for an "Aryan cosmology" to challenge the "Jewish" theory of relativity. Hörbiger was famous for his nonsensical retorts to scientists who challenged his theory, and after the

a zone in which the state of the earth's axis causes a coupling of radiating axes in space and, therefore, the formation of "shooting stars."[18] The name "shooting star" is therefore very accurate. The different distances of the atomic formation points from the celestial bodies is typically dependent on the radii of the celestial body.[19] The length of the spirals is very great, since the interval between spiral-axes at the point of atomic formation is very small. According to this rule, there are still natural atomic formation points in the Earth's atmosphere originating from far-distant celestial bodies.

A spiral chamber always results from the division of its spiral into at least one electron.[20] The effluent spiral of surface energy from a celestial body can be captured by a radiating axis of another celestial body that finds itself in the vicinity of a denuded radiating axis, and this former radiating axis becomes itself partially denuded and attracted to the celestial body that is then located in the vicinity of this denuded radiating axis. *Cosmic radiation consists of these denuded radiating axes.* Similarly, overlapping spiral-waves can shoot out across the atomic formation point. Since then the spirals of the conductive axis are missing, free electrons are formed from these aborted spiral-particles as negative electrical quanta, then subject to the Law of Attraction.[21] Where the atomic formation point resides in the vicinity of other celestial bodies, an increased and more varied formation of atoms occurs, because the number of crossing rays there is significantly greater. An increase in radiation emits from celestial bodies (sun, planets, moon) coming ever closer to this kind of celestial body. The surface of a planet also plays a great role as a mirror, and through these influences the spirals

---

fall of Nazi Germany the theory disappeared into obscurity.

18 The Leonids are a meteor storm associated with the Tempel-Tuttle comet, a periodic comet that appears at intervals of 32-34 years, first seen in 1366 CE but not confirmed as periodic until the Tempel/Tuttel discovery in 1865. The earth passes through the meteoroids left by the comet's tail; their appearance usually peaks in November. They are called the "Leonids" because they appear to originate in the constellation Leo. The Earth may not encounter the particles immediately left by the comet, however—for example, the Leonids observed before 2010 are still left over from the 1533 CE perihelion of the comet.

19 The author here uses the Latin derived *Radien* but supplements it with the native German *Halbmessern*; only *Radien* has been translated, as otherwise the text would read "due to the radii (radii)." The author's appeal to the native German points to his intended audience; not only those uneducated in the science he was describing, but those who would favour the German form over the Latin.

20 Here the author uses the term *Spiralgang*, which is a German medical term for the cochlear duct. Admittedly, translation of this term was a bit difficult, resulting in the rather awkward "spiral chamber."

21 A "quantum" (pl. "quanta") is a physics term referring to "the smallest amount possible of any given substance."

of distant celestial bodies are torn from their spiral-axes; thus the spiral-axis becomes free, and cosmic radiation is formed. Atomic formation points that have fallen into some already-existing matter come to mind, of course, because an atom is formed that is somehow coupled, a molecular rearrangement in matter that is in some way and to some extent already found. Certain star positions can thence lead to something like the explosion of a munitions dump, and, even afterwards, can possibly cause changes in the properties of each material, depending on which material the atomic formation point falls in.

It must first be shown if there is atomic fallout in free space. In contrast, the atoms of a denser body can go into atomic decay where a nucleus is no longer able to maintain equal positive charge against negative reaction. This includes the case of the Radium atom. The atom is then dissolved into radiation; if this dissolution of the atom is meanwhile able to produce a new element, this element will nevertheless remain only partially resistant to absorbed radiation, which likewise is now indicatively in a different material state, but is at once also dissolved in the very same manner by which it was dissolved before—namely radiation.

Stray Electrons

The electron (or many electrons) is compelled in the atom to circle the nucleus, but as we know, the so-called electrical and magnetic processes are chiefly explained by the movement (electrical current) and aggregation (voltage) of free electrons. The electron, then, is a true globetrotter, a vagabond. I said as much in the title of this section, *vagabundierenden Elektronen*.[22] Thus the question presents itself: how do electrons become free? Electrons can become free through radioactive processes, such as if an atom disintegrates (as in β-rays). However, just as much as electrons become free through the disintegration of an atom, they also become free through the formation of an atom, or, in other words, if an atomic formation event becomes hindered or prevented. Where a celestial body's effluent spiral is decomposed through other interrupting influences on its way to regular atomic formation points, then free electrons (and free spiral-axes) arise. These influences have especial frequency and strength in their occurrence within the area of a solar system and in the vicinity of a celestial body (the sun, a planet, or a planetoid) as in the magnetic and atmospheric shell of a planet (e.g. the Earth). The surface spirals and spiral-axes will often be dissolved near standing celestial bodies, at least in the individually gathering trends, into free electrons and free radiating axes. Thus it is that free stray electrons are constantly formed in the earth's atmosphere, as in the magnetic field of the earth, and they

---

22 *Vagabundierende* can be translated as "vagabond," "vagrant," "stray," etc.

therefore suffuse. We are therefore surrounded by naturally free cosmic electricity.

The number of relatively steadily forming electrons must naturally become varied within a solar system in periods of especial solar events. Stray electrons can be united under certain influences and within certain relationships to hollow spherical structures within certain circumstances within electrical entities (ball-lightning, balls of light, et cetera). The stray electrons become attracted to positive fields (possibly also from a human body with positive charge [polarization]).

Independent Radiating Axes (Cosmic Rays)

Where free electrons are formed, celestial-derived and spiral-related radiating axes become denuded. The radiating axis now continues to move by itself along its original path. The denuded spiral-axis has either already attracted an electron in the empty magnetic shell of the earth and therefore creates a hydrogen atom (or many electrons and, influenced by other radiating axes, more atoms) or it ties itself with free atoms and other independent radiating axes in the atmospheric layer—*or* the spiral-axis enters into the Earth unconnected as a cosmic ray, in order to finally somehow be bound here or to move across the earth. The spiral-axis will always be driven toward its natural destination, to penetrate through its original atomic formation point—whence the strong penetrating force of cosmic rays comes.

The original path is fundamentally innate to the radiating axis, but the direction can be changed through lateral assaults of other stronger influences. Independent radiating axes can also be so influenced that they, especially arriving within the atmosphere of a planet, are transformed into short spirals. Whether still within a spiral or having become free, the radiating axis of a spiral forever persists as an interrupted ray whose individual parts along its length can be changed, especially in greater distance from the emitting celestial body. Portions of the radiating axis and the spiral chamber, though, always remain relative to one another.

Formation of Free Atoms in the Atmosphere

In the atmosphere of the Earth (or other planets) atom formation that unites Earth radiation (radiation emitted by living things or objects) with free electrons can also occur along the aforementioned original path. Likewise, rays can originate in the Earth or from certain creatures (where locally the same radiating paths always prevail according to a rule, e.g. with physical regeneration) or from objects, encouraging atomic formation along their course.[23]

Further insights will be added to this tract in subsequent volumes of the *Marby-Runen-Bücherei*.[24]

Final Consideration of the above Project for a Holistic Science of Radiation

Ultimately, all radiation and each wave is indeed only the means by which material and immaterial space are felt, and the means by which both their boundaries and their mutual remoteness, depending on their condition, interact with one another.

What radiates from a celestial body (or a sphere) is indeed not "energy," but rather the means by which these celestial bodies (or spheres) in surrounding space would be felt. From sensation (feeling), therefore, everything has become what energy is, what matter becomes and was. Just as in us a feeling initiates defence or affection, sympathy or antipathy, just as upon us and in us our perception of the things around each of these produces a sort of echo, so is it also in the world of "inanimate things," though we are compelled to let this last notion drop.

A thorough, in-depth consideration of the emergence of matter from the mutual perception of space—of which the first state before a celestial body begins to emerge must have been a current (*Rune!*)—leads us not only to recognition of that which we describe as "world soul," "planet-soul," "human soul," "animal soul," "vegetable soul," etc., but also to the recognition of the very existence of the soul.

I write this last part for those who are so far advanced that they are able to grasp the great *völkische* wisdom. They who cannot understand may put the thought aside for now; they will someday mature and the wisdom will be revealed to them.

Our Practical Application of the Conclusions of Radiation Science

That *feeling* is the primal source of the development of energy and matter proves to us the calculative results of radiation science, if we know how to correctly in-

---

23 Original: (*dort, wo örtlich immer dieselbe Strahlrichtung vom Orte aus herrscht, z.B. bei körperlichen Neubildungen*).
24 This single line was its own section in the original, with "Further Insights" being the heading, and the subsequent fragment below it.

terpret them. The means by which material and non-material space is perceived leads to the creation of events—as well as of matter and to corresponding design. *Because we, too, have a material body, we thus exist, whether consciously or unconsciously, with our ability, our evocation and creator of new trends and new forces that cause any occurrences and establishment of matter and structures around us. Thus comes into being the means by and the level at which we toughen our bodies with achievement of stronger sense of feeling and the direction in which we apply increased radiation, decisive for our destiny and the prosperity of our environment and our offspring.*

The starting point of all of us, setting energy in motion, is our feeling. This, the electrical entity that is formed before our birth, has a cosmic origin and also created our bodies, just as it also brings them to maturation, to departures and to enlightenment. Fragmentary knowledge about this voltage field has been preserved from the glorious days of our ancestors to the present day. The Church calls this electrical entity a "soul" and claims to want to "save" it. Harmonization of the electrical entity and its massive power surges is necessary in order than man be made in the image of God, which is only possible if anxiety, which must always cause disharmony and weakness, is avoided.[25]

Disharmonious electrical entities consume themselves by themselves, while weak electrical entities are absorbed into other electrical entities, which a true church should know—and a true church would act accordingly. Those who spread anxiety, even if they call their work "religious" or "scientific," are murderers of the soul.

Who makes it impossible that the electrical entity of another to strengthen itself and come to full effect, but instead endeavours to weaken it places himself in the way of the Creator, for Man is, considering his bodily, organic, and spiritual as a body of evidence, *the single being which to the World-order is the avatar of the Alfather* and his greatest instrument after immutable laws. Keen, clear senses of a natural foundation, a sharp, open mind and a firm, stronger Will to the Good, to Benefit, and to Development are the foundation not only of life, but also eternal life.

Thus, clearing senses, making sense of experiences, testing knowledge, targeting a goal, and strengthening the will must be taken step-by-step. All of these de-

---

25 *Furchtgedanken* is an odd choice here, and can be translated as "anxiety," "hesitation," and a number of other things. It appears as a word translating "dread" in Shakespeare's *Lucretia* (translated from *The Rape of Lucrece*); here, though, it could realistically be meant as "paranoia."

mands, however, merely summarize a tradition: Rune-lore in applied Rune-exercises. Training in those sensations, thoughts, bodily distractions, expression of words, movements, and emanations of the Will which Rune-lore opens to us in Rune-exercises and in Rune-gymnastics is not just a path, but the path, which transverses and consecrates our whole daily work, no matter what it is, and also the daily sacred tasks, which crowns us and, through us, God's creative work. *Out of feeling, thinking, and willing to force*, and applied *in Rune-gymnastics to consequence and construction!* Thus do we create not only in God's name, but also according to his Will, as instruments, but nevertheless as knowing instruments! And *this knowledge is the greatest happiness that any man can desire!*

Essays and Poems

Things are founded in the gods. Even during the phases of cultural upheavals, mix-ups, conquests, or times when culture loses its strength and its holding power in man's living situations, it is still the gods, often concealed and unborn gods, who are the cultural dominating principles wherein things are founded. Man's task is to search for them. Even during the 'Twilight of the Gods,' gods—concealed or withdrawn—carry the meanings and the realness of things.
—Vincent Vycinas, *Our Cultural Agony*

Huuetstêneslioth:
Lay of the Whetstone

Þorbert Línleáh

The following poem was composed in 2006 CE for the occasion of a Midsummer *blót* held to honor the thunder god himself. A poetic retelling of Thor's battle with Hrungnir, it was first composed in the Old Saxon language using historical meter and alliteration and then translated, sometime later, to Modern English. At the time it was the longest Heathen poem to be composed in continental Old Saxon, rather than Anglo-Saxon, since the Reawakening began.

Ôstar tô Etonhêm Allfadar fôr.	Eastward to Giant-home All-Father fared.
Strangna strîdigna stêneton hê motida.	Strong strife-seeking stone-giant he met.
Hros uuið hros orett hôfidgeld alsô weddi	Horse against horse challenge head price as wager
Etonhêm tô Ôsgard all dag rêd sia	Giant-home to God-field all day rode they
Uuôdenes gast in uuînseli sat	Woden's guest in wine-hall sat
hêlag halla Hringo drank mikil	holy hall Hrungnir drank much
Oberdrank eton egislîc uurisi	Drunk giant horrible giant
Thaulês Thuris thanclês eton	Thewless giant thankless giant
Baluuuord tô benken balugast hê sprak	Bale words to bench fellows baleful he guest spoke
Ôsgard tô bigraban Êso tô slahan	God-field to bury Gods to slay
Frûun end Sibbia fiund niman	Freyja and Sif fiend to take
"Ginôg is ginôg!" namom Thuneres	"Enough is enough!" Thuner's name
Regan hriop hlûdo radur giskuddid	Gods called out loudly heaven trembled
Thrakagaru Thuner Thrûthhêmes hêrro	Battle ready Thuner Strength-home's lord
uurêðmôd uuîgbald Uuôdenes barn	Wroth battle-bold Woden's son
halla ingeng Hringon starroda	Hall entered at Hrungnir stared
Êsono alo Eton drincandi	Gods' ale Giant drinking
Fagar Frûa fiundes horn fulliendi	Fair Freyja fiend's horn filling
"Huuê mid hêr godo halla inlathoda	"Who among noble gods invited into hall
Unhêlagum Etone Unuuerðum Thurise?"	Unholy giant unworthy giant?"
"Grimmes gast ik bium grið ik hebbiu.	"Grim's guest I am grith have I.
Skild end skarpstên scaft brang ik ni.	Shield and sharpening stone spear brought I not.
Ôtho in Etonhême ôs mahta ik slahan.	Easily in Giant-home god would I slay.
Greotgard thâr at god lêt ûs fehtan."	At Gravel-field god let us fight."
Êsono-Thuner orett andfeng	God-Thuner challenge accepted
Hrêosân Hringo an hros farlêt	Corpse-soon Hrungnir on horse departed
Thurisos Thing held thimmuuerk rekoda	Giants held Thing dark work prepared
Klei siu giskôp craftagum etone	Clay they shaped mighty Giant
thria mîl brêda thrîuuo sô hôh	Three miles in breadth thrice as high
Mistkalfe thigida mergu herta	Mist-calf received mare's heart
Lungar lîkhamo lîhtlîc sebo	Powerful body weak disposition
Mistkalf makoda managna uuatar,	Mist-calf made much water
huuand Tandgristo hêl Tandknago lam	When Tooth-grinder hale Tooth-gnasher lame
Uuedaruurhtio Uuinddrohtin brâhta	Weather-wright Wind-lord brought
Thuneres thegan Thioalfo also.	Thuner's servant Thialfi also.
Hringos herta hardstên thriaham	Hrungnir's heart hard-stone three-cornered
starkmôd strîdful stedifast it held.	Stark and strife-full steadfast it held.
foran ran Thioalfo fêkni râd hê gaf.	Ahead ran Thialfi false counsel he gave.

Huuetstêneslioth

"Undar erðu ôs nu cumid."	"From Under earth god comes."
On skild stôd scaðo skarpstên garuuues	On shield stood harmful-one sharpening stone ready
Blindandi bliscmo bibondi galm	Blinding lightening quaking roar
Rôdbardes regantorn radur opanoda	Redbeard's divine wrath heaven parted
Ôs end eton orloggitouuas	God and giant war-tools
Uuurpun tesamna in uuîghetie	Hurled together in war-hatred
Hêlag hamur huuetistên teslôg	Holy hammer whetstone smashed
Ôses missiburi ên skerd thruhstac	God's misfortune one shard pierced
Blicsmodrohtines bragenpanna	Lightening-Lord's brainpan
Thrûthuuangun theotgod Thuner libod	Strength-meadow's Almighty-god Thuner survived
Hringos hôfid hamur dôd findan	Hrungnir's head hammer did find
Ubilas etones êndagon quam	Evil eton's end-day came
Ferahlôs fiund tô folda drôs	Lifeless fiend to earth dropped
Maguiung Thioalfo Mistkalf slôg ôðo	Youthful Thialfi slew Mist-calf easily
Obar hamuruualdo Hringos bên fell	Across hammer-wielder Hrungnir's leg fell
Ênag Megino mahtigist ôs	Only Magni mightiest god
Thuneres sunu thria wintro barn	Thuner's son three winter's child
Êsono konsta hebbean etones lið	Of Gods could giant's limb lift
Etones ehu Allfader uuelda	Giant's horse All-Father wanted
Jû hildihlôth nem Hamuruualdos barn	Yet battle-bounty received Hammer-wielder's son
Galdor Grôa sang godcunnnies rûna	Galdors Groa sang god-kind's mysteries
Huuetstên tô lôsien hnifel tô bôtian	Whetstone to loosen forehead to heal
Theotgod Thuner thankful hê uuas	Mighty god Thuner thankful he was
"Sinhîuuan sîð ended sôð ik rekkiu	"Spouse's journey ends truth I reckon
Êtrige aha obar ik wôd	Venomous river I waded across
bar ik in birile baldna Êrendel	in basket bore I bold Aurvandil
hrîmuunda tâ hîuuaman farlôs	Rime-wounded toe husband lost
tâ Êrendeles tungal ik giscôp."	Aurvandil's toe star I shaped."
Sô glad uuas Grôa galdor siu fargât	So glad was Groa galdor she forgot
Hêlag hôbid huuetistên inbîdid	Holy head whetstone remains in
Êson âbolgie angimâli skerpid	The God's fury the scar sharpens
Thuneres thrâuuerk Thurisos dôðos.	Thuner's misery and Thurs' deaths.

The Natural Order and the Ensouled Folk

Stephen M. Borthwick

The Natural Order

One of the central identifiers of Heathenry, be it of the ancient or the contemporary variety, and one of the principle differences between it and the secular worldview and Abrahamic religions is a recognition of the spiritual significance of the natural world. There is a shared connexion felt between contemporary Heathens and our ancestors, especially of Germanic Heathenry, in our relationship to nature and the natural world in which we once lived without the refuge of concrete and steel that the Western world has gifted to the world in the form of the megalopolis. For folkish Heathens, however, this love of nature is different than the thinly-veiled materialism of the environmentalist movement or the occultic fascination with some "Earth Mother" concept like that native to the neo-pagan and Wiccan "religions." Rather, there is a true harmony with the natural and supernatural world in Ásatrú, a recognition of the necessity of our folk to use the natural world, and also of our natural drive toward civilization that has given rise to urban living, but nevertheless a respect for the natural incarnation of our Gods, a holy realm which, though material, has intense spiritual significance.

This is not to say that the proper Heathen understanding of the natural world is entirely material, or even mostly material. The Natural Order is far more than just "nature" in the mundane understanding. Rather, it is recognition of one's place, a recognition of a very real order of divine origins, a hierarchy inherent to nature, of which we are a part. It is an organic concept, one as ancient as the folk itself, which is native to the folk. It is a fundamental difference between an organic faith like Ásatrú and world religions like Christianity and Mohammedanism. In the West, religion, meaning here Christianity, has always posed the question, "why am I here?" Christianity has answered it definitively, but as Christianity broke up into various sects and eventually began to be replaced with a secular worldview, or by other, new religions, the phrasing, and the nature, of the question, remained the same in the West: "why am I here?"

The answer posed by Ásatrú is simple, and direct; it is found in the lore, in the belief native to our ancestors and to our faith of fate, of destiny. To fulfill one's destiny, though, one would need to know what one's destiny is. The Ásatruar, therefore, does not concern himself with the question "why am I here?" but rather, "what is my place?" Rather, the Heathen seeks a place in the natural order; just as "why am I here?" is the central question to Western religion, as it has been for centuries, "what is my place?" becomes the central, the deciding, the driving question of Heathenry.

Before, though, a place can be found in any order, it is absolutely necessary to identify and understand what the order is. What, then, is the natural order? This is a question that has been pondered by many, and we are not by far the first to consider the question. The natural order, as a natural structure, must encompass all things in nature—it must be reflective of what is seen in nature. This means, principally, a balance; it means both a physical *and* a metaphysical order, one which encompasses the individual, the folk, and the spirituality which unites them. This order is something permeating in nature—most obviously, it is apparent in a material sense, allowing man to see the categories and divisions to which observers of both the ancient and contemporary variety gave names of a general and rudimentary nature—bird, dog, tree, flower—and of a more specific and refined nature—raven, crow, oak, beech. It did not, after all, take Darwin to recognise that there is more than one kind of finch, or see the difference between the various kinds of oak, or recognize that, while incredibly similar, the plants we today call Baldr's brow and daisies were in fact different kinds—or, as the language of latter days has it, different species.

In addition to the differences that scientists have recently seen in the division of kingdom, division, class, order, family, genus, and species, revealing the intricacy of material nature's beauty as it takes new shape over the millennia, the order also applies to other revealed categories—such as those of inferiority and superiority, and of dominion and subjection. These latter categories are far more spiritual—and, subsequently, far more significant, than their previously mentioned purely material counterparts, and they reveal far more about our own species, our own kind; they reveal things that contemporary times have sought to extinguish —who, for example, is fit to rule and lead, and who is fit to be ruled, to follow, and to fall in defeat. This is not merely a question, of course, of raw power, but also one of spiritual sensitivity, of wisdom and intelligence—indeed for those who have only raw power and no access to higher Truth are undoubtedly those least fit to lead men. Unfortunately, the ancient order of rulership has seen itself supplanted in modern times because of the spiritual poverty of the time in which we are forced to live. Rather than the rule of the best, the rule of raw power dictates contemporary hierarchies—he with the most buying power, with the most political power, with the most military power. There is a reason for this—a reason why the ancient caste and class system of our ancestors has been supplanted by a contemporary vulgar system of wealth and power.[1]

---

[1] Cf. Plato, *The Republic*.

Once more, less well known, the class system finds itself reiterated in nothing less than our own ancestral lore. The *Rígspulá*, or "List of Ríg," lists four classes of men born of the bloodline of the god Ríg, who is Heimdallr disguised. His three sons are Jarl, Karl, and Thrall, which are three classes: the noble warriors, freemen, merchants and farmers, and laborers and slaves. The greatest of these, Jarl, was recognized by Heimdallr/Ríg as a man, and told "to get ancestral land."[2] His youngest son, Konungr ("Kon the young"), whose name is actually the Old Norse, *konung*, meaning "king," is not just taught the runes, like his father, but masters them, a sign in our lore always denoting highest leadership and direct relation with the divine.[3] Thus the priestly scholar, born a warrior-king, is the highest class—just as in the Hindu caste system. It is in fact, this social order of the ancient Germanics that would become Christianized and twisted into the class system of feudal Europe.

The roots of the decline of this structure can be found among our ancestors themselves, and in the aforementioned relationship with the material natural world they had. The ancient, timocratic societies of the ancient Germanic tribes, the Celtic peoples, and even the Spartan city-state eschewed coinage, feeling it was a corrupting influence.[4] Tacitus, the great Roman historian of the Northern tribes, was so struck by the Germanic disdain for coinage in his work *Germania*:

> Silver and gold have been denied them by the Gods, whether as a sign of favour or of anger I cannot say. Yet I would not claim that no veins of silver and gold exist in Germany. After all, who has searched for them? They lack the necessary interest in their possession and use. One can see among them silver vessels given as presents to their envoys or chiefs which are put to the same use as earthenware ones. All the same, those who live nearest us recognise the value of gold and silver for trade...[but] the people of the interior, being simpler and more old-fashioned, use barter.[5]

Tacitus was amazed at the practices of the Germanic tribes, especially this practice which seemed to pervade Germanic society. The Germanics, like other organic, warrior societies, regarded all metal, be it iron or gold, as equal, only worth anything for its practical or aesthetic use; wealth was determined by merit,

---

2 *Rígspulá* in *The Poetic Edda*, trans. Carolyne Larrington, *Oxford World's Classics*, (USA: Oxford University Press, 2009), 36:5.
3 *Rígspulá* 43:1, 44.
4 "Timocracy": from the Greek words τιμή (*timē*), meaning "honour", "worth", or "merit" and κρατια (*kratia*) meaning "government" or "rule".
5 Cornelius Tacitus, *Germania*, trans. A.R. Birley (Oxford: Clarendon, 1999), 39.

not by material possessions. Likewise, this shunning of material wealth must carry through to contemporary Heathenry, since it is the spiritual category determined by merit and honor which is the highest, far above capital and commodity, in importance to the Heathen.

This is of course not to say that the Germanic peoples drove material wealth out entirely; indeed the Norse merchants were and are renowned for their savvy, and the Viking raiders likewise for their greed: such desire for material wealth did most certainly exist, though not among the highest classes. For these, continuing through into the Viking Age, material wealth was sought not for itself but, rather, because one's loyal retainers deserved reward for their loyalty, and so land, and goods, and precious metals were given to them. Great riches, however, were never a warrior's want or desire: only dragons and giants, those creatures of death, chaos, greed, and evil, ever kept hordes of gold for themselves.[6]

The centrality of this virtue to the wealthy is littered throughout Skaldic poetry in the form of dozens of kennings referring to Kings and Jarls: "ring-breaker," "gold-giver," "disposer of gold," etc. Never does material wealth overcome honor; never would the miser or the modern tycoon ever be a respected man, for they lacked this virtue, this mark of honor. Thus it was honor and merit which supported this Konung-Jarl-Karl-Thrall caste system of our ancestors, just as it was merit that denoted and maintained the early Hindu caste system. Even this social order, however, is ultimately a material reflection of the natural order spoken of thus far. There is a separate, spiritual aspect of this order, of which the material incarnations are reflective and from which they derive.

A Spiritual and Intellectual Order

The spiritual order of the natural order is necessarily the highest order—it is what separates the natural order of Heathenry from secular orders established on purely social bases. The order on a spiritual level presents itself throughout Western thought, both of Germanic and non-Germanic origins. Just as there is a hierarchy of the merit of individuals and souls revealed in the caste system, so too is there a hierarchy of ideas—a hierarchy of knowledge and Wisdom which stretches from slave knowledge—the crafts—to the highest knowledge, the Truth bestowed by Yggdrasil upon our Alfather, and equally bestowed upon those who imitate His ways and His everlasting quest for knowledge. This hierarchy of knowledge is best developed by the Philosopher, Plato, student of the pre-eminent Greek mind Socrates.[7]

---

6 Cf. *Fafnismál*
7 Pre-eminent because his work survives the most intact; there is great value to be

The Natural Order and the Ensouled Folk

The appearance of a hierarchy of knowledge is found illustrated in Plato's *Republic*, but also elsewhere, as in *Phaedo,* in which he develops the nature of the Forms more. The theory of the forms is founded on a hierarchical epistemology illustrated in Plato in the form of the "Divided Line," a fixture in all studies of Classical philosophy from the most basic to the most developed. It will seem, because of the structure we have made here, that the divided line reflects the caste system previously discussed, but one must bear in mind that this is meant to be an understanding of higher things, divorced from and transcendent of the material world in which the caste system exists. There are two Divided Lines; the first is illustrated by Plato himself in *Republic*, the second is a construction taking Plato's understanding of different kinds of knowledge to apply these forms of knowledge to the caste system described above, which will show that there is a correlation to be found between the Platonic *Weltvorstellung* and our ancestors' *Weltwirklichkeit*.[8]

First, a summary of Plato's own Divided Line may be in order. Socrates (the main character of *Republic*, itself a philosophical dialogue) is discussing with his protégés the difference in perception—a central theme to the text. He constructs as an example to them a Divided Line, in which the different levels of human perception are listed. It is illustrated in Figure 1.[9] The line is first divided in two: the visible and the intelligible. The visible is then divided itself between "images"—the imagined or conceived—and "originals"—the actual or perceived. The intelligible is then divided between what we might term "scientific" and "philosophic" inquiry, the former of the category of investigation which is dependent on hypotheses formed from and investigating those things which belong

---

found in earlier writers as well, especially Heraclitus, the so-called "weeping philosopher," who, aside from being significant in his own right, was heavily influential on the German philosopher and historiographer Oswald Spengler, whose thought has generated a number of interesting readings of our lore and understandings of the teleology of Heathenry.

8　The English language lacks the proper terms to describe these philosophical concepts—the closest one might get is "understanding of the world" or "imagining of the world" or "conception of the world" and "material reality of the world" or "actuality of the world" or even "realization of the world". The former is an understanding of "why", a metaphysical theory that imagines how the world is shaped, while the latter is the material reality, an actual construction that shapes the world, as described in the caste system. The German words themselves are original constructs; we appeal to German here because it is, from a practical standpoint at least, a superior tongue for such philosophical expressions. In addition, unlike Greek, which is also a superior tongue in such cases, German also remains close to our own ancestral tongue.

9　Plato, *The Republic*, trans. G.M.A. Grube and C.D.C. Reeve (Indianapolis: Hackett, 1992), 183:26.

to the visible sphere, and the latter the category of investigation which does not use the visible, either imagined or actual. Perhaps a better way of describing it would be to say that the intelligible segment is the difference between physics and metaphysics, while the visible segment is the difference between imagining and observing.

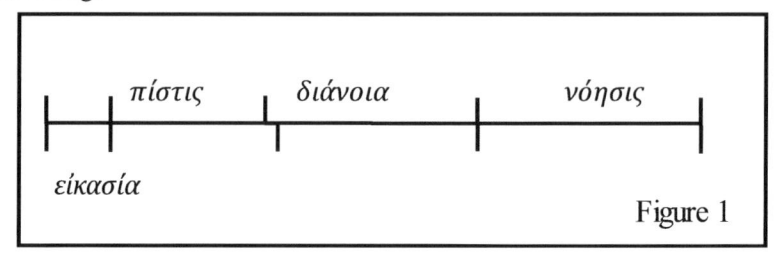

```
         |  πίστις    |  διάνοια      |   νόησις      |
|--------|------------|---------------|---------------|
  εἰκασία
                                                Figure 1
```

There then arise four categories on the line itself: Imagination (εἰκασία—*eikasia*), Belief (πίστις—*pistis*), Knowledge (διάνοια—*dianoia*), and Understanding (νόησις—*noēsis*). Imagination is almost exactly as the word suggests; it is the capacity to and the act of imagining beings and actions in the mind. Belief is somewhat more difficult: it can perhaps better be phrased as "opinion"; to fully understand what is meant here would require a full exposition into Platonic thought, which is most certainly a digression not worth making. One should imagine "opinion" as being a claim to knowledge of which one cannot be sure; to see things in the world is only to see them as they appear—Plato's Socrates supposes that the fundamental nature of the thing is obscured by the apparent nature; therefore, to behold something's apparent nature—*pistis*—is only to *opine*, not actually to *know*.[10] This is why "Imagination" and "Belief" belong to the Visible half of the line. Knowledge, on the other hand, is the certitude that testing and questioning produce; it is investigation into the actual nature of the thing based on the apparent nature of the thing. Thus it produces something higher than opinion, but lower than the highest perception, which is Understanding. Understanding is achieved only through investigation—in rough translation—of the actual nature standing by itself. In other words, it is investigation of things in their pure form; indeed, Plato uses the term "Form" to describe this purity.

This is the original Theory of the Divided Line. Using Socrates' various forms of knowledge spoken of throughout the text, however, it is possible to construct a new divided line to similar effect but using different categories. Rather than looking at perception of the world, as Plato's original Divided Line does, this divided line will look at potential for understanding of the world. To do this, it is necessary to discuss the different kinds of knowledge that appear in *Republic*.

---

10 Plato, *The Republic*, 182.

The lowest form of knowledge for Plato spawns the lowest form of man: *technē* (τέχνη), technological skill, or, literally, "art." This "art" should be understood as the root of "artificial" not a form of aesthetics. It is a craft, a skill, an ability to make or unmake, do or undo something physically. All men have some form of technological skill, and therefore know *technē*. It is the lowest form and farthest from Truth, able only to imitate. The caste born of this level of knowledge are the slaves, themselves unable to grasp anything more than mere craft, fit only to be common laborers and craftsmen.

We see already the four-fold caste system articulated in the Hindu and Germanic cultures taking shape in Platonic epistemology, but it takes more than one parallel to make a system. Figure 2 illustrates the divided line, showing the distances one must travel from the lowest to the highest form of knowledge. As one can see, above *technē* is *doxa* (δόξα), or "opinion"; more properly, it denotes discernment and ability to appraise superior from inferior, especially in terms of goods and services. To see such a thing elevated perhaps might strike the contemporary man as odd if he takes for granted the discerning ability of all human beings—many simply cannot do it. This did not escape Plato or his students, who elevated those who had the capacity for opinion and appraisal above those who lacked the ability for such a thing. To continue the parallel, let us ask: what is the primary skill of the merchant, the buyer and seller of wares? Is it not appraisal, of discernment, opinion, and persuasion? All of these things are those things directly associated with *doxa*.

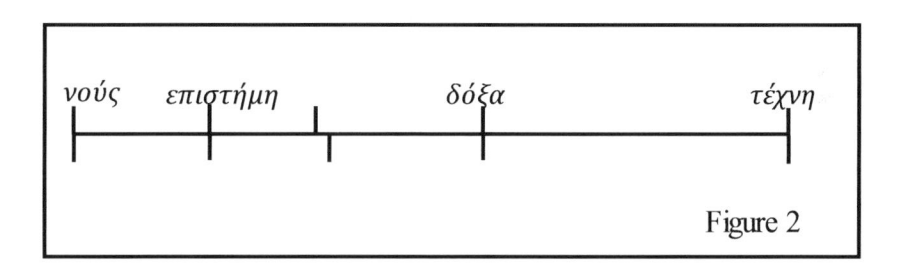

| νούς | επιστήμη | δόξα | τέχνη |

Figure 2

As displayed in Figure 2, *doxa* and *technē* are roughly the same distance from each other; the next step up from *doxa*, however, is significantly closer to the highest form of knowledge than any other form of knowledge. Above the ability to make and appraise is *epistēmē* (επιστήμη), which is "understanding," "knowledge," or "science."[11] This is perceived knowledge; it is scholastic understanding—it is the understanding of things that are greater than merely the practical

---

11 Of course, "knowledge" and "science" here are practically synonyms, since "science" itself comes from Latin *scio,* meaning "to know."

and merely the substantive. Only a few have the perception necessary to access this sort of knowledge; some have the ability to access some of it—they are not relegated to the realm of *doxa*, but are likewise not able to fully access *επιστήμη*. Aristotle would develop a concept that may be useful for making sense of this—*endoxa* (ἔνδοξα), which is *doxa* that has been made into tradition by authority figures. In short, the customs and law handed down by the Konung, the lawspeaker, the *goði*, and obeyed by the warrior class. Herein resides, for argument's sake, the separation of the warrior, the doer of deeds, the *Jarl* and the scholar, the thinker, the priest, the *Konung*.

The Forms

One will notice no discussion has yet been made of the highest point on the second divided line. This is *nous* (νοῦς), which to Plato represented both the immortal (for him, rational) part of the human soul and also the highest form of knowledge, the Greater Forms and the Form of Good. This is not the mundane, a realm in which the other three kinds of knowledge reside (much like the first three segments of the original Divided Line all share connexion to the Visible World). Rather, this highest point, wisdom, should be understood to be divine. Thus we see that the natural order discussed so far is alive here in Plato: an order of both the mundane and the divine, of both the human and holy. In Platonic thought, the *nous*, and its counterpart *noēsis* can be identified with Plato's Forms, which can be discerned by us as *idea* (ἰδέα) or *eidos* (εἶδος), both from the proto-Indo-European "weid-", meaning "see" or "discern."[12] Later philosophers would make a juxtaposition of the forms as they appear to us—as *phainomena* (φαινόμενα)—and the Forms in their pure state—as *noumena* (νοούμενα).[13] The Forms in their pure state, however, are not discernable by the senses—in short they cannot be accessed through the means made available by *epistēmē*.

Plato expresses the *nous*, the Forms, as the natural order in its pure state, mentioned elsewhere as the Truth inherent to Yggdrasil, that same Truth and higher wisdom sought after by the Alfather. In the Platonic dialogue *Phaedo*, in which his Socrates says:

> And the earth itself is set in heaven, a pure thing in pure surroundings, in which the stars are situated, and which most of those who usually describe such things name "aether"; it's from

---

12 In the words of David Gallop, "the 'theory of the forms'…is a modern collocation which does not correspond to any wording of Plato's own, but which usefully picks out a *leitmotif* recurring in many of his dialogues." Plato, *Phaedo*, trans. David Gallop (Oxford: Clarendon, 1999), x.
13 Cf. Immanuel Kant, *Critique of Pure Reason*, Book II, Chapter 3.

> this that these elements are the dregs, and continually flow into the hollows of the earth. Now we ourselves are unaware that we live in its hollows, and think that we live above the earth—just as if someone living at the bottom of the ocean were to think he lived above the sea, and seeing the sun and the stars through the water, were to imagine that the sea was heaven, and yet through slowness and weakness had never reached the surface of the sea, nor emerged…and seen how much purer and fairer it really is than their world, nor had heard this from anyone else who had seen it.[14]

Let us not make the mistake, either, of thinking that Socrates speaks in purely material terms. Like in the other Platonic dialogues, when Plato's characters discuss, and especially when Socrates speaks, they speak in allegories and metaphor—the "hollow" into which Socrates places humanity is a spiritual hollow, not a physical hollow:

> Living in some hollow of the earth, we think we live above it, and we call the air "heaven," as if this were heaven and the stars moved through it; whereas the truth is just the same—because of our weakness and slowness, we are unable to pass through to the summit of the air; for were anyone to go to its surface…if his nature were able to bear the vision, he would realize that this is the true heaven, the genuine light, and the true earth. For this earth of ours, and its stones and all the region here, are corrupted and eaten away, as are the things in the sea by the brine.[15]

The Forms incarnate themselves before us as this earth, just as the fish sees things through the surface of the water and they are corrupted, so too in Plato's vision the imitators of the Forms in our world are "corrupted and eaten away" compared with the Divine World—a concept not foreign in the lore itself, for it is the imperfect and corroded nature of the world, with its evil, lies, treachery, etc. which makes the purging fire of Ragnarök necessary. Admittedly, after Ragnarök it remains unclear whether the new world is purified, since Níðhögg survives along with many of the Gods, but it is clear that the world is admitted in the lore as being imperfect and in need of purging fire. Plato merely takes this notion of an imperfect world and proposes a perfect world of the Forms. Rather than think of this as another world, as we envision the Nine Worlds, perhaps it is better to consider it *part* of this world, but completely inaccessible to the human mind de-

---

14 Plato, *Phaedo*, 69.
15 Ibid.

pendant on knowledge discerned from what is perceived either in the mind or by the senses.

Having discussed and explained the Forms, at least partially, enough has been said to provide a decent foundation of the Platonic vision of the spiritual aspect of the natural order. The key is that for Plato (and his mouthpiece Socrates) it is men's desires which define their potential. The castes described above, for example, exist because members of each caste have different desires in their lives. Plato's Producers (merchants and workers) desire material wealth, and are entirely worldly-minded, craving material things, chief among them money. The Auxiliaries, the warrior class, desire honour and glory—things which are abstract and cannot be measured in material price, and which can only be attained through fulfillment of duty. Finally, the Guardians, the scholars, philosophers, and priests, desire wisdom, a craving found in the very word to describe their work—*philosophia* (φιλοσοφία), from *philos* (φίλος), meaning "love" (cf. "biblio**phile**") and *sophia* (σοφία), meaning "wisdom" (cf. "**sophi**st"). Desire is a driving force in Plato's Cave, because for Plato *desire* is the ruler of the soul, and the entire discussion of his *Republic* is, ultimately, rulership.

Significance to Heathenry

Rulership, though, is not the concern of theology; theology is the exploration of the relationship to the Divine. In this sense, the discussion of desires is very important. The desires of the Gods define their relationship to us. Óðinn is the highest God, the ruler God; what is his desire? Is it not knowledge and wisdom?

> I know that I hung on a windy tree,
> nine long nights,
> wounded with a spear, dedicated to Odin,
> myself to myself,
> upon that tree of which no man knows
> whence the roots run.
>
> No bread did they give me, nor drink from a horn;
> downwards I peered,
> I took up the runes—screaming I took them,
> then I fell back from there.[16]

So runs *Hávamál* 138-139, the core passages of the most holy book of Ásatrú, and arguably the foundation of our very faith. The name Yggdrasil itself comes

---

16 *Hávamál*, 138-139.

from this ultimate act of sacrifice that defines Óðinn's character—*Yggr*, meaning 'the Terrible One," one of the many names of Óðinn listed in the *Gylfaginning*, and "*drasil*" meaning "steed" or "mount." Thus is Yggdrasil named—"The Terrible One's Steed," or "Óðinn's Mount"—such that Yggdrasil itself is defined by this ultimate act on the part of the High One.

Thus do the Gods themselves reflect the social hierarchy derived of the natural order: the God of wisdom, of poesy (our ancestors' vehicle for history and tradition), and of magic (supernatural power—let it not be corrupted as "magick" or other such contemporary nonsense) is the chief of all Gods. It is no mistake that it should be His Son who is second to him, the Giant-slayer, Þórr, the greatest warrior of the Gods.[17] No God is of the lower castes—the slaves, the labourers, the merchants—which reflects the distance those of these classes are from the holy, and why they, like their higher counterparts, are fit for their role. Plato's understanding of the various forms of knowledge, and the difference in classes based on desire, is heavily reflective of these spiritual realities, which is what makes it so useful in illustrates the Natural Order of Yggdrasil to which even the Gods are subject in our Faith. Specifically, it illustrates that the Natural Order is not just a material order but a spiritual and intellectual order as well, and in so doing illustrating its totality and completeness.

It is this completeness which lends the order its holy nature. The word "holy" does not sound like the word "whole" for no reason—the words are similarly derived. "Holy" is a concept native to our people, it is a word which was adopted into the Christian lexicon and altered in the process. Here, too, is evidence that our ancestors shared Plato's understanding of the world as corrupted and incomplete—for "holy," the German *heil*, is a cognate of "whole," "hale," "heal," "healthy," and "hail," the latter a wish of good health. Ultimately, the concept is one of completeness and of totality, a totality which mundane things and environs lack. Thus it is that the natural order is holy because it is whole, it is spiritual and material, metaphysical and physical, reflected in society, in nature, and even among the Gods. Our relationship as humans to this order, however, is unique. Like the Gods, we are able to ignore it or alter our culture and society to no longer reflect it; unlike the Gods, we are ignorant and arrogant enough to actually

---

17 Of course, there should be no confusion on one point: no singular, steady, and universal pantheon was ever established amongst our ancestors; the Gods they worshiped depended largely on individual tribes and specific environment. Using Óðinn and Þórr to illustrate this point suggests no requirement to worship either, or suggestion that all of our ancestors did worship one or the other—after all, if the cult of either were universal, it would defy the natural order that insists on lower castes existing. It makes sense that only those with the inherent intellect and natural ability to recognize the natural order should worship according to that order.

employ this ability, and we are wrights of our own destruction when we do.

Plato speaks of education to spawn the philosopher-king, for as he said famously, "until philosophers rule as kings in cities or those who are now called kings and leading men genuinely and adequately philosophize, that is, until political power and philosophy entirely coincide...cities will have no rest from evils, Glaucon, nor, I think, will the whole human race."[18] This is not to say that the Platonic understanding of "evil" or even his understanding of "philosopher" need necessarily be adopted by our people, but this famous Socratic saying is of immense value because it is the declaration that until the natural order is properly recognized, the evils of the world will continue to multiply. Our ancestors took for granted that the natural order was recognized and would remain so—this is how they preserved an organic society and organic faith until the coming of Christianity.

It was with the earliest conversions of our folk that the corruption of the natural order began to creep—for the Christian quest after the afterlife encourages rejection of this world as utterly corrupted and completely divorced from divinity. It sees the world not in a hierarchical structure, but dualistically. There is good and evil, corrupt and pure, the Divine and the mundane; there are no grades in between them except those which are seen in the material world, and since they belong to the material world they are completely material. This understanding was never explicitly stated; no decision was suddenly made that the natural order observed by our ancestors was suddenly going to vanish—rather, it is reflective of a changing psychology of the people, such that it ceased to be the wise and noble liege who gathered riches only as a means and became the affluent noble who sought riches and opulence as an end alone. The word "noble" ceased to be a revered adjective and became a mundane noun, to denote a social class with more material wealth than any other.

It should be understood that this state of affairs has nothing to do with Christianity being a greedy or inherently evil religion—rather, it is because the dualism of Christianity, which was organic for the Hebrews and their Semitic brother-folks was introduced into an organic order to which it was essentially foreign. For other folks, among them the Hebrews, a dualistic order is native, and it is best; for others, it is not native, and it is therefore not best. The folk to which we belong is independent, it is its own, but it has its own earliest incarnation as well. Just as once there were only a few incarnate souls, so too once there were only a few incarnate folk-souls. Just as the oak, when it is at its mightiest, its greatest height, drops acorns, formed of itself and carrying nothing new within them except potential to replace, in unique forms, the old oak, these ancient folks, too planted

---

18 Plato, *The Republic*, 148.

seeds in the soil, and from them sprung the folks which we know. There is wisdom of this to be found in the ambiguity of Ragnarök: Ragnarök is yet to be, but it has also already been. The Indo-European, or Aryan, folk has come to pass, it has known its Ragnarök, just as the Semitic folk has, and the Turkic folk has, and the African folk has. It is the saplings grown of their acorns which constitute the folks we know today, many of which have been pruned by outside forces, interfering with and hindering their growth, as Christianity and Mohammedanism have done. It is therefore the return to our ancestral faith, the faith organic and native to our folk, which shall once again allow it to grow and mature as it should, to its fullest extent and richest potential. Recognition of the natural order is part of this return to the organic faith of our ancestors.

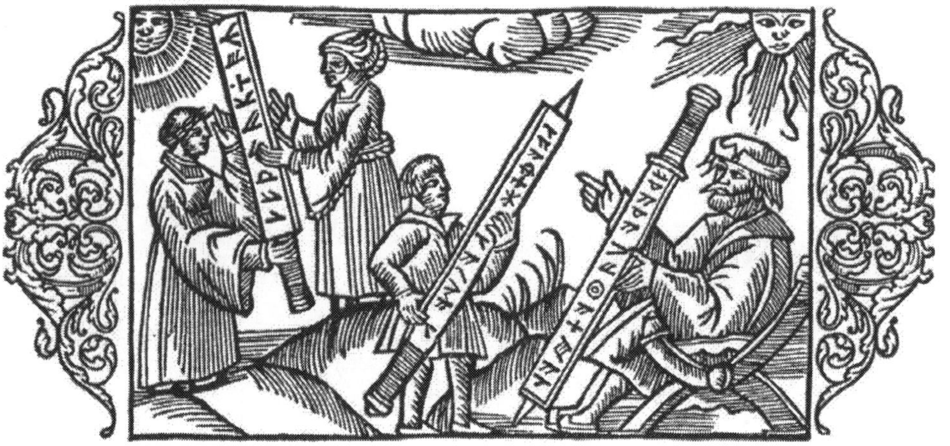

The Emergent Hierarchy:
An Evolutionary Recasting of Neoplatonic Polytheism[1]

Christopher A. Plaisance

Religion will not regain its old power until it can face change in the same spirit as does science.[2]
—Alfred North Whitehead

Introduction

This is a paper in the philosophy of religion, which draws upon a rich network of cross-connections between Classical Neoplatonism, archetypal psychology, and evolutionary neurotheology. The paper's thesis is that the Aristotelian reversal of the top-down, Neoplatonic vector of ontological dependency found in the writings of Bruce MacLennan serve as a foundation to rework Neoplatonic metaphysics and theurgy into forms which are rooted in the principle of emergence, rather than emanation, and thus arrives at an understanding of polytheistic theology which is not only compatible with, but fundamentally tied to, the process of evolution. This argument is explored in turn by first examining the essentialism and emanationism that originates with Plato. This train is then followed forward several hundred years to Plato's commentator, Plotinus, who developed Platonic philosophy into the four-tiered hierarchy of Neoplatonism. This treatment of the Classical Neoplatonists is rounded out with a review of Iamblichus, for his expansion of Plotinus's emanative scheme and insistence on the primacy of theurgic praxis. We then leap forward more than a thousand years to the psychology of Carl Jung, whose theories of the archetypes of the collective unconscious are shown to be a modernization of Neoplatonic metaphysics and theology. The paper then turns to the contemporary work of Bruce MacLennan, who analyzes this correlation between Neoplatonism and Jungianism in light of recent developments in evolutionary neurotheology and the emergent Aristotelian response to

---

1 This paper, minus the final, "Epistle to the Heathen," section was submitted as the author's BA thesis in the American Military University's philosophy program. It draws on two previously written papers: "The Hierarchical Cosmos: Occult Theology as a Direct Continuation of Neoplatonism" (to be published in the forthcoming *Occult Traditions* volume of the *Primordial Traditions* book series) and "The Ubiquity of Prehension: Panpsychism as a Solution to the Mind-Body Problem" (to be published in the second volume of *KannenBright: Concordia University Undergraduate Journal of Theological Studies*).
2 Alfred North Whitehead, "Religion and Science," *The Atlantic*, August 1925.

Plato's emanative essentialism. Finally, the paper, building upon MacLennan's reformulation of the core Neoplatonic process of contingency—which he principally explores in terms of the relationship between mankind and the Gods—extrapolates this Aristotelian recasting into a complete philosophical picture, which takes into account the effect that this reformulation has on the constitution of and interrelations between all levels of the metaphysical hierarchy. The resultant structure is one which presents a view that necessarily entails a panexperientialist foundational ontology, a series of polytheistic middle layers, and a culminating panentheistic vision of the whole—all of which is driven in a bottom-up manner by the principles of evolution and emergence.

As this work is principally a critique of two of Neoplatonism's core ideas, it befits us to begin with definitions of these two terms and a foray into their genesis. The first point to be made is that the fundamental orientation of Neoplatonic metaphysics can be characterized as *top-down* in nature.[3] A quick way to explain this is to do so in contrast with modern physics, whose orientation is thoroughly *bottom-up*. So, although contemporary physics and Neoplatonism both begin with the layer of reality that presents itself to the senses and both have in common a predisposition to produce theories which conceive of that layer as being one of many, each mode of investigation operates from a different pole. The physicist, seeing the ultimate causes of perceptible phenomena in the increasingly miniscule and atomized layers below (e.g. bodies are composed of cells, which are composed of molecules, which are composed of atoms, etc.) "proceeds 'downwards' by penetrating the subtleties of material or physical structures of the universe."[4] His orientation begins with the ultimate at the *bottom* of the cosmic hierarchy and proceeds *upwards* in the eventual constitution of every day objects; thus, we call this a *bottom-up* kind of metaphysics. In contrast, the Neoplatonist sees the material world as a whole, and views it as the *end* of a chain of contingency whose ultimate source sits far *above* the sensible world. For the Neoplatonist, the world of matter is conceived of as being the final result of a *downwardly* directed process, and is thus referred to as a *top-down* metaphysical model.

While the idea of this differentiation in the constitutive vector is indeed reversed between these two schools of thought, there is another key difference between the way in which top-down and bottom-up models treat the successive layers as being formed. Being our default metaphysical model, we understand the physical-

---

3   Pauliina Remes, *Neoplatonism*, (Berkeley, CA: University of California Press, 2008), viii.
4   Ibid., ix.

ist position that we begin with a bottom layer of *some* sort of atomized[5] sub--atomic particle, and from there simply build up larger structures by putting together particles like a child puts together Lego blocks. The Neoplatonist, had a completely different conception of what process led to the current state of the material world as we experience it. Since the kind of constructivism that the "building block" model presents is fundamentally bottom-up, the top-down metaphysics of the Neoplatonists necessarily explains things in vastly different terms. The particular word used to describe the way in which the hierarchies in the Neoplatonic cosmos are constituted has become known as *emanation*. In brief, this doctrine can be summed up as the principle that the universe has a single originating source, and that this source is "the most perfect thing we can imagine since there is no cause 'above' it. This one cause would generate something else by the necessity of its perfection, and the generated thing would be inferior to it."[6] This process then repeats at each level below the source, with each emanating layer being a poorer reflection of the one upon which it is contingent. At each layer the universality and singularity of the source decreases, and particularity and multiplicity become more strongly manifested. This process continues until the bottom of the hierarchy is finally reached: the material world.

Platonic Roots

Any treatment of Neoplatonism must begin with, at the minimum, a brief exploration of the formational system upon which it is largely a hermeneutic: Platonism. While a full treatment of Plato's philosophy would extend far beyond the boundaries imposed by this paper's size and scope, it is incumbent upon us to examine how the aforementioned principles of top-downism and emanationism originated—and their origins lie with Plato (428–348 BC). Both concepts are inseparable from Plato's doctrine of the Forms, making it a necessary point of reference in the present investigation of Neoplatonism. The English word "Form" (generally capitalized in connection with Plato) is used to translate two terms which Plato used for the same concept: *eidos* (εἶδος—"that which is seen," "form," "shape," or "figure") and *idea* (ἰδέα—"the *look* of a thing, as opposed to its reality").[7] The theory of Forms is outlined most clearly in the *Republic*, where

---

5   Unless referring to the proper atoms of modern physics, any use of terms derived from this root (e.g. atomic, atomized, etc.) refer to the principle of discrete, indivisible units of substance called *atomos* (ἄτομος—"uncut, unmown, indivisible") by Leucippus and Democritus. As a further note, all Greek orthographic and etymological notes are derived from Liddell and Scott's *Greek-English Lexicon*, 7th ed. (Oxford: Oxford University Press, 2000).
6   Remes, 44.
7   Frederick Copleston, *Greece and Rome*, vol. 1 of *A History of Philosophy*, (London: Search Press, 1946), 164.

Plato demonstrates his theory as a solution to the problem of universals.[8] To do so, he takes the example of a bed. The bed made by a carpenter, Plato argues, is "only *a* bed;" it is a particular instance of something that we recognize as belonging to the overarching type of phenomenon called Bed.[9] The particular bed of the carpenter is however "a somewhat dark affair in comparison to the true" Form of the Bed.[10] What he means by this is that the Form of an object is the perfect, universal—the bedness that makes the discrete bed recognizable as such—of which instantiated particulars are but an imperfect reflection. This is the root of the principle of emanation, of the notion that the sensory world of phenomena is the lower tier of a dyadic cosmos—a level of existence in which the plurality of instantiation radiates forth from a unity of conception. Each Form is a monadic unity; its nature is singular. All plurality that exists in the perceptible world is due to the reflective emanation of the Form as it shines from the upper level down into the lower. It is as if each Form were a star. The star casts light that is reflected in a myriad of imperfect ways as it penetrates the atmosphere. Yet these disparate reflections are all manifestations of *one* perfect source: the Form. Thus, under Plato's system the *essence* of the thing being considered is ontologically prior to the existence of the thing itself. This top-down orientation of Platonic metaphysics is the source of the Neoplatonic postulations that reality is both *layered* and that the vector of ontological dependence which leads from the upper to the lower is *unidirectional*.

A second element of Plato's thought that needs examining in order for the Neoplatonic hermeneutics to be brought into the proper context is that of the demiurge (δημιουργός—"one who works for the people," "framer," or "maker"). This term was, in Plato's day, commonly used to refer to craftsmen and artisans. In the dialogue *Timaeus*, the demiurge is described as "he who framed this whole universe of becoming."[11] If all existent phenomena are the resultants of pro-

---

8   Roughly speaking, the problem of universals concerns the relationship between universals (e.g. the idea of redness) and particulars (e.g. concrete instances of red). The Platonic position described above derives particulars from universals. Aristotle reversed this flow, positing that universals were dependent upon particulars. Both positions fall into the modern taxonomic grouping of *realism*, in that they both treat universals as being real in a metaphysical sense. In contrast to realism is *nominalism*, which treats universals as mere names for artificial groupings of phenomena (Michael J. Loux, *Metaphysics: A Contemporary Introduction*, 3rd ed., [New York: Routledge, 2010], 17–18, 41).
9   Plato, *Republic*, trans. G.M.A. Grube, rev. C.D.C. Reeve, in *Plato: Complete Works*, ed. John M. Cooper, (Indianapolis: Hackett Publishing Company, Inc., 1997), 596e–597a.
10 Ibid., 597a.
11 Plato, *Timaeus*, trans. Donald J. Zeyl, in *Plato: Complete Works*, 29d–29e.

cesses which are contingent upon antecedent processes, it is natural to suppose that at the root of this causal chain is a singularity that is the uncaused first cause —a being Plato's student Aristotle (384–322 BC) described so famously as the "unmoved mover" (οὐ κινούμενον κινεῖ).[12] The demiurge then, acts as the prime rational cause that initiates the ordering of the chaos that Hesiod describes as existing prior to the shaping of things by the Gods.[13] This notion of there being a *singular* source that *all* resultant order was contingent upon is the source of the One around which all Neoplatonic thinkers center their metaphysical hierarchies. The demiurge is distinct from the God of scholastic theism in a very important respect: he is not a creator *per se*, but is a shaper as the very word demiurge implies. The Greeks had no conception of *ex nihilo* creation. Something must always come from something else, there is no nothingness that exists apart from God; there is only the fluxating chaos that was ordered into actuality by the demiurge. Although in Plato's metaphysical system, there is but *one* ordered layer of reality for the demiurge to shape, the Neoplatonists had no trouble transforming this to suit the increasing complexity of their cosmic manifold. Furthermore, Plato is somewhat ambiguous as to whether or not the demiurge is ontologically primary.[14] Owing to this, the Neoplatonists who followed in his wake ascribed various upper levels of the celestial hierarchy to the demiurge, with some granting him the ultimate position of the One,[15] and other relegating him to the penultimate role of the uncreated second emanation.[16]

Plotinian Metaphysics

After Plato's death, there developed a dedicated tradition of exegetical and eise-

---

12 Aristotle, *Metaphysics* in *Introduction to Aristotle*, ed. Richard McKeon, (New York: The Modern Library, 1947), 285.
13 Hesiod, "The Theogony of Hesiod," in *Hesiod, Homeric Hymns, Homerica*, trans. Hugh G. Evelyn-White, Loeb Classical Library (Cambridge, MA: Harvard University Press, 1995), 87.
14 "Ontological dependency is a relation—or, more accurately, a family of relations—between entities or *beings*," as ontology (ὄντος—"that which is," and -λογία—"a suffix denoting the study of the preceding prefix") is the study of *being* (E. Jonathan Lowe, "Ontological Dependence," *Stanford Encyclopedia of Philosophy*, http://plato.stanford.edu/entries/dependence-ontological/ [accessed May 27, 2011]). In such a system of relations, those things which *depend* upon other beings for their existence and/or identity. The antecedent being to which these beings are dependent is ontologically prior. That which is ontologically *primary* is that which depends upon nothing for its existence and is, through the chain of dependency, that upon which *all* depends.
15 Copleston, 476.
16 Ibid., 467.

getical hermeneutics centered around his dialogues.[17] The full flowering of this interpretative tradition was realized in the philosophy of the Neoplatonists, a lineage of thinkers who flourished between the 3rd and 6th centuries throughout the Hellenistic world. Plotinus (204–270) was an Egyptian thinker whose "teaching and writings...form the backbone of Neoplatonic philosophy."[18] His writings, collected by his student Porphyry as the *Enneads*, detail the foundational doctrines of Neoplatonism. As principally a commentator on Plato, there is much in his thought that is shared in common with his antecedent, yet there is equally much innovation and development of root ideas found in Plotinus as well. The commonalities include:

1. That there is a first principle.
2. That there exists a plurality of metaphysical layers, each with corresponding entities.
3. The idea that "the metaphysically prior is always more powerful, better and more simple or unified than the metaphysically lower."
4. That reality is permeated by mind and intelligibility.
5. That the perfection of the top of the hierarchy leads to an upwardly directed striving in those beneath.[19]

There are, however, numerous ways in which these common ideas were modified by the Neoplatonists. For the purposes of this paper, the most important distinctions are the differing ways in which Plato and Plotinus conceived of the layering of reality. Plotinus, and the Neoplatonists such as Porphyry (234–305 AD), Iamblichus (245–325 AD) and Proclus (412–487 AD) who followed him, adhered to a cosmology composed of four or more emanations. The original Plotinian system comprised of:

1. *To Hen*, The One (τό ἕν—"the one")
2. *Nous*, The Intellect (νοῦς—"mind" or "perception")
3. *Psuchē*, The Soul (ψυχή—"breath," "life" or "spirit")

---

17 Hermeneutics, from the Greek ἑρμηνεύω (*hermeneuō*—"translate" or "interpret") is the art and practice of interpreting, among other things, texts. Within hermeneutics, two methodologies may be distinguished, ἐξήγησις (*exegesis*—"to lead out of") and εἰςήγησις (*eisegesis*—"to lead out"). Exegetical hermeneutics pull their interpretation out of a text *from* cues that are within; the eisegetical mode of analysis interprets the text by applying externally formulated ideas *to* it (*An Introductory Dictionary of Theology and Religious Studies*, ed. Orlando Espin and James B. Nickologg, [Collegeville, MN: Liturgical Press, 2007], c.v. "exegesis/eisegesis" and "hermeneutics").
18 Remes, 19–21.
19 Ibid., 7–8.

4. *Phusis*, The Physical (φύσις—"the nature or natural qualities of a thing")[20]

The One[21] is also identified by Plotinus as *theos* (θεός—"god, both in the general and particular sense") and sits at the very top of the series of hypostases (ὑπόστασις—"that which settles at the bottom"), or emanations, that proceed downwards from it. In contrast to the Classical theists who would follow him, Plotinus did *not* identify the One with being. Indeed, Plotinus saw the One as transcendent *to* being; for, "being is varied and many, whereas the One is absolute simplicity, and hence is not among beings but beyond being."[22] The One is uncaused, like Plato and Aristotle's demiurge. As Plotinus tells us, if it were itself caused by *anything* then it would not be the ultimate metaphysical category —and thus must be self-caused.[23] While Neoplatonic metaphysics *are* monistic in that the One is both the highest category *and* is the source of all emanations secondary, tertiary and quaternary to it, it is important to note that this is *not* the kind of illusory vision of plurality and temporality we find in the ontologies of the Eleatics such as Parmenides (5th century BC) or Zeno (ca. 490–430 BC). Rather, the descending levels of reality are *real*, but are generated by and contingent upon the levels immediately higher. Thus, the One does not *immediately* generate *all* levels beneath it, but births the layer directly under it, which in turn does the same, etc.[24]

In dealing with the One, we witness the emergence of the earliest Western form of *panentheism*. As a theological theory of divine identity, it is best understood in context with the two other overarching theological positions: Classical theism and pantheism. Classical theism, we may say, is a grouping of theological positions which assert that God is "transcendent, self-sufficient, eternal, and immutable in relation to the world; thus he does not change through time and is not affected by relation to his creatures."[25] This is distinguished from pantheism, which we shall define as the position "that God is identical with everything," that deity is imminent, contingent, temporal and mutable in relation to the world, because the two are one and the same.[26] Seeing that these two theologies are

---

20 Ibid., 58.
21 For clarity's sake, I have capitalized the emanations as proper nouns.
22 Remes, 49.
23 Plotinus, *Enneads* in *Neoplatonic Philosophy: Introductory Readings*, eds. John Dillon and Lloyd P. Gerson, (Indianapolis, IN: Hackett Publishing Company, Inc., 2004), 176.
24 Remes, 53.
25 John W. Cooper, *Panentheism: The Other God of the Philosophers*, (Grand Rapids, MI: Baker Academic, 2006), 14.
26 Robert Audi, ed., The Cambridge Dictionary of Philosophy, 2nd ed., (Cambridge:

wholly different in every respect, where does that leave panentheism? Panentheism positions itself as an intermediary view between the extremes of Classical theism and pantheism. It is distinguished from pantheism, linguistically, by the inclusion of the *-en* suffix,[27] which amounts to "the belief that…God includes and penetrates the whole universe, so that every part of it exists in Him."[28] This leads us to treat panentheism as a theology which bridges several of the gaps existing between Classical theism and pantheism by affirming that God is at once immanent *and* transcendent—that he is in possession of attributes which are both eternal and temporal, immutable and mutable. "The One is both infinite and utterly transcendent, yet it includes or contains everything that emanates from it"[29] by means of all things which emanate from a higher level *participating*[30] in the higher layers.

Immediately emanating from the One is the Intellect, which is identified by Plotinus as the Platonic world of Forms.[31] This secondary level of hypostasis is that of being.[32] As mentioned earlier, in Neoplatonic metaphysics being emanates from the One, which is henologically prior to it.[33] The ideal world of the Intellect is characterized by a plurality of Forms, which are the "true or real beings" from which all material beings emanate.[34] In this regard, we may consider Neoplatonism to be in line with contemporary realism in that universals and ideas are

---

Cambridge University Press, 1999), s.v. "pantheism."

27 The term *panentheism* is a Hellenization of a word coined by Karl Krause (1781–1832): *Allingottlehre*, both of which literally translate as "all-in-God-ism," (Cooper, 26).

28 Frank L. Cross and Elizabeth A. Livingston, eds., *The Oxford Dictionary of the Christian Church*, 3rd ed., (Oxford: Oxford University Press, 1997), p. 1213.

29 Cooper, 39.

30 Participation referring to the way in which lower layers are reflections of the upper. Just as a particular horse participates in horseness, so do all things participate in the One.

31 Plotinus, 74.

32 It should be noted that just as post-Plotinian philosophers disagreed on the placement of the Demiurge within the hierarchy, so did they disagree on whether Being occupied the first or second *hypostasis*. Plotinus and Porphyry adhered to the view described above, while Iamblichus and Proclus identified the One with being (Gregory Shaw, *Theurgy and the Soul: The Neoplatonism of Iamblichus*, [University Park, PA: The Pennsylvania State University Press, 1995], 113).

33 Here we must use *henology* in place of *ontology*, as *ontos* (ὄντος—"being") is not the ultimate category involved, with that honor going to *hen* (ἕν—"one"). As mentioned previously, ontological priority takes *being* as its foundational idea. If, as is the case with Plotinus, being itself is dependent upon yet *another* category, then we must phrase our terminology around that upon which being depends.

34 Remes, 54.

real metaphysical entities which exist independent from particular, instantiated conceptions of them in a mind.[35] However, just as the Neoplatonic schema differs in that it does not place the world of Forms as the ultimate metaphysical layer, it *also* differs in that it does not place the perceptible world directly beneath the Forms. In the Neoplatonic system there is a further, intermediary realm that affects the emanative transition from ideal to actual. In Classical Platonism there is, it seems, an abyss that yawns between the ideal Forms and the actual instantiations. Plotinus sought to naturalize this by positing a transitional layer betwixt the two.

This third level is that of the Soul.[36] As each hypostasis brings us closer to the human experience, it is unsurprising that the Soul level "even more emphatically than the Intellect sounds like something human."[37] The Soul functions as an intermediary step between the atemporal realm of the Intellect and the wholly temporal Physical reality. Thus, while the Soul itself is not strictly temporal, it is the agent through which flux comes to be. The actions of the Soul create temporal succession and give this succession a directional vector that is responsible for producing the perception of time as a continuum in the fourth and final emanation.[38] As in so much of Greek thought, we find that ensoulment is *not* a particular feature that is limited to humanity. Rather than the kind of bifurcation between man and the world that humanism espouses, the Neoplatonists naturalized the *psuchē* and espoused a panpsychist[39] position in which Soul was participated in by *all*.[40] Furthermore, for Plotinus, the Soul was the animating principle that brought life to the inanimate forms. He saw life and change as being fundamentally entwined, which is why they both have their genesis in the same emanatory layer. The specific term for the agent of Neoplatonic panpsychism was the *psuchē kosmou* (ψυχή κόσμου—"world soul").

As the panentheism that pervades Neoplatonism does not *necessarily* imply panpsychism, a self-contained argument which demonstrated the continuity of the *psuchē* throughout the world was made. All that is required of a panpsychist position is that all individual things—at the lowest ontological level—posess

---

35 Ibid.
36 Ibid., 55.
37 Ibid.
38 Ibid., 56.
39 Panpsychism, from the Greek roots *pan* (πᾶν—"all" or "everything") and *psuchē* (ψῡχή—"mind, "breath," or "spirit") is the position that all things have a mind or mind-like quality. While for some schools of thought this quality is more specifically mental in nature, in the case of Neoplatonism, it is Soul.
40 David Skrbina, *Panpsychism in the West*, (Cambridge, MA: The MIT Press, 2007), 61.

some mind-like quality. Neither panentheism, pantheism or Classical theism necessitate that mind or soul pervade *all* levels of the cosmos. Neoplatonic panentheism would only *require* it at the level of the whole.[41] Yet, in typical top-down fashion, we *begin* with the idea of a World Soul, and then proceed downwards to extrapolate this principle to the particulars who participate in this universal. The argument which seeks to demonstrate this all-pervading *psuchē* is found in Plato's *Philebus*.[42] Roughly summarized, the argument proceeds as follows:

1. All material bodies—to include everything from insects, to humans, to the universe at large—are solely composed of the four elements.
2. Human material bodies are connected to higher level psychic forms.
3. The fact that the human body is composed of the four elements entails that it is in possession of a *psuchē*.
4. Therefore, the cosmos as a whole is in possession of the same—in the form of the World Soul.
5. And, since *psuchē* is "a general quality of objects composed of the four elements, one may conclude that…"
6. *Psuchē* is an attribute of *all* materiality.[43]

Thus we can see, from this argument, a line of reasoning that allows for the participation of the material world in *psuchē* in two ways: both as individual atomic bits of matter, and as a cosmic whole. This hearkens back to the panentheism found in the topmost layer of the hierarchy in which the divinity exists both as a singular unity *and* as the unfolding series of emanations below. This dyadic mode of the constitution of metaphysical entities is something which rears its head continually in Neoplatonic thought, and will be particularly noticeable when we come around to the discussion of Iamblichean theology.

The fourth tier of the cosmic ladder is the Physical world of materiality and sense perception.[44] This world is the culmination of the emanative process. As such it demonstrates both the greatest unfolding of the potentiality of the One into actuality and at the same time is the farthest from the perfection of the One. While we are all too familiar with our experience of this level of reality, it will do much good at this point to step back and examine just how this emanative schema explains the experience of sensory phenomena in the final layer. Let us take as an example a brown horse that we witness running across a field.[45] The horse appears as a unified being that is able to be identified as such due to its participation

---

41 Ibid., 39.
42 Plato, *Philebus*, trans. Dorothea Frede, in *Plato*, 29a–30b.
43 This six-point breakdown of Plato's argument was formalized in Skrbina, 39.
44 Remes, 58.
45 This example is taken from Remes, 58–59.

in the principle of unity that is at the top of the metaphysical ladder: the One. Its *whatness*, that aspect of its intelligible structure that identifies it as participating in *horseness*, its being a reflection of the ideal Form of the Horse is owed to the second emanation: the Intellect. The horse is also *alive* and is driven by an internal impetus to strive onwards and persist in time as a being whose goal is to actualize its potentiality. This animating core is caused by the third layer: the Soul. Finally, we come back to our immediate experience of the *thatness* of this *particular* horse as an imperfect representative of the ideal Form that we hold in our minds of what a Horse really is. This horse before us has myriad imperfections: it limps slightly, its color is not as pure as it could be, etc. This is product of the culmination of the emanative process. The imperfect, temporal multiplicity that shines down from the perfected One.

Iamblichean Theology

Upon the foundation laid by Plotinus, Iamblichus—an Assyrian Neoplatonist who was a student of Plotinus' protege and biographer Porphyry—greatly expanded the system to better incorporate and synthesize the religious doxa and praxes[46] of the Hellenic world. Where Plotinus' metaphysics were *implicitly* pagan, yet focused almost exclusively on the unity of the One, Iamblichus' were much more strongly polytheistic, placing great emphasis upon the differentiation within the medial layers of the cosmic hierarchy. Just as Thales before him,[47] Iamblichus' world was one that teemed with Gods. Following the fourfold emanative cosmological scheme detailed above, Iamblichus presents us with a four-tiered theology to match:[48]

1. Gods (θεοί)
2. Daimones (δαίμονες—"Gods, generally" or "the links between Gods and men")
3. Heroes (ἥρως—"inferior local deities" or "patrons of tribes, cities, etc.")
4. Human Souls (ψυχαὶ ἄχρατοι—lit. "undefiled or immaculate person")

However, far from this being the *only* division, Iamblichus delineates a myriad of interwoven subdivisions within these four hierarchies, displaying the Neoplatonic tendency to multiply the metaphysical layers with their analyses. The first class,

---

46 *Doxa* (δόξα) and *praxis* (πρᾶξις) refer to the binary components of "belief and practice" or "dogma and ritual," that characterize religion.
47 "There are some, too, who say that soul is interfused throughout the universe: which is perhaps why Thales supposed all things to be full of gods," (Aristotle, *De Anima*, trans R.D. Hicks, [New York: Cosimo Classics, 2008], 33).
48 John M. Dillon, Introduction to *Iamblichus: The Platonic Commentaries*, ed. and trans. John M. Dillon, (Leiden: E.J. Brill, 1973), 49.

The Emergent Hierarchy

the Gods, are first divided into two classes, the *perkosmioi* or *enkosmioi* (περκόσμιοι, ἐγκόσμιοι—"cosmic") Gods, which he refers to as being material and immaterial.[49] The "material Gods are those that contain matter within themselves and give it order, but the entirely immaterial Gods are removed from matter and transcend it."[50] These two divine modalities of manifestation reflected Iamblichus' doctrine of a distinction between *participated* and *unparticipated* aspects of an entity.[51] To use part/whole terminology, the unparticipated face of an entity is that which is the whole in and of itself, without relation to the parts. The participated aspect is that which is the whole as constituted by its relations with the parts. An example of this principle in action might be an atom. As a monadic individual, the atom exists as an unparticipated unity. As a participated entity, it exists as a process of relations between several protons, neutrons and electrons. Furthermore, in typical Neoplatonic fashion, Iamblichus postulates a *third* level of Gods between the cosmic and hypercosmic. It was the Neoplatonic urge to mediate between extremes—the law of mean terms—that led Plotinus to develop the two additional hierarchical layers between the original two of Plato; Iamblichus carries this impetus further and thus achieves a system that is closer to a smooth transition between levels than was Plotinus'. This intermediary class of Gods were called *apolutoi* (ἀπολυτοι—"liberated"), and consisted of those Gods which served a mediating function between the cosmic and hypercosmic deities.[52]

Even application of the law of mean terms—which postulates that between any two terms there exists an intermediary term—along with the distinction between participated and unparticipated entities led Iamblichus to further sub-divide the daimōnic level into a triad that mirrors those of the Gods above: archangels (αρχάγγελος—"chief or principal angel"), angels (άγγελος—"messenger" or "one that announces"), and daimones.[53] This process was again replicated at the heroic layer leading to the following trinity: sublunary archons (ἡγεμονικοί ἄρκοντος —"authoritative or leading rulers"), hylic archons (ἔνυλοι ἄρκοντος—"material rulers"), and heroes.[54] As it was the final, consequent state of being, the physical layer of the hierarchy was *not* sub-divided in this manner. Thus, the resulting theological chain of emanation was stratified as such:

1. Demiurge
2. Hypercosmic Gods
3. Liberated Gods

---

49 Shaw, 135.
50 Iamblichus, *De Mysteriis*, trans. Gregory Shaw, in *Theurgy and the Soul*, 217: 4–8.
51 Remes, 70.
52 Shaw, 135.
53 Dillon, 51.
54 Ibid.

4. Cosmic Gods
5. Archangels
6. Angels
7. Daimones
8. Heroes
9. Sublunary Archons
10. Hylic Archons
11. Human Souls

The intermediary classes, the daimonic and heroic triads, "bind together in a continuous link from highest to lowest and make indivisible the community of the universe" that exists between the Gods and the Human Souls.[55] The daimones "serve the will of the gods, make manifest their hidden goodness, and give form to their superior formlessness."[56] If a God is the *being* of whatever sphere of the cosmos is being considered, then the corresponding daimones would be the Forms and ideas that that being takes as it gathers shape in its emanative descent into the material world. Further down the chain are the *heroes*, beings who are "more akin to the gods, but still far inferior to them."[57] The heroes are thus the *active* agents who directly interface between the æthereal realms above and the material spheres below. If we say that the daimonic entities "represent the lowest extension of the gods, one could say that the heroes represent the highest degree of the soul," making the plenum[58] between the highest and lowest emanations a fluid continuum.[59] So, while the daimones serve a principally downward, emanative function, the heroes serve an upwardly directed *theurgic* place in the hierarchy, making their role less cosmological and more soteriological.

Theurgy

Up to this point, we have spoken only of the top-down cosmological vector of dependency that most strongly characterizes Neoplatonic metaphysics. There is, however, another vector that begins at the bottom and ascends through the plenary levels of the hierarchy. This act of rising formed the praxis which operated within the parameters laid down by the emanative schema. Theurgy (θεουργία —"divine rite") was seen by Iamblichus as an activity wholly distinct from theo-

---

55 Ibid., 49.
56 Ibid.
57 Ibid.
58 In this context, we may define a plenum as a completely filled space, the opposite of a vacuum.
59 M. Alan Kazlev, "Iamblichus' Hierarchy of Spiritual Entities," http://www.kheper.net/topics/Neoplatonism/Iamblich-beings.htm (accessed May 29, 2011).

logy. "For theology was merely *logos*," a way of *speaking* about the Gods, "and however exalted, it remained a human activity, as did philosophy."[60] Theurgy, however, was the veritable work of the Gods—work whose goal was to rectify the imperfections of man's state in the final emanation by elevating the soul to the levels of the Gods themselves. Theurgical rites emerged from the innate orectic impulse to rectify the imperfect state of multiplicity and to return to the henologically prime state of unity and perfection.[61] The end result, the *magnum opus*, of the theurgic process was termed *henōsis* (ἕνωσις—"oneness" or "union").[62] *Henōsis* was thought of as the culmination of the climbing of the emanative ladder—the final state resulting from the reversal of the hypostatic transformation. The means by which this result was obtained was via the invocation of the various Gods who inhabited the realms above the physical emanation. The purported ability of the theurgist to call down the divine into the material sphere at first, however, appears pregnant with a problem: if the vector of dependence is unidirectional and strictly proceeds from the upper levels to the lower, how is it that beings in the lowest sphere could exert any influence over those in the higher layers? In Neoplatonic theology, the divine is clearly "not a self-evident part of human nature, but a thing over and above it."[63]

That being the case, how does the theurgist accomplish his task? Iamblichus was quick to resolve this problem. What he proposed was that rather than attempting to command or control the Gods, that theurgic praxes managed to shape the soul of the seeker so that the higher beings would deign to descend.[64] The difference, then, is that the Gods are invited into the receptacle that the theurgist—by the correct practice of meditation, prayers and rituals—has transformed himself into. The term Iamblichus uses for this preparation is *epitēdeiotēs* (ἐπιτηδειότης—"fitness, suitableness"), and refers to the aptitude of the theurgist to receive the God being invoked.[65] The process, then, is similar to the means by which one prepares an object to "better reflect a particular color of light; a golden object does not 'compel' yellow light to appear, but it allows the presence of the yellow in the white light to become manifest."[66] So do the theurgic rites prepare the soul to

---

60 Shaw, 5.
61 Ibid.
62 Ibid., 51.
63 Remes, 171.
64 Iamblichus, *On the Mysteries of the Egyptians*, in *Neoplatonic Philosophy: Introductory Readings*, eds. John Dillon and Lloyd P. Gerson, (Indianapolis, IN: Hackett Publishing Company, Inc., 2004), 229–230.
65 Shaw, 86.
66 Bruce MacLennan, "Evolution, Jung, and Theurgy: Their Role in Modern Neoplatonism," http://web.eecs.utk.edu/~mclennan/papers/EvolutionJungTheurgy-long.pdf (accessed May 29, 2011), 19.

better receive the omnipresent Gods by reshaping himself into a proper vessel. He is like a lightning rod which, by virtue of his very constitution, naturally calls down the fire from the heavens. Through theurgy, man is able to bridge the gap between all the emanations, elevating his soul into the form of a hollow tube—a tube through which the divine influence is free to flow. This interfusion of the Gods of the upper emanations into the lower has, in its initial phases, the effect of raising the theurgist's soul to the level of the Gods: in other words, *theōsis* (θέωσις—"divinization" or "deification"). It is only with the completion of the theurgic process that the *theōsis* of the medial levels reaches the final state of *henōsis*: perfect union with God.

This final point, about *theōsis* being a necessary bridge between material existence and *henōsis*, is particularly important as it marks yet another advance that Iamblichus made away from Plotinus. "Unlike the system of Plotinus, where the soul could transcend its hypostasis and attain union with the One, Iamblichus fixed the soul in its ontological rank."[67] The beginning and end states in each system are nearly identical, but Iamblichus' belief that the emanations could only be transcended one at a time was a far cry from Plotinus' position—which echoes Plato's—under which the soul could rise from the Physical to the One in a single bound. Indeed, due to each emanation's being ontologically dependent upon the one *directly* preceding it, Iamblichus reasoned that the soul's ascent *must* follow a path that mirrored the descent. In theological terms, "the soul could not rise to the paternal Demiurge alone."[68] To climb to the top of the hierarchical ladder, "the soul had to be assimilated to the Whole, and this was accomplished only by honoring 'all the gods.'"[69] Although there was certainly no disagreement between Plotinus and Iamblichus on the fact that theurgy invariably led to the One, the latter reasoned that the gradation of the emanative process necessitated a similarly graded mode of ascent, in which the theurgist worked his way ever upwards—beginning with the heroic triad, passing on to the daimonic, then through the Gods, culminating with the *henōsis* with *the* God: the Demiurge.

The means by which this unification with the higher powers was achieved was manifold, but three principal methodological groupings can be identified. Key among all is the idea of the *sunthēmata* (σύνθηματα—"signatures," "symbols," or "signs"). The theory behind this term is that since the Gods occupy a high position in the ontological hierarchy and are relatively few in number, there are necessarily a number of different types of material objects which participate in the Gods. In the course of theurgic rituals, "such objects served as receptacles of the

---

67 Shaw, 79.
68 Ibid., 156.
69 Ibid.

gods because they preserved an intimate relation with them and bore their 'signatures'...in the manifest world. As such they were pure specimens of the divine presence in matter."[70] Just as the daimones are hypostases of the Gods, and heroes are hypostases of the daimones, so are the material fingerprints of the Holy emanations from above. In that way the physical symbols that have been historically associated with the various Gods of pagan pantheons were thought to be directly in lineal contact with the Gods they are proper to. Thus, by means of these *sunthēmata* did Iamblichus postulate that the theurgist could "procure...an indivisible communion with the Gods," to awaken within himself the latent participatory modality proper to that deity.[71] Examples of these symbols are nearly innumerable and everything from Óðinn's association with ravens, to Zeus' connection with the oak tree were explained via the *sunthēmata* concept.

Since the theurgist's work began in the physical emanation, the principal theurgic rites are largely material in nature—dealing with the *sunthēmata* occupying the final level. Most common among these was the practice known as *telestikē* (τελεστικη—"consecration"), in which divine images (e.g. statues, paintings, etc.) were specially prepared to function as receptacles for the Gods they represented by the offering by the priests of *sunthēmata* proper to the God.[72] "Thus the image may function as a focus for contact with the god, allowing the theurgist to make inquiries, petitions, vows, pacts, etc."[73] This was, again, much less of an act of "calling down" the Gods and much more of tuning the material object into the correct wavelength to pick up the divine signal that was already being broadcast. As such, once the deity deigned to possess the object, it became "a mean that functioned both as a projection of the soul's powers and as an image of the powers of the god revealed in a single coherent form."[74] The idol became, for a time, the living material *body* of the God being invoked.

A second extremely common theurgic practice was known as *katochē* (κατοχή —"a holding fast," "detention" or "possession by a spirit"), in which the vessel prepared for the God's descent is not an inanimate object, but a person.[75] While this operation could be performed by one person alone, it was typically done in a pair, with one person functioning as the recipient and the other as the operator. It

---

70 Ibid., 48.
71 Iamblichus, *De Mysteriis*, 235: 5–9.
72 Algis Uždavinys, "Metaphysical Symbols and Their Function in Theurgy," *Eye of the Heart: A Journal of Traditional Wisdom*, vol. 2, (2008): 50.
73 Bruce MacLennan, "Individual Soul and World Soul: The Process of Individuation in Neoplatonism and Jung," http://web.eecs.utk.edu/~mclennan/papers/ISWS-TR.pdf (accessed May 31, 2011), 15.
74 Shaw, 167.
75 Ibid., 87.

was common for the recipient to be a child, as it was believed that "prepubescent children are less likely to be possessed of sexual complexes and personal daimones, and therefore less likely to color the divinity's voice with their own unconscious or subconscious content."[76] The success of an attempt at *katochē* was dependent on two factors: the suitability of the receiver, and the hieratic power of the operator.[77] While it was certainly possible for one theurgist to be skilled enough in *both* arts to affect a true possession (as was the case with many of the oracles), it was apparently a much more widespread practice for the experienced theurgist to specialize in the latter skill. In fact, this was such a widespread practice that it continued through the Medieval theurgical texts into modern times. One of the best documented examples of this practice comes from the journals of John Dee (1527–1608) and Edward Kelley (1555–1597), who conducted a decade long series of skrying sessions with entities who identified themselves as Enochian Angels.[78] During these operations, Dee performed the active role of performing the hieratic invocations, while Kelley performed the passive role of receiver.

Now, the above two procedures could both be characterized as *lower* theurgy, for the *sunthēmata* involved are invariably material, and function from the position of the lowest hypostasis. There existed, however, a *higher* theurgy as well that functioned on a completely noetic level and was bereft of material tools.[79] The principal method by which this type of theurgy was carried out was by means of the *augoeides ochēma* (αὐγοειδὲς—"starry, luminous" ὄχημα—"vessel," "anything that bears or supports," or "chariot")—the body of light. Also known as the *augoeides sōma* (σῶμα—"the body of a man"), the body of light seen by Iamblichus as the means by which the theurgist ascended beyond the material world, into the realms of the heroes, daimones and Gods. It was conceived of as a "spherical body gained in theurgic rituals...[and] the perfection of this aetheric and luminous body effected the soul's immortalization."[80] Through elevating his soul within this spherical vessel of starry light, the theurgist was able to become Godlike, and transcend from his position of particularity into the Gods' realm of universality. By these means, he would rise, penetrating each layer of the hierarchy, until the eventual attainment of *henōsis* was achieved.

Christian Neoplatonism

---

76 MacLennan, "Individual Soul and World Soul," 15.
77 Ibid., 16.
78 *John Dee's Five Books of Mystery*, ed. Joseph H. Peterson, (York Beach, ME: Red Wheel/Weiser LLC, 2003), 19–21.
79 Shaw, 190.
80 Shaw, 52.

After the end of the Classical period and the passing of the philosophical torch to the thinkers of Western Europe, Neoplatonism re-emerged from its Pagan origins in two forms. First among these is the phenomenon of Christian Neoplatonism. In the intervening years between the peak of the activity of Plotinus, Porphyry, Iamblichus, Proclus, etc. and the thoroughly Catholic theologies of Augustine of Hippo (354–430) and Thomas Aquinas (1225–1274), there were a handful of transitional thinkers who were responsible for Christianizing Neoplatonic philosophy and theology. Foremost among these was a man now known as the Pseudo-Dionysius, a late 5th century theologian and philosopher about whose personal life extremely little is known.[81] Within the confines of our current discussion on divine hierarchies, his most important work was the tract *De Coelesti Hierarchia*, a highly influential work which adapted the Neoplatonic emanative schema to Christianity. It was through this work of the Pseudo-Dionysius that the Gods, daimones, heroes and pure souls of Iamblichus and Proclus were translated into the Christian experience—turning the Neoplatonic entities into varying types of Angels.[82] What he presents us with is a nine-fold order—three classes, each with three sub-classes—that emanates forth from God:

1. The Godhead
2. The First Triad[83]
   1. Seraphim (שְׂרָפִים—"burning ones")[84]
   2. Cherubim (כְּרוּבִים—"winged angel")
   3. Thrones (θρόνος—"seat" or "throne")
3. The Second Triad[85]
   1. Lordships (*dominatio*—"dominions")
   2. Virtues (δύναμις—"power," "force" or "virtue")
   3. Authorities (*potestas*—"powers")
4. The Third Triad[86]
   1. Principalities (*principatūs*—"rulers")
   2. Archangels
   3. Angels

---

81 As an aside, he is called the *Pseudo*-Dionysius because during the following centuries he was confused with the authentic Dionysius the Areopagite, an Athenian convert of St. Paul (Frederick Copleston, *Medieval Philosophy: From Augustine to Duns Scotus*, vol. 2 of *A History of Philosophy*, [New York: Image Books, 1993], 91).
82 Pseudo-Dionysius, *On the Heavenly Hierarchy*, in *Dionysius the Aeropagite, Works (1897)*, trans. John Parker, (London: James Parker and Co., 1987), 110.
83 Ibid., 121.
84 Latin and Hebrew etymologies were gleaned from the *Online Etymological Dictionary*: http://www.etymonline.com
85 Ibid., 124.
86 Ibid., 126.

This proved to be such an influential schema that it was adopted by Thomas Aquinas in his *Summa Theologica*, thus becoming canon.[87] While the specific contents of the hierarchical configuration varies from thinker to thinker, the same four-tiered pattern was replicated well into the late Medieval and early Renaissance grimoires such as the *Lemegeton*, which provided the theurgist with exhaustive lists of individual angels within these hierarchies and detailed rites to attract their influence and cajole them into descending to the material plane.[88]

Furthermore, outside of the importation of Angelic hierarchies, Neoplatonism had a tremendous impact on the development of Christian panentheism during the Middle Ages and Renaissance. Johannes "Meister" Eckhart (1260–1327) was chief among the proponents of Plotinus, putting forth numerous sermons in which he delineated that God, as the One, extended into pure transcendence and was "something that must necessarily be above being."[89] This position elevates the One, which Eckhart termed Godhead, above the God of the trinity: "God and Godhead are as different as heaven and earth."[90] Nicholas of Cusa (1401–1464) was another thinker who, by the route of Eckhart, was a fervent proponent of Neoplatonic theology, and worked towards the formulation of a theology rooted in the conception of God as not being *beyond* being, but as the "One Absolute Maximal Being."[91] He, following Duns Scotus (1265–1308), "then conjoins Being and Infinity," which results in a deity which "must include all beings and differences," being at once immanent *and* transcendent.[92] It was not, however, until the Italian Renaissance that the Neoplatonic texts which had been lost during the Dark Ages were rediscovered and translated into Latin by Marsilio Ficino (1433–1499).[93] It was Ficino's work that reopened the doors into the Classical world which gave rise to the varied systems of belief that we now group under the heading of Western Esotericism. Contemporary Christian panentheism owes a

---

87 Thomas Aquinas, *Summa Theologica*, Volume 1, Part 1, trans. Fathers of the English Dominican Province, (New York: Cosimo Classics, 2007), 533.
88 The second part of the book, "The Art Theurgia Goetia," begins with an exposition of the hierarchical structure (Joseph H. Peterson, Introduction to *The Lesser Key of Solomon: Lemegeton Clavicula Salomonis*, [York Beach, ME: Weiser Books, 2001], 57–58).
89 Eckhart, *Sermon 17*, in *Meister Eckhart: An Introduction to the Study of His Work with an Anthology of His Sermons*, ed. and trans. James Clark (New York: Thomas Nelson and Sons, 1957), 205.
90 Eckhart, *Sermon 12*, in Clark, 183.
91 Cooper, 53.
92 Ibid.
93 Nicholas Goodrick-Clarke, *The Western Esoteric Traditions: A Historical Introduction*, (New York, NY: Oxford University Press, 2008), 36.

tremendous intellectual debt to Plotinus, as the genealogy of this concept certainly demonstrates. It is not, however, with Christian Neoplatonism that this paper's thesis is concerned. Rather it is to the contemporary revival of *Pagan* Neoplatonism that we must turn our gaze.

Archetypal Psychology

Carl Gustav Jung (1975–1961) was a Swiss psychoanalyst who founded the discipline of analytical psychology and was responsible for the introduction of concepts such as the collective unconscious, archetype, and complex to the contemporary psychological vocabulary. A colleague of Sigmund Freud (1856–1939), Jung adapted two of Freud's most revolutionary ideas and transformed them into the contemporary system of Neoplatonic psychology that is now associated with Jung and his students. The first of these notions was that the *psuchē* is *not* a monadic unity, but is rather a *plenum* of several distinct minds—or, alternatively, *layers* of mind. Freud developed a tripartite structure to describe mentality, consisting of the id, ego and superego. The id was seen as the mind that consisted of primordial instincts and drives; it was the animal mind that was largely inaccessible to every-day consciousness. It was within the id that Freud believed all of the chaotic, disordered and instinctual thoughts and desires arose.[94] The ego was viewed as the center of one's sense of self. It was the mind from which rational judgments and behaviors emanated, and functioned as a mediating agent between the animalistic id and the outside world.[95] Lastly, the superego was treated as the mind's *conscience*, and was constantly attempting to sway the ego away from the id's influence into more socially conventional modes of behavior—for, the superego was, more so than an of the three, intimately conditioned by the ego's social relationships.[96] Just as the id is the brute *description* of what the self instinctively begins as, so is the superego the *normative* complex that attempts to mold the instincts into something more suitable for the society within which the superego developed. And, it is in the midst of this psychic tug of war that the ego finds itself refereeing. The second idea that Jung borrowed from Freud was that of the unconscious mind. In the 19th century, theories of unconscious mental dimensions *were* already somewhat commonplace when Freud published his seminal *The Interpretation of Dreams* in 1899. However, despite Freud's initial dabbling in the idea of a two-fold division between the conscious and unconscious mind, his work in this area laid the groundwork for his eventual development of the id,

---

94 Sigmund Freud, *New Introductory Lectures on Psycho-Analysis*, standard ed., ed. James Strachey, (New York:W.W. Norton and Company, 1990), 91.

95 Freud, "The Ego and the Id," *The Essentials of Psycho-Analysis*, ed. James Strachey, (London: Vintage, 2005), 450.

96 Peter D. Kramer, *Freud: Inventor of the Modern Mind*, (New York: Harper Collins, 2006), 172.

ego and superego triad—of which the first and last members represent mental functions of which the conscious ego is largely unaware, making them *de facto* unconscious minds.[97]

It was from this background both in Freudian theory and the hands on heterophenomenological research into his patients' minds—and autophenomenological research into his *own*—that Jung came to develop his theories. Like Freud before him, Jung treated the *psuchē* in plenary rather than monistic terms, and like Freud as well, he acknowledged that the conscious mind is but one island amidst a sea of unconscious minds. However, it is with this concept of the unconscious that Jung makes a decisive break with Freud, for in Jung's system there are two divisions of unconscious minds: the individual unconscious and the collective unconscious. In his own words, Jung differentiates the two as such: "The collective unconscious is a part of the *psuchē* which can be negatively distinguished from a personal unconscious by the fact that it does not, like the latter, owe its existence to personal experience and consequently is not a personal acquisition."[98] So, whereas the contents of the individual unconscious consist of things of which we have at one time been conscious, "the contents of the collective unconscious have never been in consciousness, and therefore have never been individually acquired, but owe their existence exclusively to heredity."[99]

This is to say that our individual, personal unconscious is largely composed of memories and complexes that are unique to each person. There may be similarities between John Jones' and Mary Smith's personal unconscious minds based on similarities of biology, environment, culture, etc.—yet they would in no wise be *identical*. Each individual's life, the life that shapes the personal unconscious, is a necklace strung from pearls of events that can never be wholly replicated in the life of another. The *collective* unconsciousness on the other hand, is pre-existent and is of an "impersonal nature which is identical in all individuals."[100] Jung treated the collective unconscious as a universal layer of the *psuchē* which was common to all mankind and was a source of inborn mental attributes. The collective unconscious can be said to be a collection of "modes of behavior that are more or less the same everywhere and in all individuals."[101] It is for this reason

---

97 Henk de Berg, *Freud's Theory and Its Use in Literary and Cultural Studies: An Introduction*, (New York: Camden House, 2004), 49.
98 C.G. Jung, "The Concept of the Collective Unconscious," in *The Archetypes and the Collective Unconscious*, The Collected Works of C.G. Jung, vol. 9, part 1, trans. R.F.C. Hull, eds. Read, Fordham, Adler and McGuire, (New York: Princeton University Press, 1959), 42.
99 Ibid.
100 Ibid., 43.
101 Jung, "Archetypes of the Collective Unconscious," in *The Archetypes and the Col-*

that we may say while the individual unconscious is the property of *a* man, the collective unconscious is the property of *all* men; it is as integral and universal a part of humanity as is our four limbedness, our configuration of organs, or our division into two genders. Just as these physical characteristics are—excepting deviations caused by accidents of environment and circumstance—patterned after a seemingly *ideal* human Form, so did Jung's research indicate that the same mental analogs were similarly derived. Indeed, it was Jung's position that the archetypes of the collective unconscious were the factors which were primary and *gave rise* to the secondary conscious psychic contents.[102] To use the philosophical vocabulary, we would say that the individual unconscious is *ontologically dependent* upon the collective unconscious, just as the conscious mind depends upon the unconscious.

The governing forces of which the collective unconscious is composed were called *archetypes* by Jung. It is important to note a distinction at this point. Both the individual *and* collective unconscious ought not be thought of as mental analogs of some kind of spatial dimension within which archetypes and complexes exist. Rather, it is more in line with Jung's thought that the totality of the unconscious minds consisted of these constitutive entities. In other words, each may be thought of as a true plenum, in which there is no "space" which is not occupied by a body—bodies which are in this case the archetypes or complexes. In this way, rather than thinking of the archetypes as extended *in* the collective unconscious, we can view the collective unconscious itself *as the extension* of the archetypes. But, what *are* the archetypes? Identifying them with the various Gods and Goddesses of the world's mythologies, Jung wrote:

> They form a species of singular beings whom one would like to endow with ego-consciousness; indeed they almost seem capable of it. And yet this idea is not borne out by the facts. There is nothing in their behavior to suggest they have an ego-consciousness as we know it. They show, on the contrary, all the marks of fragmentary personalities. They are mask-like, wraithlike, without problems, lacking self-reflection, with no conflicts, no doubts, no sufferings; like gods, perhaps, who have no philosophy…Unlike other contents, they always remain strangers in the world of consciousness, unwelcome intruders saturating the atmosphere with uncanny forebodings or even with the fear of madness.[103]

---

lective Unconscious, 4.
102 Jung, "The Concept of the Collective Unconscious," 43.
103 Jung, "Conscious, Unconscious, and Individuation," in *The Archetypes of the Col-*

The Emergent Hierarchy

The archetypes are the *sources* of our individual instincts—the shadowy hegemons from which the particularities of our mental complexes emanate. For all of the universal modes of instinctive human behavior, there is an archetype that sits above the conscious layer of actualization as a causative agent in the murky realm of unconscious potentiality. As Jung sees it, not only are our particular mental instincts *dependent* upon the archetypes, they are also *governed* by them —which is to say that in addition to the archetypes being the *genetic* causes of our individual unconscious contents, they also function as downwardly determinative influences upon the developmental patterns of behavior manifested by the particulars which emanate from them. It is from these psychic universals that the unconscious complexes which are particular to each individual emanate.[104] They are the manifestations of the archetypes as they descend from universality into the particularity of the individual. It should also be mentioned that "it is a mistake to think the archetypes are 'merely psychological,' with the implication that they are in some way imaginary and subjective. Rather, they are objectively real in that they are *empirical*, *stable*, and *public*."[105] Their empirical nature can be seen from the fact that their "existence and character can be inferred from their effects in experience;" in other words, by observing innate behaviors among humans, we can induce that there exists a set of common, archetypal, behavior patterns which govern the manifestations of these particular expressions.[106] Their stability can be seen in the relative impermeability of human instinct. And their public nature stems from the fact that they are shared in common by all—making them accessible to each member of the species, not a select few.

If the reader finds himself thinking that this schemata is all too familiar, there is no need to worry—*it is*. The psychic structures described by Jung, as uncovered from his psychoanalytic research, correspond almost exactly to the hierarchies and emanative vectors of ontological dependence and downward causation of the Neoplatonists. This can be explained in two ways. Firstly, those who advocate the truth of the metaphysical models described by both would likely say that Jung's *discovery* of the structures of the unconscious and its strong resemblance to that of Neoplatonism was an inevitability, as anyone engaging in psychonautic phenomenology is *bound* to uncover the same truths—just as any astronomer is bound to discover the same stars and constellations as any other who utilizes the same methodology. It is for this reason that Jungians often refer to the collective unconscious as "the objective psyche."[107] Secondly, the strong similarities can

---

lective Unconscious, 287.
104 Jung, "The Concept of the Collective Unconscious," 42.
105 MacLennan, "Evolution, Jung, and Theurgy," 4.
106 Ibid.
107 Ibid.

also be understood as reflections of Jung's having been *profoundly* influenced by Platonic and Neoplatonic philosophy. Jung makes no secret of this, and in his preliminary definition of the archetype, he notes that the term itself "is an explanatory paraphrase of the Platonic εἶδος," or Form.[108] Even the very word, archetype, "occurs as early as Philo Judaeus, with reference to the *Imago Dei* (God-image) in man," then later "in the *Corpus Hermeticum*, God is called τὸ ἀρχέτυπον φῶς," (*to archetypon phōs*—the archetypal light) and then in the writings of the Medieval Neoplatonist, Dionysius the Areopagite, "immaterial archetypes," are referenced in regards to the celestial hierarchy.[109] Additionally, "although Jung cites Neoplatonists infrequently, he was inspired at an early stage of his career by the Neoplatonist scholar Friedrich Creuzer, who later edited the works of Plotinus, Proclus, and Olympiodorus."[110] All of this is in addition to the secondary influence to Neoplatonic ideas that Jung received from his exhaustive investigations into Gnosticism and Alchemy—both of which are heavily indebted to Neoplatonism. By means of comparison, the relationships between the terminologies of the Neoplatonists and Jung can be represented as such:

Neoplatonic Emanations	Neoplatonic Entities	Jungian Emanations	Jungian Entities
The Intellect	Gods	Collective Unconscious	Archetypes
The Soul	Daimones	Individual Unconscious	Complexes
Physical	Human Souls	Consciousness	Ego

To be sure, this model necessitates a slight reconfiguration of Plotinus' system to suit Jung's model, yet the impact of the former upon the latter is undeniable. In each system, there is a series of descending hypostases that proceed from universality to particularity in a gradated fashion. Furthermore, each of these emanative layers, in both systems, are composed of plena of entities which are beyond the reach of normal consciousness. We might further chart out a list of metaphysical commonalities shared by the two systems. Each model shares in common the ideas that:

1. The *psuchē* is both plenary in nature, and that this plenum is hierarchically organized in a vertical manner.
2. The layers of the hierarchy are populated by entities who, the further one

---

108 Jung, "Archetypes of the Collective Unconscious," 4.
109 Ibid.
110 MacLennan, "Evolution, Jung, and Theurgy," 3.

proceeds from the egoic point, increase exponentially in the degree of their abstraction from the mode of consciousness/materiality.
3. Both the vectors of ontological dependence and causation/governance proceed downward, in a strictly unidirectional fashion.
4. Knowledge of the archetypes is not gained empirically, but is inborn—transforming encounters with archetypal forces not as discoveries, but as remembrances of what has been forgotten in the *psuchē*'s descent from universality into particularity.

These parallels do not end as the descriptive level of Jung's psychological models, but continue with his soteriological methodology: the process of individuation. The term individuation is defined by Jung as "the process by which a person becomes a psychological 'in-dividual,' that is, a separate, indivisible unity or 'whole.'"[111] This procedure, which is essentially soteriological, begins from the natural position within which we find ourselves: that of misinterpreting the conscious ego as, not only the center, but the *totality* of the self. Indeed, the ego is, in Jung's model, both dependent on and governed by the archetypes—"the unconscious is the mother of consciousness."[112] As Jung wrote:

> Just as consciousness arises from the unconscious, the ego-centre, too, crystallizes out of a dark depth in which it was somehow contained *in potentia*. Just as a human mother can only produce a human child, whose deepest nature lay hidden during its potential existence, so we are practically compelled to believe that the unconscious cannot be an entirely chaotic accumulation of instincts and images. There must be something to hold it together and give expression to the whole. Its centre cannot possibly be the ego, since the ego was born out of it into consciousness and turns back on the unconscious, seeking to shut it out as much as possible.[113]

Just as the theurgist finds himself to be a fragmentary façade of the One, so does the Jungian analyst find his ego to be but one body orbiting a mysterious center —a single member of a vast system. In each case, the aspirant finds himself humbled before the towering immensities that are the Gods.

The method by which the individuation process proceeds is two-fold, consisting of both *analytic* and *synthetic* functions. "First, it requires a person to break up

---

111 Jung, "Conscious, Unconscious, and Individuation," 275.
112 Ibid., 281.
113 Ibid.

(i.e. analyze and make conscious) the prevailing state of unconscious identification with extraneous figures and psychic contents...Second, after a person has made some headway with analysis, individuation requires paying careful and continuous attention to the emergence of the Self. This is the synthetic aspect of individuation and requires heeding the spirit of the unconscious."[114] The analytic portion of the individuation process is largely concerned with breaking the illusion that the *persona* (the complex which the ego identifies with) is *the* Self and recognizing it as *a* self.[115] This runs perfectly parallel to the Neoplatonic teachings on the *anatropē* (ἀνατροπή—"upside down") nature of the soul, in which the theurgist was taught to recognize that the identification of his soul with his individual, material self was false—that the true soul was far greater and more inclusive than the anatropic self.[116] It is vital, during this phase of the individuative process when the analysand disassociates the self from the persona, that he *not* replace that association with an archetype. "If a person succumbs to this temptation, the result is grandiose inflation (a "mania personality"). One becomes convinced that one is a prophet or a wise sage, a culture hero or demon lover, or another myth-sized figure, and an identity is forged from a psychological content that is archetypal."[117] Yet again, this runs parallel to the injunctions that the theurgical aspirant not succumb to the spiritualistic type of possession that the *goēs* (γόης—"sorcerer") were known for. There is, in both systems of praxis, a distinction between the kind of unhealthy obsessive possession that takes over a person—where the possessing force can be said to *ride* them—and the previously described *katochē*, where the theurgist's intent was to nourish "the intuitive mind and greatly [enlarge] the soul's receptacles for the Gods."[118] In the former, the self is completely taken over by the possessing force, bringing the quest for individuation/*henōsis* to a halt. In the latter, the temporary and *intended* identification with not one, but *many* Gods is seen as a necessary component of the synthetic processes.

As the process of individuation depends on the synthesis of the conscious and unconscious dimensions of the *psuchē*, "individuality cannot manifest fully until the invisible, unconscious elements of the personality that lie outside the range of the ego complex are brought into the open."[119] In other words, once the analysand has realized that the persona and ego complexes are *not* the Self, he must then en-

---

114 Murray Stein, "Individuation: Inner Work," *Journal of Jungian Theory and Practice* vol. 7, no. 2 (2005), http://www.junginstitute.org/pdf_files/JungV7N2p1-14.pdf (accessed June 5, 2011), 2.
115 Ibid., 4.
116 Shaw, 145.
117 Stein, 5.
118 Shaw, 87.
119 Stein, 10.

gage in the process of synthesizing *all* of the complexes and archetypes that comprise the individual and collective unconscious into a unified, harmonious whole. Just as this is the "higher" goal of Jungian synthesis, so was it the path towards *henōsis*. As the theurgist ascended upwards through the realms of the daimones and Gods, he had to gradually expand his soul to accommodate the synthetic sequence of *theōses* of "all the Gods" that led to the final goal of unity.[120] In neither case is the path upwards a straight shot to the end goal. The path is necessarily a slow process of assimilating and incorporating *all* of one's various complexes and archetypes into a harmonious, systemically organized One. It is only when this is accomplished that "the whole individual emerges"[121]—that "unification with God"[122] takes place.

From Emanation to Emergence

Throughout his writings, Jung tantalizingly hints at two different ways in which we can understand the archetypes. At times, he is forthright with his insistence that they are identical with Platonic forms,[123] yet at other times "he suggests that innumerable repetitions of typical forms of experience had resulted in the archetypes being somehow present in the structure of our brains."[124] The problem between the mutual acceptance of *both* propositions at face value is that we now know that there is a fundamental distinction between the ways in which phylogenetic groups emerge from ontogenetic[125] individuals and the way in which Platonic particulars emanate from universals. What this realization has led to is for a new breed of Jungian analysts to rework certain "problem" areas of Jung's psychological model to bring the system in line with the contemporary understandings of the emergence of human mentality gleaned from the disciplines of ethology[126] and evolutionary psychology. The resulting system—which is most clearly articulated in the contemporary works of Anthony Stevens and Bruce

---

120 Shaw, 156.
121 Stein, 12.
122 Remes, 171.
123 Jung, "Archetypes of the Collective Unconscious," 4.
124 David Ray Griffin, "Archetypal Psychology and Process Theology: Complementary Postmodern Movements," in *Archetypal Processes: Self and Divine in Whitehead, Jung, and Hillman*, ed. David Ray Griffin, (Evanston, IL: Northwestern University Press, 1989), 40.
125 Ontogeny is the individual development of an organism throughout the course of its life cycle. This is contrasted with phylogeny, which is the "evolutionary origin and development of a species," (Anthony Stevens, *Archetype Revisited: An Updated Natural History of the Self*, [Toronto: Inner City Books, 2003], 355).
126 Ethology being the zoological sub-discipline specializing in the study of animal behavior in its proper environmental context.

MacLennan—is a neurotheological[127] approach to archetypal psychology that, by recasting the emanative vector of ontological dependence into one of *emergence*, arrives at a reformulation of polytheistic theology which not only concurs with the Neoplatonic/Jungian model of *what* hierarchical levels exist, but combines this with a Darwinian explanation of *how* these layers of reality are formed. This marks a radical shift from the Platonic conception of emanative essentialism to a more Aristotelian theory of emergence which, by resisting the pitfalls of orthogenesis,[128] is able to cast off the nascent supernaturalism of the former and enjoy the consistency of the naturalism that is the logical conclusion of the latter.

This being the case, what precisely does this shift from emanationism to emergentism entail, and for what reasons is it necessary? Emergentism's roots lie with Aristotle's solution to the problem of universals. Where Plato treated the particular as being ontologically dependent on the universal, Aristotle took the contrary position.[129] Rather, he invoked the primacy of *substance*—of the particular—over that of the Form. While disagreeing heartily with Plato's essentialism, he is also clear to sidestep the nihilistic dangers of nominalism,[130] which results in the position we now know as *Aristotelian realism*, where the existence of the Forms is ontologically dependent on the substances.[131] In other words, for Aristotle, horseness as the essence of all horses cannot exist independently of *actual* horses. Its existence as a formal essence is wholly dependent upon its being actualized in particular individual horses. He believed that there was a "principle of growth" within organisms that was responsible for the qualities or form that would later emerge. Aristotle called this *entelechy* [ἐντελέχεια], the internal principle of growth and perfection that directed an organism to actualize the qualities that it contained in a merely potential state."[132] That is to say, for Aristotle, each individual contained a seed that was replete with the internalized Form of the or-

---

127 Neurotheology "is a unique field of study and investigation that seeks to understand the relationship specifically between the brain and theology, and more broadly between the mind and religion," (Andrew B. Newberg, *Principles of Neurotheology*, [Burlington, VT: Ashgate Publishing Company, 2010], 1).
128 Orthogenesis is a teleologically oriented take on evolution which understands the evolutionary process as purposefully directed towards the actualization of a final goal. Notable proponents include Jean-Baptiste de Lamarck and Pierre Teilhard de Chardin (Pierre Teilhard de Chardin, *The Phenomenon of Man*, trans. Bernard Wall, [New York: Harper & Row, 1959], 108–109).
129 Aristotle, *Metaphysics* trans. W.D. Ross, in *The Complete Works of Aristotle*, vol. 2, ed. Jonathan Barnes, (Princeton, NJ: Princeton University Press, 1984), 1038^b1–15.
130 Ibid., 1038^b25.
131 Ibid., 1038^b25–30.
132 Philip Clayton, "Conceptual Foundations of Emergence Theory," in *The Re-Emergence of Emergence: The Emergentist Hypothesis From Science to Religion*, eds. Philip Clayton and Paul Davies, (New York: Oxford University Press, 2006), 5.

ganism, which pulled it towards the actualization of this potentiality—towards its perfection as an instance of the Form. This was *the* original impetus behind biological science, and for millennia after Aristotle, the idea that both ontogeny and phylogeny were teleologically oriented reigned supreme. As Aristotle's metaphysics were heavily dependent on sequential causation, the Demiurge, who sat at the very *bottom* of the Aristotelian cosmos as the *first cause*, set in motion the *telos* (τέλος—"goal" or "purpose") that governed all of creation. It was not until the triumph of Charles Darwin that teleologically driven theories of evolution were finally put to rest.

In the contemporary sense, then, what then do we mean by *emergence*? At their root, emergentist theories stand in contradistinction to the notion of *reduction*—the idea that all natural phenomena can be explained via a single set of descriptive laws. This is not to say that emergentism is somehow *anti*-science. Quite the opposite is true. It is, rather, an attempt to delimit the domains proper to each mode of explanation based on the level within the emergent hierarchy being dealt with. In other words, it stands opposed to the view that, given proper data, *all* phenomena could be reduced to the formulæ of physics. The emergentist sees complex systems which emerge from simpler constituent systems to be wholly differentiated from their antecedents and thus not reducible to them. For example, a natural philosopher in Isaac Newton's day would likely have believed that, given sufficient data, the thought process of a person could be predicted with absolute certainty by the laws of physics. However, these

> limitations to the programme of reduction*ism*, understood as a philosophical position about science, do not affect everyday scientific practice. To do science still means to try to explain phenomena in terms of their constituent parts and underlying laws. Thus, endorsing an emergentist philosophy of science is in most cases consistent with business as usual in much of science.[133]

In terms of a formal definition of emergence, there are four features that constitute the emergence process:

1. Ontological Monism
2. Property Emergence
3. Irreducibility
4. Downward Causation[134]

---

133 Ibid., 1
134 Ibid., 2.

Ontological monism is a theory of substance which proposes that "all of reality is in essence either a single entity of a single kind of entity."[135] Monism stands apart from dualism, which is the position that there are *two* primary substances, and pluralism, the notion that there are *many* substances which are mutually differentiated. Dualism has its roots in Plato's essentialism, but found its full flowering in the Enlightenment with René Descartes' (1265–1308) famous dichotomy between the *res cogitans* (mentality) and *res extensia* (materiality).[136] Pluralism originated with the Pre-Socratic Atomists, Democritus (470–360 BC) and Leucippus (5th century BC), but is generally absent in contemporary philosophical discourse.[137] Monism, then, presents itself in three forms: materialism, idealism and neutral monism. Materialism (or physicalism) is the position that the sole substance of which all is composed is *material* in nature—that no matter how far we break things down, the very *bottom* of the metaphysical hierarchy is some form of matter.[138] Idealism, materialism's twin, is the exact opposite, putting forth the thesis that *thought* is ontologically primary. Originating with Parmenides, idealism also became extraordinarily popular in the Enlightenment, branching off into the metaphysical idealism of Bishop Berkeley (1685–1793), the transcendental idealism of Immanuel Kant (1724–1804), absolute idealism of Johann Fichte (1762–1814), and the personal idealism of John McTaggart (1866–1925).[139] While the process of emergence can be said to occur in any of the varieties of ontological monism, it is with the third variant, *neutral* monism, that this paper will demonstrate is most in keeping with MacLennan's reformulation of Neoplatonism. Neutral monism is an intermediary position between physicalism and idealism, proposing that the fundamental "stuff" of reality is neither mind nor matter, but is some sort of psychophysical substance that is at once both and neither—that mentality and materiality are in some way flip sides of the same ontological coin.[140] The most developed contemporary form of neutral monism is the *panexperientialism* of Alfred North Whitehead (1861–1947) and the process philosophers who followed in his wake.

Monism is, regardless of the particular type, an essential feature of emergentist theories for the reason that emergentism seeks to explain those very differences that are taken as ontologically primary in nature by dualists and pluralists *as emergent processes*. In other words, where a Cartesian sees consciousness and matter as intrinsically separate, neither being the source of the other, the emer-

---

135 Skrbina, 8.
136 Ibid., 13.
137 Copleston, *Greece and Rome*, 72.
138 Daniel Stoljar, "Physicalism," *Stanford Encyclopedia of Philosophy*, http://plato.stanford.edu/entries/physicalism/ (accessed June 9, 2011).
139 Skrbina, 10–11.
140 Ibid., 11–12.

gentist sees conscious neural systems as emergent properties of layer upon layer of processes, each emerging from a bottom foundation of monism. Thus might the emergentist explain that consciousness is a process that emerges from neurobiological process, that neurobiological processes emerge from chemical processes, that chemical processes emerge from physical processes and that physical processes (if the thinker is a physicalist) are ontologically prime and are the *source* upon which all higher tiers are dependent. The same chain of deconstruction could be replicated for idealist and neutral monist theories as well, but the line of reasoning is the same. Emergence explains what *appear* to be fundamental differences by means of *property emergence* (the definition's second point). This can be explained further by the following. For any emergent property (P) of an object (O), there are four conditions which hold true:

1. That P supervenes[141] on the properties of the parts of O;
2. That P is not a property of any of O's parts;
3. That P is distinct from any of O's structural properties'
4. That P exerts a downwardly directed determinative influence upon the behavioral patterns concerning O's parts.[142]

This above example demonstrates the third point of our definition of emergence, that the emergent property is irreducible to the system's components from which it emerges. It is this point of the definition which *necessitates* that one adopt the presupposition "that reality is divided into a number of distinct levels or orders," which is "in stark contrast to what we might call 'New Age holism,'" where the whole is treated more as a flat plane—what Willard Quine (1908–2000)called a desert landscape—than the branching, tree-like structure of an emergent hierarchy.[143] Thus, according to this point, not only are the metaphysical structures themselves not directly reducible to their constituents, but also are the forms of causality associated with these structures similarly non-reducible. Animal behavior proves to be *the* paramount example of this principle of non-reducibility. While the individual cells of which any creature is composed can be demonstrated to behave in a regular fashion by the laws of biology, the individual creature which emerges from this mass of cells cannot be described by means of the same rules. The behavior of a cat demonstrates a degree of complexity that can in no wise be directly reduced to the behaviors of its component parts. On their own, these parts behave in one way, but their assemblage into the organic

---

141 The term "supervene" is defined by Dictionary.com as "to take place or occur as something additional or extraneous (sometimes followed by on or upon)," meaning that a property which supervenes on a system emerges as something additional to that system—something which none of its internal processes carry as an attribute.
142 Clayton, 3.
143 Ibid.

feline form births a new degree of complexity whose behavioral patterns are shared by none of the members of the aggregate of which it is composed. Thus, "in complex systems, the outcome is more than the sum of the parts."[144]

The fourth and final point of our definition of emergence is that of *downward causation*. This is the idea of whole-part influence, where the whole that emerges is able to exert causative influence over the parts from which it is constituted.[145] In this way, an emergent system's behavior is not only *not* determined by its parts, but the future life-courses of those very parts are governed in part by the emergent system, leading to a model of causation whose vector is *bidirectional*. This is in stark contrast to the unidirectional vector of ontological dependency that we found in Neoplatonism. Under the emergentist model, there is the bottom-up vector that describes the constitutive causes which lead to the *existence* of the emergent entity, and there are also top-down vectors of governance which describe the effects that the behaviors of the whole have upon its parts. The animal proves itself to be, yet again, a perfect example. As discussed previously the animal itself is dependent upon the cellular and organic parts from which it emerges, yet as a complex system above and beyond those parts, it has a degree of novelty of action not owned by its constituents that allows it to influence their behavior in ways that they are individually incapable of doing. The cells compose that which *is* the cat, but the cat *itself* decides where the whole will go and what it will do. The cells have no choice in these decisions made by the cat, for the whole, in this instance, exerts near complete governance over its parts.

Evolutionary Thought

Alongside emergence, the process of *evolution* is a key concept in this paper's reworking of Neoplatonism. And, as with emergence, evolutionary thinking also begins with Aristotle. Apart from being one of the two most influential Western philosophers, Aristotle is commonly regarded as "the father of all science."[146] The philosophical Aristotle was a pioneer in metaphysics, logic, ethics and aesthetics; and at the same time, the scientific Aristotle virtually created the disciplines of physics, biology and psychology. Indeed, his collected works contain more dedicated writing on zoology than they do on any one philosophical issue. While Aristotle did *not* develop any kind of formal theory of evolution, he did lay the groundwork for later thinkers to do so. Much of Aristotle's zoological work

---

144 Ibid., 4.
145 Ibid.
146 Henry Plotkin, *Evolutionary Thought in Psychology: A Brief History*, (Malden, MA: Blackwell Publishing, 2004), 13.

consisted of cataloging the ways in which animal species were different from one another and in theorizing ways in which these species groups were related to each other—coining the term *genus* to refer to related groupings of species.[147] This recognition of the facticity of the relatedness of the whole animal kingdom combined with his treatment of all extent causative processes ultimately leading back to a primary uncaused cause, the Demiurge, perfectly set the stage for the theory of evolution to be developed in full. If all current states of nature are dependent upon anterior causes, and all causes lead back to a single cause, then it follows that the chain of causation necessarily follows an upwardly branching pattern from which differentiation evolves from a singularity. While a similar line of reasoning leads from the Neoplatonic *Phusis* to the One, the difference here is that Aristotle's conception of the world's unfolding was rooted in emergentism rather than emanationism. This necessitates that the combined differentiation and relatedness among phyla are the result of a bottom-up chain of events in which the complexity of the material world is conceived of as being dependent on further *material* rather than *ideational* causes. In other words, that there exist a number of related species in the world is not owed to a downwardly directed causative vector leading from the Forms, but stems from the branching of one biological group into several.

While this notion of biological evolution was not *specifically* worked out in detail by Aristotle, it was upon his work that all subsequent inquiries into the field would be made. It would not, however, be until the early 19th century that evolutionary thought would once again be pursued. This revival came at the hands of Jean-Baptiste de Lamarck (1744–1829). It was with his 1809 publishing of *Philosophie Zoologique* that Lamarck put forth his theory of evolution. While revolutionary at the time, we now know that Lamarck's orthogenetically driven theories were largely incorrect. His initial assumptions "were that organisms are always wonderfully adapted to their environments, but also that environments constantly change in time. From these it followed that the organisms themselves must be able to change in time."[148] Thus, under Lamarck's theory, *all* biological change is in *response* to environmental change imposing an evolutionary imperative upon the organism. In this way, he viewed *all* physical adaptions as having developed in direct response to environmental pressures, giving them a distinct *purpose*. So, while these evolutionary changes were passed on via the line of genealogical descent, no adaptive change came from within the organism itself; all was directed externally. Evolution was the organism's adaptions to its form done so with the express purpose of increasing survivability in a changing world.

---

147 Aristotle, "History of Animals," trans. d'A.W. Thompson, in *The Complete Works*, 486ª15–20.
148 Plotkin, 22.

The point about *purpose*, what Aristotle called *telos*, is important. This is what designates Lamarckian evolution as a teleologically driven theory. "It is essentially a theory of *progress* by way of the interplay of specified processes of environmental change, organismic needs and activity giving rise to changes within organisms that are passed across generations."[149] This emphasis on evolution as a process of *progress* continued well into the late 19th century and, due to Herbert Spencer's (1820–1903) popularizations, became a dominant force in that period's philosophy of science. Within this framework "species may be placed along a linear scale…from simple creatures to the more complex."[150] This notion of the evolutionary vector being completely linear in nature led to the popular idea that the transitions from simple unicellular organisms, to vertebrates, on down to the more "elevated" animals such as man represented a purposeful progression that was directed towards the end of the emergence of intelligence. Taken to its logical extremes, this orthogenetic position was fully fleshed out in the mid-20th century by Pierre Teilhard de Chardin (1881–1955), who equated the evolutionary process with the emergence of consciousness,[151] thus treating man as the tip of the arrow of the vector of evolutionary ascent.[152] As the orthogeneticists saw things, if the *purpose* of evolution is to evolve organisms into increasingly complexified forms, and as the goal of this complexity is the rise of consciousness and intelligence, then mankind simply *must* be the current pinnacle of evolutionary progress.

This theory of externally directed progress was not, however, to triumph. The evolutionary theory of Charles Darwin (1809–1882) has since been demonstrated countless times over as the more truthful explanation of phylogenetic change. Just as Lamarckian evolution was "driven wholly by external forces of change, which mediated by the altered needs and activities of organisms, became *impressed* by these external changes upon the malleable substrate of the organism and then transmitted to offspring," so did Darwin completely contrast this by proposing that differences and variations in the biotic kingdom were "caused by events internal to each organism and occur in advance of and unconnected with changes in the world."[153] This view of the evolutionary process as driven by *selection* rather than impression was a complete deviation from Lamarck's model of linear ascent. If change occurs, as Darwin theorized, due to natural selection then it follows that the only *telos* that could be said to be affecting the process would be particular to each organism.

---

149 Ibid., 23–24.
150 Ibid., 25.
151 Teilhard, 243.
152 Ibid., 224.
153 Plotkin, 34.

This shift from an externally directed purpose to one which is internally directed completely strips Darwinian theory of the top-down mechanism of the orthogeneticists and naturalizes the picture into one in which evolution is a thoroughly bottom-up process of emergence. In other words, under the orthogenetic model a *single* change in the outside environment impressed changes upon the organisms within it, the Darwinian theory transforms this into a process by which undirected "changes are incorporated into an integrated bodily structure and function better suited to survival and reproductive competence (fitness), and somehow transmitted to offspring."[154] So, while the Lamarckian theory may speak of higher and lower species, the Darwinian model only speaks of difference and change. It is a theory of *process* rather than *progress*. Thus, the overall picture transforms from a pyramid, with man at the very top, to a tree, with innumerable branches reaching outward in all directions. Following Darwin's revolution, our understanding of the mechanism by which organisms evolve was dramatically increased by Gregor Mendel's (1822–1884) discovery of the genetic heritability of traits, and James Watson (b. 1928) and Francis Crick's (1916–2004) understanding of the role of DNA in transmitting genetic information from one generation to the next. While an in depth discussion of the discoveries of these men would prove interesting, it would stray far from this paper's thesis. It will suffice to say that the discovery and subsequent mapping of the human genome has proven to be of the utmost importance in understanding how Darwinian selection occurs.

In short, the current understanding of evolution involves four mechanisms. Natural selection, which was Darwin's original conception of evolution's "how," deals primarily with the evolutionary fitness of an organism.[155] That is to say that the genetic contribution made by any organism to the following generation is dependent upon its ability to do two things: survive and reproduce. Therefore, those organisms which are more likely to do both of these are more likely to pass on their traits to future generations than are organisms which fail at either. The second mechanism is *genetic drift*, which is the tendency that alleles[156] have to

---

154 Ibid.
155 Nicholas H. Barton, et al., *Evolution*, (New York: Cold Springs Harbor Laboratory Press, 2007), 464.
156 The term allele is defined by *The American Heritage Science Dictionary* as, "Any of the possible forms in which a gene for a specific trait can occur. In almost all animal cells, two alleles for each gene are inherited, one from each parent. Paired alleles (one on each of two paired chromosomes) that are the same are called *homozygous*, and those that are different are called *heterozygous*. In heterozygous pairings, one allele is usually dominant, and the other recessive. Complex traits such as height and longevity are usually caused by the interactions of numerous pairs of alleles, while simple traits such as eye color may be caused by just one pair."

change on their own, in the absence of external selective forces.[157] In other words, due to genetic drift, given identical environments, two separate groups of organisms which began with identical genomes would eventually drift apart into two distinct genotypes.[158] The third means by which evolutionary change occurs is gene flow. This is the kind of interchange of genetic information that occurs when previously separate groups intermingle.[159] For example, during the course of any tribal migration from one region to another, the tribe in question is often subsumed by, or itself subsumes, another tribe. The admixture of these two genotypes results in the emergence of a genotype which is distinct from each of the two by virtue of having received genetic material from both. The final evolutionary mechanism is mutation. Mutations are similar to the allele changes in genetic drift, but most often occurs in concert with natural selection.[160] Mutation would be the genetic way in which a species which originally evolved in a normal environment gradually tends to lose pigmentation and eye sight when transported to a lightless environment. A primary example of this would be the blind, pigmentless lobsters recently discovered deep within the hydrothermal vents on the floor of the Pacific.[161]

The Blank Slate

The discoveries of these methodological means by which evolutionary change occurs in population groups revolutionized Darwin's original findings, giving scientists insight into how microevolution on the genetic scale eventually translates into macroevoluton on the scale of animals such as birds, reptiles and humans. However, although these breakthroughs were primarily interpreted in terms of physical adaptions, a cotemporal exploration of the evolution of *mind* was being undertaken by a handful of dedicated individuals. The development of evolutionary psychology was, initially, met with disapproval from the behavioral psychologists of the early 20th century. The reason for this was the primacy that a particular epistemological theory had gained over the centuries: that of the *tabula rasa*. Like so many ideas in contemporary philosophy, the *tabula rasa*, or "blank slate," is a concept which arose out of Aristotle's critiques of Platonic metaphysics. Intimately tied to the theory of the Forms, was Plato's doctrine of *anamnēsis* (ἀνάμνησις—"a calling to mind," or "recollection"). In the *Phaedo* dialogue,

---

157 Barton, 418.
158 The complete genetic makeup of an organism (its *genotype*) can be contrasted with its physical makeup (its *phenotype*).
159 Mark Ridley, *Evolution*, 3rd ed., (Malden, MA: Blackwell Science Ltd., 2004), 359.
160 Ibid., 172.
161 E. Macpherson, W. Jones and, M. Segonzac, "A new squat lobster family of Galatheoidea (Crustacea, Decapoda, Anomura) from the hydrothermal vents of the Pacific-Antarctic Ridge," in *Zoosystema* 27, no. 4 (2006), 709–710.

Plato explains "that what we call learning is recollection,"[162] for while we certainly do acquire some sort of knowledge about particulars, that core of any given particular that truly reflects the universal from which it emanates is not learned of by empirical observation. The knowledge of it is *remembered*, for, since the kinds of rational truths that Plato believes can be innately known via rememberence are *formal* truths (e.g. the principle of two similar objects being the same *type* of object, mathematical truths, etc.) that cannot *not* exist, they have been present in the mind eternally. That they are largely forgotten is, Plato would say, a symptom of the soul's descent from the world of the Forms into the material body. Thus, for Plato, all "learning" of that category of rational truths was never truly the learning of something new, but was always the clarifying of that which was obscured by the mists of the material hypostasis, making his approach to epistemology the precursor to modern Cartesian rationalism.

For Aristotle, however, the process by which the mind obtained knowledge of truths was rooted more fundamentally in empiricism than rationalism. The term *tabula rasa*, which literally means "uninscribed tablet," is an epistemological orientation that Aristotle developed to suit his critiques of Platonic metaphysics. If Plato's rationalism is the natural consequence of emanation metaphysics, so, Aristotle reasoned, must empiricism be the epistemological cognate to emergentism. In what is the first psychological text, *On the Soul*, he writes:

> If thinking is like perceiving, it must be either a process in which the soul is acted upon by what is capable of being thought, or a process different from but analogous to that. The thinking part must therefore be, while impassible, capable of receiving the form of an object.[163]

Later in the same chapter, he concludes this thought with:

> What it thinks must be in it just as characters may be said to be on a writing-table on which as yet nothing actually stands written: this is exactly what happens with thought.[164]

In other words, what Aristotle is saying is that the process of thought is wholly receptive in nature. The mind is, at birth, a completely blank slate upon which experiences write themselves. This transmission of external data to our internal memory bank is the foundation upon which all subsequent doctrines of empiri-

---

162 Plato, *Phaedo*, trans. G.M.A. Grube, in *Plato*, 73b.
163 Aristotle, *On the Soul*, trans. J.A. Smith, in *The Complete Works*, 429^{a}10–15.
164 Ibid., 429^{b}1–430^{a}1.

cism rest. It stands in direct contradistinction to the rationalist thesis that some—if not *all*—truths can be known in the absence of the mind experiencing something outside itself. Indeed, although empiricists may concur with rationalists that certain types of truths (e.g. mathematical, logical, etc.) *are* eternally so, yet they would disagree that these truths can be known without their being experienced in some fashion. For example, while a rationalist might argue that upon seeing two things which are equal in some respect, such as two sticks of equal length, we *recognize* the facticity of their equality by virtue of recalling the intrinsically known Form of "the Equal."[165] Whereas, the empiricist would argue the counter position that such knowledge of Forms emerges from repeated exposure to instantiations.

While empiricism *currently* forms the bedrock of popular epistemology, after Aristotle's passing it was forgotten for over a thousand years. In the Middle Ages, much of the disputes between Aristotle and Plato were reenacted in a Catholic setting by Thomas Aquinas and Bonaventure (1221–1274) respectively. However, it was not until John Locke's (1632–1704) restatement of the empirical thesis that the *tabula rasa* concept reemerged from the hoary antiquity of the Classical world to take its place as the epistemology of natural science. In his widely influential *Essay Concerning Human Understanding* he phrased his position as:

> Let us then suppose the Mind to be, as we say, white Paper, void of all Characters, without any *Ideas*; how comes it to be furnished? Whence comes it by that vast store, which the busy and boundless Fancy of Man has painted on it, with an almost endless variety? Whence has it all the materials of Reason and Knowledge? To this I answer, in one word, From *Experience*: In that, all our Knowledge is founded; and from that it ultimately derives it self.[166]

This notion that *all* knowledge is necessarily *a posteriori* became firmly entrenched in the philosophies of science which followed in Locke's wake. And, although psychology as a proper discipline did not emerge until centuries later, by the time it *did*, it took the *tabula rasa* as a given. This was the epistemological foundation of *behaviorism*, one of the first major schools of psychological thought. Behaviorism was an early 20th century train of psychological thought which revolved around the premise that *all* behavior and thought in an individual

---

165 Plato, *Phaedo*, 74a–b.
166 John Locke, *Essay Concerning Human Understanding*, ed. Peter H. Nidditch, (Oxford: Oxford University Press, 1975), 104.

was entirely owed to external conditioning stimuli.[167] This was the origin of the *nurture* side of the still raging "nature vs. nurture" debate regarding the human mind. Thus did the behaviorists adopt so extreme of an interpretation of Locke's *tabula rasa* that the very notion of such things as human instincts was denied—favoring the position that all "instinctive" behaviors were the results of postnatal conditioning. One of the intellectual leaders of the behaviorist movement, James B. Watson (1878–1958) famously stated:

> Give me a dozen healthy infants, well-formed and my own specified world to bring them up in and I'll guarantee to take any one at random and train him to become any type of specialist I might select—doctor, lawyer, artist, merchant-chief and, yes, even beggar-man and thief, regardless of his talents, penchants, tendencies, abilities, vocations, and race of his ancestors.[168]

This insistence upon the primacy of nurture over nature formed the basis for "the passionate opposition to human ethology and sociobiology expressed by Marxists psychologists and sociologists who are mythologically committed to the belief that human nature is unstructured and that all human behaviors arise from conditioning by social agencies."[169] If human thought and the consequent behavior which stems from that thought is literally a blank slate at birth that can be inscribed with *any* set of pseudo-instincts, then this fuels the fires of those authoritarians who would see whole population groups programmed to behave in a particular way. This triumph of behaviorism stood upon the corpse of the abysmal failure of theories of human instinct that were rooted in Lamarckian thought. Yet, with the inevitable seeping of Darwinian ideas into psychological circles a contemporary challenger to the *tabula rasa* soon arose.

The refutation of pure empiricism in psychological epistemology would not, this time, be found by returning to a strictly Platonic rationalism. Rather, the response came from the blending of ethology and psychology that resulted in the emergence of evolutionary psychology. Now, at the time of behaviorism's reign, the idea that *non-human* animals' behaviors were largely (if not wholly) determined by biological instincts was taken for granted. Darwin himself defined instinct as:

> An action, which we ourselves require experience to enable us to perform, when performed by an animal, more especially by a

---

167 Plotkin, 58.
168 James B. Watson, *Behaviorism*, (Chicago: University of Chicago Press, 1924), 104.
169 Stevens, 259.

very young one, without experience, and when performed by many individuals in the same way, without their knowing for what purpose it is performed, is usually said to be instinctive.[170]

This is to say that, for example, when turtles swim to the shore to lay their eggs, they are not doing this because they have observed and learned this behavior from external sources. Their drive to do so comes solely from within; it is an inborn behavioral pattern that is common to all members of the species. This type of instinctive behavior, in Darwin's conception, also avoids the Lamarckian problem of teleology. The turtles do not swim ashore because they have some sort of *a priori* knowledge of what a beach is or why it is beneficial to their genetic continuance to lay their eggs there, yet due to countless generations of "selection acting *a posteriori* upon variant egg-laying behaviors had resulted in a particular species-typical behavior as an adaption for laying eggs."[171] Thus, what initially appears to be some kind of Platonic *a priori* knowledge is explained to be *a posteriori* selective criteria which have been, via heredity, transformed into something resembling an *a priori*. That is the nature of instincts and mechanism by which they operate and evolve.

Working off of this theory of instincts, that certain varieties of animal behavior related to survival are performed without conscious purpose, Konrad Lorenz (1903–1989) founded the discipline of ethology in the 1930s. As the study of animal behavior in a natural environmental context—as opposed to previous methodologies which primarily relied upon the investigation of either dead animals or of live organisms in a laboratory environment—the ethologists were quick to discover that there are direct linkages between elements of animal behavior and the environments within which the animal evolved; this relation was termed "the environment of evolutionary adaptiveness."[172] However, within psychology and philosophies of mind, the Cartesian idea of human exceptionalism—which bifurcated the world into one group, humans who were free willed and capable of novel behaviors, and another, all others whose behavior was determined by physical, chemical and biological laws—reigned supreme. This position, called philosophical libertarianism, that we humans have absolute free will and are capable of responding in whatever way we choose to whatever situation presents itself to us, stems naturally from the ego's experience of itself as a conscious agent. The widespread pre-philosophical belief in the absolute truth of this position which underlies most people's conception on themselves proved to be a bul-

---

170 Charles Darwin, *On the Origin of Species*, 6th ed., (New York: Mentor Books, 1958), 228.
171 Plotkin, 35.
172 Plotkin, 93.

wark against the application of ethology to psychology, for fear that such a combination would inevitably lead to a form of genetic determinism in which *all* of our thoughts and behaviors were pre-programmed in our genes.[173] Fortunately, the picture, as uncovered by evolutionary psychologists, is not a completely "nature" answer to the "nurture" of the behaviorists.

Beginning with Lorenz's key discovery about the environment of evolutionary adaptiveness, a new school of psychologists began analyzing human behavior through the lens of ethology. Although they did take into account the fact that humans, as do *all* animals, display a wide range of behaviors which *are* instinctive, they did not espouse a strong form of genetic determinism. Rather, they conceived of instincts as releasing mechanisms for *patterns* of behavior or experience, the activation of which was dependent upon certain environmental cues. This differentiates the instinct as an inherited mode of functioning rather than an inherited idea.[174] To explain this, a physical corollary may be helpful. Take breathing for example; it is an involuntary biological pattern of activity that all humans must breathe. This behavioral pattern is inherited and is a necessary function related to our respiratory and circular systems. However, *within* this inherited pattern of behavior, we have the ability to consciously shape certain aspects of this behavior's manifestation. We can choose to breath fast, slow, or to hold our breath. In times of duress, unconsciousness, etc. our instinctive mode takes over and breathing is automatically regulated to suit the present environmental cue (e.g. slow elongated during sleep, staccato during physical exertion, etc.). We do not *learn* to breathe; it is an instinct. Yet, we *can* learn how to control our breath, as any athlete or *yogī* will tell us. In this same way is our performance of more complex behaviors such as mating, parenting, etc. *guided* by instinctive patterns yet not wholly determined by them. In this way, we might think of instincts as like rivers. We can canoe down a river and, to a degree, control where amidst the waters we travel, yet we are at once constrained both by the spatial dimensions of the riverbed (the patterned mode of behavior) *and* the forward flowing course (the biological imperative to perform instinctive actions which relate to our survival). In this way, the epistemology of the evolutionary psychologists is neither Platonic nor Aristotelian, but is rather a synthesis of the two, incorporating both a phylogenetically determined set of behavioral matrices that are expressed ontogenetically as well as the ability for previously unknown information to be learned empirically and for novel behavior to be exhibited within pre-structured modes of expression.

MacLennan's Synthesis

---
173 Stevens, 9.
174 Ibid., 18.

Within this overarching backdrop of emergentism, evolution and the nature/nurture problem, we may now begin to explore the system of thought which is this paper's central concern: Bruce MacLennan's synthesis of Classical Neoplatonism, Jungian psychology, and the theories of emergence and evolution into a single explanatory model. To begin, let us reexamine the relationship between Jungian archetypes and the instincts. Jung maintained that "the archetypes are the unconscious images of the instincts themselves, in other words, that they are patterns of instinctual behavior."[175] He identified the archetypal with the instinctual so strongly that we might go so far as to say that "the hypothesis of the collective unconscious is, therefore, no more daring than to assume there are instincts."[176] MacLennan takes this correlation of Jung's and expands its meaning to account for our new found understanding of the origin of instincts as described by evolutionary psychology. MacLennan examines Jung's distinction between the *internal* and *external* aspects of archetypes. The external manifestations are the instinctual behaviors that are observable, quantifiable, etc. The internal aspects are the archetypal images themselves.[177] So, if we take, for example, the Mother archetype, the external aspect would be that universal set of instinctive behaviors that mothers display towards their infant children. The internal manifestation of this would be the various mother deities of the world's religions. To the outside observer, the actualization of this dynamic pattern of instinctive behavior simply appears as normal actions appropriate to the situation, yet for the mother, "when an appropriate *releasing stimulus* activates the instinct, you may feel you are living a myth or that you are possessed by a spirit with its own agenda."[178] The releasing stimulus in this case would be the correlative instincts that the child is born with. Evolutionary psychology tells us that children are genetically endowed with the predispositions to appropriately interact with the world through the family structure, and that its earliest instincts are largely geared specifically towards activating the maternal archetype of its own mother.[179] Thus, in a situation like this, a newborn, whose mind is more unconscious than conscious, operates nearly entirely in the mode of the Child archetype, which in turn serves as the releasing stimulus to activate the Mother archetype. The two have a psychic relationship that is one of mythic symbiosis—their instinctive behavior reenacting the universal myths of the Great Mother and the Holy Son (e.g. Frigga and Baldr, Isis and Horus, Mary and Jesus, etc.).

---

175 Jung, "The Archetypes of the Collective Unconscious," 44.
176 Ibid.
177 MacLennan, "Evolutionary Jungian Psychology,"
　http://web.eecs.utk.edu/~mclennan/papers/EJP.pdf (accessed June 15, 2011), 2.
178 Ibid.
179 Stevens, 107.

Now, this conception of archetypal possession is none too different from Jung's, except in the fact that MacLennan (following Stevens' lead) specifically advocates the position that the archetypes are *evolved* portions of our minds—something Jung likely would not have *disagreed* with, but never personally espoused. It is this evolutionary origin of the archetypes that serves as the necessity for MacLennan's reversal of the vector of ontological dependency which leads to the constitution of the archetypes. He explains this via the connection between the genome and the unconscious. An individual's genome is the sum total of that person's genetic makeup, a sequence of millions upon millions of bits of genetic data all stored within the nucleus of each cell of one's body. Each person's genome is the *seed* of their archetypal world. This is, again, not strict genetic determinism, for even though an acorn can only grow into an oak tree, so is the individual tree's pattern of actualization affected by environmental conditions.[180] In the same way the *ontogenetic* seed that is an individual's genome necessarily develops within a *phylogenetically* determined pattern, yet within that pattern the unfolding is affected by the environment (both physical and interpersonal) within which this development occurs. This governance of the ontogenetic *psuchē* (the individual unconscious) by the phylogenetic *psuchē* (the collective unconscious) still lines up nicely with the Neoplatonic and Jungian theory of emanation. However, evolutionary understandings of the relationship between ontogeny and phylogeny render this thesis null in two ways.

First, the Neoplatonic conception of the Forms was that they were *eternal* and *unchanging*. An evolutionary understanding of instincts fundamentally precludes this as a possibility. To be sure, such things are *relatively* unchanging, yet change *does* occur on an evolutionary time table (on the order of a hundred or more generations). "Thus the archetypes are not innate *images*, as it is often supposed, but *dynamic forms* shaping perception and behavior."[181] This is so because "the genome is not a fixed essence, but a time-varying form."[182] This admission of dynamism does not change the fundamental *nature* of the archetypes. Under this view they are still empirical, stable and public. Yet, the notion of stability must now be seen as an extremely slow moving type of flux rather than Plato's ideal fixity. If change and adaption are constant factors in the evolution of a species, the instincts that form the unconscious backbone of that species' behavior must be in just as constant an evolutionary state of flux as are their phenotypical[183] attributes. When considering only the external behavioral aspects of the arche-

---

180 MacLennan, "Evolutionary Jungian Psychology," 5.
181 MacLennan, "Evolution, Jung, and Theurgy," 2.
182 Ibid., 15.
183 Where the genotype is the genetic profile of an organism, its phenotype is the outward manifestation of the active portions of this genetic code—in other words, one's physical characteristics.

types, this may seem, nowadays, like a given and no big deal. However, when the internal aspect is taken into account, such a reformulation has tremendous theological consequences. If the Gods are the *products* of evolutionary processes, then they are neither unchanging nor eternal. Their existence and forms are intrinsically linked to humanity's phylogenetic development. Far from being atemporal, they are *in process*—something which is quite far indeed from Plotinian and Iamblichean theology.

The first objection raises the second. The relationship between ontogeny and phylogeny—the evolution of individuals and of population groups—"must avoid *essentialism*, the notion that there is an 'ideal kind' for each species."[184] Although the human genome is connected to the individual genome in a way that mirrors the Platonic relationship between the Form of the ideal man, *Anthrōpos* (Άνθρωπος—"*man* generally"), the vector of ontological dependence is not the same. MacLennan tells us that the phylogenetic Form of man is "an Aristotelian abstraction from particulars...rather than an eternal Platonic essence."[185] In other words, the genome as a thing unto itself *emerges* from the individual genotypes of extant actual humans at any given time. The individuals do not *emanate* from the genomic universal; the converse is true. In this way we see that rather than men being dependent upon Man, Man is only capable of emerging from men and cannot, as an idea, exist without them. This shift from Platonic to Aristotelian vectors of dependence *does* keep in tact the basic "shape" of the Neoplatonic cosmos, but the way in which they are related to one another is drastically altered. In other words, MacLennan's recasting of Neoplatonism still admits a realism which manifests as a multi-tiered hierarchy of metaphysical layers. The change is in the bottom-up reversal of the ontological vector of dependence.

This, again, has staggering theological ramifications. As we remember, according to the Classical Neoplatonists, man, quite literally, came *from* the Gods. The downwardly directed emanative vector ensured a logical way of understanding this in a sense that at once incorporated the long held Pagan notions of this relationship consisting of:

1. Hereditary descent from the Gods.
2. The dependency of the material world upon the celestial.
3. The governance of mankind by the Gods.

Though it may seem that MacLennan's reversal necessarily negates all three of these propositions, it is really only the second that is fundamentally incompatible

---
184 Ibid.
185 Ibid.

with an Aristotelian recasting of the emanative vector into one of emergence. Let us begin with the third point. As mentioned in the paper's section on emergence, *downward causation*, is a hallmark feature of *all* emergent processes. Thus, we do know that phylogeny *does* govern ontogeny (e.g. individual humans, regardless of particularities, develop into *humans*), thus would the collective *psuchē* govern the behavioral unfolding of the individual *psuchē*. The internal cognate to this relationship is that we, as individuals, are governed—via the emergent process' downward causation—by the Gods. They are in positions of spiritual authority over us such that our behaviors, attitudes, emotions and thoughts are beholden not only to their subtle guidance (*viz.* the large scale governing of ontogeny by phylogeny), but also to their possession at critical times (*viz.* the activation of particular archetypes by corresponding release stimuli). The first point, the near universal Pagan belief that the Gods sit at the top of humanity's family tree, is upheld by this large-scale phylogenetic governance. Not only is an individual's personal ontogenetic development an acorn which has budded off of the phylogenetic tree of Man, such is true for mankind as a whole. In a very real way, MacLennan's recasting makes this hereditary connection to the Gods that much *closer*. In the past, it was only thought that such a link was made in the misty days of anthropogenesis. Yet, under MacLennan's view, the divine creation of man occurs with *each and every* ontogenesis. The anthropogenic myths in which Óðinn, Hœnir and Lóðurr bequeath life upon driftwood,[186] or Yahweh's breathing of life into dust[187] are not, under this restructuring of Neoplatonism, *historical* events that happened at some discrete point in the past. Rather, they are to be seen as processes which are continually occurring in the beginning of every ontogenetic process. The creation of man by the Gods is not something that *happened*; it is something that is *happening*.

In this way, not only does MacLennan's Neoplatonism *not* strip the Gods of their divinity by recasting them as ontologically dependent upon humanity, but, quite the opposite, it *increases* their dominion. Another point which MacLennan's theology resolves rather nicely is that of the goodness of the Gods. Following Plato, Plotinus identified the One the Form of the Good.[188] In this way, lesser hypostases, the Gods, were seen as rarified and differentiated manifestations of the Good. This, however presents a dramatic problem in that the Gods, as described in the myths of the world and as experienced autophenomenologically during the grips of instinctive possession not only often *do not* comport themselves in accord with Plato's idea of the Good, but also tend to be at odds with one another

---

186 *Völuspá* in *The Eddas: The Keys to the Mysteries of the North*, trans. James Allen Chisholm, http://www.woodharrow.com/images/ChisholmEdda.pdf (accessed June 15, 2011), 5.
187 Genesis 2:7.
188 Remes, 39.

(e.g. the wars between the Olympians and Titans, or the Æsir and the Jötnar). MacLennan's solution to this is to conceive of the Gods *not* as *absolutely* good, but as anthropocentrically good, in that "they have promoted the survival of our species."[189] In a way, they are "beyond good and evil," for such terms are culturally conditioned superego complexes; the archetypal Gods are not bound by cultural mores and "serve their own ends, which may not be ours, and their inclinations may not conform to contemporary standards of morality, or promote our individual interests."[190] As beings which comprise the *collective* mind of mankind, their interests must necessarily be concerned with the long term survivability of that collective. Sometimes this may overlap with that of the individual or a particular culture, but oftentimes it does not.

One point further brought up by MacLennan that somewhat clashes with the sensibilities of the Classical Neoplatonist is the notion that the Gods relate differently to different types of people. Under Plotinian and Iamblichean Neoplatonism *theōsis* was the reception of the divine by the properly prepared human soul. Under that model the Gods existed independently of humanity and would likely be experienced similarly by all people able to attain the same level of *theōsis*. However, evolutionary Jungian psychology tells us that there are significant differences in the human experiences of archetypes, and that this differentiation is most strongly typified in the the male/female dichotomy.[191] Jungians explain these differences by means of the Anima and Animus archetypes. All humans are divided, sexually, into two genetic groups: those bearing XX chromosomes (women) and XY chromosomes (men). This genotypical variation is the root of phenotypical dimorphism, the psychosomatic variations that differentiate men from women.[192] However, "everybody carries qualities of the opposite sex, not only in the physical sense of contrasexual genes, hormones and anatomical vestiges, but also in the psychological realm of attitudes, feelings and ideas."[193] Jung discovered that the psychic manifestations of these were archetypal, with men carrying a feminine archetype called the *Anima* and women a masculine archetype known as the *Animus*. The presence of these contrasexual archetypes within each person was seen by Jung as the means by which potential mates were instinctively driven to comprehend the numinous *otherness* of the opposite sex. "Thus the whole nature of man presupposes woman, both physically and spiritually. His system is tuned to woman from the start," and *vice versa*.[194] The physical aspect is self explanatory, human biology necessarily presupposes two op-

---

189 MacLennan, "Evolution, Jung, and Theurgy," 16.
190 Ibid.
191 MacLennan, "Evolutionary Jungian Psychology," 6.
192 Ibid.
193 Stevens, 76.
194 Jung, *Man and His Symbols*, (London: Aldus Books, 1964), 50.

posite sexes in order for genetic continuation to occur. It is, for our purposes, the *internal* aspect that is far more interesting. Stevens tells us that the intense attraction that is felt by a man towards a woman occurs when she is seen to be the embodiment of his Anima. Because of this she may *seem* to him to be "more beautiful, more numinous than any other woman around—often to the stupification of his friends who completely fail to understand what he sees in her."[195] This is one of the most commonly experienced instances of what Jung called *archetypal projection*, where one party (in this case, the man) is possessed by an archetype. That archetype, in turn, projects upon a person with whom the man is relating (in this case, the woman) the archetype that complements the one doing the possessing.[196] This process of projection is not *limited* to the Anima and Animus, but it is this projective mode that can be so utterly striking that we still refer to it in opaquely mythic terms as having been struck by Cupid's arrow. This instinctive mode of behavior in which the whole of one's being becomes entwined around the numinosity of another might be called the Eros archetype (after the Greek God of erotic love), but as this is a case in which archetypal variation between population groups is expressed, we cannot accurately speak of this kind of divine intervention as being caused by a *single* God, but by a *pair*—with each party being under the influence by one.

Delving further into this notion of differences in hierophanies[197] between individuals, we come to MacLennan's treatment of the *daimones*. As mentioned previously, Jung equated *complexes* (the constituents of the individual unconscious) with Neoplatonic daimones. In MacLennan's terms, the place held by the daimones as intermediaries between the Gods and men can be described via evolutionary mechanisms as "networks of associations…[that] are created by intense or repeated activation of the archetypes in the ontogenetic psyche," making each archetype "a nucleus for complexes, which constellate around the *universal* archetypal core, but incorporate *individual* associations, formed according to the laws of similarity and contiguity."[198] In this way, MacLennan applies the principle of emergence equally to complexes as well as archetypes. The only difference here is that the emergence of the two levels is not strictly upwards. The emergence of the complexes as formed from interactions between the individual and the archetypes seems to necessitate a prior emergence of the latter. So in this way we have a vector of ontological dependence which, between man and the Gods is directly upwards, but for the daimones leads both up from man and down

---

195 Stevens, 76.
196 Stevens, 180–181.
197 Hierophany, from the Greek ἱερός (*hieros*—"holy") and φᾰνερός (*phaneros*—"open to sight" or "visible"), meaning the experience or manifestation of the holy or holiness.
198 MacLennan, "Evolution, Jung, and Theurgy," 10.

from the Gods, meeting in the middle. Yet, this dual sourced ontological dependency does not place them higher than *both* in the metaphysical hierarchy, but betwixt the two, since they are in a way similar to a quale[199] that emerges not from a collection of like organisms, but between the interaction of two different objects. So, in this way we can think of the archetypes as being biologically conditioned by the collective genetic structure of man, while the complexes are conditioned by the interplay between that universal structure and its individual constituents. This being the case, the daimones take on attributes from both sides of the spectrum, making them *individualized* entities which mediate between men and the Gods. And, like archetypes, complexes behave as if they were independent, autonomous beings, making the internal experience of them take on a *numinous* quality similar to that of an archetypal experience.[200] And, like the Gods, they are more than capable of participating in the activities of both possession and projection.

MacLennan identifies several important complexes which bear mentioning in this evolutionary context. The first is the *ego complex*, the conscious mind. As noted before, this is just *one* complex among *many*. Certain evolutionary pressures have pushed it to the forefront of our recognition in the internal daimonic hierarchy, but "the ego is not in charge, nor should it be."[201] The complex that both MacLennan and the Classical Neoplatonists believe *ought* to be treated as dominant is the higher self. "The Higher Self comprehends the totality of the archetypal field, and therefore it comprehends all the archetypes."[202] The ego is no more to be confused with the higher self than a limb is to be confused with the totality of a person. The higher self is the *ontogenetic* complex that emerges from the plenary collections of complexes which constitute our individual unconsciouses. Just as the Neoplatonists conceived of a transcendental Demiurge sitting atop the pyramid shaped emanative hierarchy, so does the higher self sit at the top of our internal daimonic constellation. As before, however, the process by which this complex is formed is emergent, not emanative, so the vector of dependence still rises upwards from the various internal complexes to this arch-complex. As it encompasses both conscious and unconscious dimensions of the *psuchē*, the higher self is *superpersonal*. The persona is yet another complex (that with which the ego identifies most strongly), which is completely transcended by the emergence of the higher self through the individuation process. This higher self

---

199 Quale (pl. qualia) is a Latin term meaning "what sort." A prime example of qualia in the everyday world would be the taste of a beverage. The metaphysical entity that is the taste itself resides neither in the tongue of the taster nor in the liquid of the beverage. It emerges as a third term as a consequence of their interaction.
200 MacLennan, 11.
201 Ibid., 12.
202 Ibid.

can, MacLennan argues, be further identified with the particular type of personal daimōn that was believed to embody a person's fate. This identification would include Socrates' daimōn,[203] the *fylgja* of the Norse,[204] the Holy Guardian Angel of the Medieval Christian theurgists[205] and many other cultural representations throughout history.

Another daimōn of extreme importance within the ontogenetic *psuchē* is the *superego*, which "may be defined as the moral complex."[206] This is the complex which functions as the center of one's sense of morality, that little voice in our heads that we often identify as our *conscience*. "This inner parental figure and moral judge perpetually strives to censor and 'jail' any aspects of the Self which it has learned through experience may prove unacceptable to significant others and result in" consequences which are anathema to the organism's evolutionary fitness in the societal environment.[207] Just as the archetypes influence our behavior as it relates to *biological* functions and processes, so do the complexes influence us within those aspects of the social sphere that are outside the realm of pure biology. Within the Neoplatonic context, this complex can be positively identified with the Neoplatonic *agathodaimōn* (ἀγαθοδαίμων—"good daimōn") or the Roman *genius*, which was thought of as a kind of moral guide which served to facilitate the person's interaction with society.[208] The obvious cognate to this, and other similarly structured complexes, are the legions of tutelary and guardian spirits that one finds at the lowest personal, levels of Pagan religious practices worldwide. These spirits are *not*, MacLennan explains, strictly limited to serving personal functions either. Indeed, superegoic complexes "may be shared by families and other groups, even entire cultures."[209] These complexes which are shared by different levels of population groups would serve as culturally conditioned mediating entities which comprise the gradated levels of the psychic hierarchy that exists between the personal and the universal. MacLennan treats *all* of these intermediary hypostases as being environmentally conditioned (e.g. by one's family, village, tribe, etc.), yet this is one of three points to follow where I question the complete descriptive accuracy of his model.

Two Layers of Archetypes

---

203 Plato, trans. Alexander Nehamas and Paul Woodruff, *Symposium*, in *Plato*, 202d–e.
204 Rudolf Simek, *Dictionary of Northern Mythology*, trans. Angela Hall, (Suffolk, England: D.S. Brewer, 2008), 129.
205 [Abraham of Worms], *The Book of the Sacred Magic of Abramelin the Mage*, trans. S.L. MacGregor Mathers, (New York: Dover Publications, Inc., 1975), 49.
206 MacLennan, "Evolution, Jung, and Theurgy," 12.
207 Stevens, 232.
208 MacLennan, "Evolution, Jung and Theurgy," 12.
209 Ibid., 10.

This first point of departure between us comes from his treatment of the ontological reality of the specific Gods of various pantheons. In a polytheistic theological setting, there are generally two ways to treat this issue: hard and soft polytheism.[210] Soft polytheism is the position which stems from Classical Neoplatonism and has been recently espoused by Jung, Joseph Campbell (1904–1987)[211] and others within this continuum of thought. Under this position, the particular Gods of culturally specific pantheons are seen as *faces* of universal Gods (e.g. Frigga, Isis, Mary, etc. are all hypostatic façades of the universal Great Mother Goddess). Hard polytheism, on the other hand, is exceedingly common among contemporary practitioners of reconstructed forms of Paganism (e.g. Heathenry, Hellenismos, Celtic Reconstructionism, etc.), and advocates the contrary position that the tribal Gods are both ontologically *unique* and non-dependent upon some collection of universal Godforms. This is compounded by the unique connection that ethnic exclusivist[212] practitioners see between a pantheon and the population group of which they are the traditional Gods.[213] While a soft polytheist necessarily sees polytheistic religiosity as universal in nature, with *all* culturally specific Gods being pathways to the true, universal Gods, hard polytheists of the ethnic exclusivist persuasion treat the connection between a people and that people's Gods as one that is private—meaning that the nature of the connection between the two precludes a member of one tribe from engaging in a relationship with the Gods of another tribe by virtue of the special relationships that exist between the Gods and their peoples. MacLennan supports a variation on the soft polytheistic theology with his view that culturally particular Gods are ontologically subordinate to and dependent upon universal Godforms by treating them as group complexes which emerge from "similar patterns of association with an archetype" shared by the group as a whole.[214] In this way, the tribal Gods of the Greeks, Romans, Celts, Germanics, etc. are seen as a sub-category of daimones which are engendered by the repeated, culturally conditioned interplay between members of the group and the universal archetypes. While this argument is, in a way, quite

---

210 Timothy Alexander, "Types of Polytheism," http://hellenismos.us/b/2010/10/types-of-polytheism/ (accessed Jung 16, 2011).
211 Campbell's soft polytheistic theory of the monomyth is delineated in exquisite detail in his *The Hero With a Thousand Faces* (Novato, CA: New World Library, 2008).
212 It ought be noted that ethnicity is, in this usage, *not* synonymous with race, but rather encompasses the shared ancestral, cultural, linguistic and religious bonds that tie an organic group together.
213 This position of ethnic exclusivism, called *folkism* by Germanic Neopagans, is explored in a more or less even handed manner in the following publication: Kveldúlf Gundarsson, ed. *Our Troth*. vol. 2 (North Charleston: BookSurge Publishing, 2007), 25.
214 MacLennan, "Individual Soul and World Soul," 22.

convincing in light of it providing a cogent explanation for the emergence of lesser daimones, it not only clashes with the orientation of hard polytheists, but is seemingly contradicted in part by an evolutionary process with MacLennan himself discusses elsewhere: the Baldwin effect.

As the superegoic complexes are largely matters of *nurture* over *nature*, being the resultant processes of "behavioral norms acquired during an individual's lifetime," it may seem, initially, to stand to reason that this would necessitate that culturally particular Gods form a subspecies of complexes rather than archetypes.[215] This position is, however, undermined by the Baldwin effect, which is an evolutionary mechanism by which socially conditioned behaviors can, over a substantial period of time, affect a group's genetic development. Named after James Baldwin (1861–1934), an early 20th century giant in the history of evolutionary psychology, the Baldwin effect can be described as such:

> Consider the simple example of a group of organisms suddenly subjected to environmental conditions which their phenotypic plasticity allows them to adapt to through ontogenetic means, perhaps by learning. It might, for instance be a learned dietary preference. These ontogenetic adaptions are not directly inherited and evolved and hence innate; the capacity for forming them, of course, is evolved and inherited. Such indirect adaptions ensure survival over enough generations for chance-based genetic changes to occur which fit with, supplement, or perhaps produce identical phenotypic effects. Eventually such genetic modification would produce the same, or very similar adaptions, and the indirect, ontogenetic adaptions become redundant. The learned dietary preference becomes innate. The initial, indirectly determined, ontogenetic adaptions provide, in effect, a scaffolding that bridges the gap to inherited and evolved direct adaptions.[216]

In other words, the Baldwin effect allows for behavioral patterns which are specific to a population group within a species to incorporate more readily genetic adaptions to their particular physical and social environments, in order to increase their overall evolutionary fitness. That is to say that this effect allows for us to consider the idea that certain population groups are now, after hundreds of generations of conditioning, genetically predisposed to learning norms particular to their group. In Jungian terms, we might say that the Baldwin effect transforms

---

215 MacLennan, "Evolutionary Jungian Psychology," 13.
216 Plotkin, 78.

the group superegoic complexes from being culturally conditioned *after the fact* to inherited complexes which are present in group members from birth. MacLennan agrees, stating that "over time, these norms will come to be less learned and more innate; in effect aspects of the culture that have a selective advantage gradually come to be genetically encoded."[217] MacLennan, however translates this into theological terms by proposing that even though the daimones are ontologically dependent and subordinate to the Gods, that the Gods learn from those particular daimones which best promote their group's welfare, thus enabling the Gods to learn from the daimones.[218] The only problem with *this* theological application of the Baldwin effect is that MacLennan is still treating the Gods involved as those of the *universal* mind. It would seem to me that such adaptions which are specific to the physical and social environments of a genetically endogamous group would engender the emergence of a new subspecies of *phylogenetic* archetypes rather than for the ontogenetic complexes to directly affect the universal collective unconscious. In such a circumstance, we are talking about the collective genome of a homogenous group being altered by a shared culture and landscape over a period of thousands of years. This kind of intraspecies evolution has no *direct* bearing on the evolution of the *human* genome, but has everything to do with the specific evolution of that population group's genome.

This is of particular importance when we conceptualize the vast spatio-temporal differences that separate different population groups within the human species. The "shrinking" of the world and the bringing together of the various population groups of the world via high speed transportation is an eminently *recent* state of affairs. For *most* of human history, groups have existed, flourished and evolved in geographically separated, endogamous societies. For instance, the Australian Aboriginals are estimated to have migrated to the Australian continent some thirty to forty *thousand* years ago.[219] Similar migration patterns were followed by the Upper Paleolithic settlers of Europe and Asia as well, creating situations in which humanity, after the African diaspora, evolved in discrete pockets for tens of thousands of years rather than as a whole. During these intervening millennia the Baldwin effect, alongside the standard methods of evolutionary selection discussed previously, would have inevitably resulted in the particularities of those peoples' landscapes—think, for a moment, of the *tremendous* difference between the endless forests of Paleolithic Europe and the eternal desert of Australia—and cultures being etched upon the genetic coding that is still with us today.[220] What

---

217 MacLennan, "Evolutionary Jungian Psychology," 13–14.
218 Ibid., 14.
219 Peter Hiscock, *Archaeology of Ancient Australia*, (London: Routledge, 2008), 22.
220 For a fuller treatment of the link between landscape, language and culture upon the development of a people's religiosity, please refer to my essay "Why I am a Heathen," in *The Journal of Contemporary Heathen Thought* 1 (2009): 9–17.

this means in connection with tribal Gods is that, taking into account the Baldwin effect's ability to encode both culture and landscape genetically, is that we might explain theological differences between peoples not as one of culturally conditioned *complexes* but as each group having slightly differentiated *archetypes*.[221] To ensure that this process I am proposing is fully understood, let us recapitulate.

MacLennan tells us that the archetypes of the collective unconscious emerge from the individual subconsciouses of humanity. Further, he tells us that the emergent process is mediated by environmental factors, in that we evolve—both genotypically and phenotypically—within an environment of evolutionary adaptiveness. Once this archetypal emergent layer has been established, the repeated interaction between the complexes of the individuals and the universal archetypes result in the bidirectional emergence of a medial layer of superegoic complexes. This bidirectional process of emergence occurs not only within individuals, but also within population groups who share behavioral norms. These group superegoic complexes then, by means of the Baldwin effect, transform the group's individual constituents—imprinting the minds of new generations with culturally particular modes of behavior. From these newly evolved members of the group, now differentiated from the unified genetically homogenous population that immediately followed our anthropogenesis, emerges a *new* collective unconscious —one that is exclusively participated in by members of the group in question. We may still speak of a *universally* collective unconscious, but in light of this group specific differentiation, it becomes something which emerges as a further layer from the archetypes of the collective unconsciouses of *various* independent groups rather than from each individual. Thus, via the Baldwin effect, we are able to account for the emergence of tribal Gods as being ontologically dependent upon their particular peoples in a way that provides a philosophically cogent account of the nature of the connection between the group and that group's Gods that is advocated by ethnic exclusivist polytheists. Thus the theological picture that ultimately presents itself is far closer to the extremely gradated model of Iamblichus than it is to the minimally tiered cosmos of Plotinus and Jung.

The Mind Body Problem

The second point where I shall break slightly from MacLennan's presentation is on the extrapolation of his reversal of the vector of dependency to ontological layers *other* than the psychic. As consistent as MacLennan's work is *within* the

---

[221] This is not to say that culturally specific *images*, Godforms, names, etc. are truly phylogenetic, but rather that broad and subtle differentiations in externalized, instinctive patterns of behavior translate into similarly differentiated, internalized archetypal forms.

psychological domains, he fails to apply the same vectoral reversal to the layers both above and below the *psuchē*. This is not at all to say that his writings *preclude* this, he merely does not explore this avenue of inquiry. As a starting point, the application of MacLennan's Aristotelian transformation of Neoplatonism to the mind-body problem proves quite fruitful. This problem, perennial in contemporary philosophy, can be stated as: "What exactly are the relations between the mental and the physical, and in particular how can there be causal relations between them?"[222] To fully grasp what is meant by this question, some background on its origin will prove beneficial. The mind-body problem as understood in a modern context arose in the middle of the 17th century from the methodology developed by René Descartes during the course of his *Meditations*.[223] Descartes began his daily meditations by seeking to discover what aspects of his experience could be doubted and which could not. In due course, he concluded that the only thing of which he could be absolutely certain was that *he existed*. His methodical doubt had led him to believe that although he could call into question sensory data received from sight, sound, touch, taste and smell—thinking that there was always the possibility that a præterhuman intelligence was feeding him false data—the very idea that this data would be fed to *him* was predicated upon the existence of Descartes as a thinking subject, in other words, as a mind. Thus, he deduced that the one piece of data which could be trusted was *non-sensory*: the *psuchē*'s experience of itself as a center of subjectivity. Neoplatonists sidestepped this in a way that emergentists cannot explicitly mimic, yet we can *certainly* rectify this gap in MacLennan's philosophy with a contemporary restructuring of the Neoplatonic panpsychism that was discussed earlier.

That being the case, let us explore how contemporary panpsychism is able to respond to the mind-body problem within an emergentist framework that is compatible with MacLennan's analysis. We can begin with the fact that while Descartes' non-sensory, experiential justification for the belief in the reality of one's mind is not only *not* a point of contention between Cartesian dualists and panpsychists, the latter often *explicitly* root their arguments in this very experience.[224] However, what *is* contested by panpsychists is Descartes' train of reasoning which leads from the known existence of mind to a declaration of mind and body being composed of distinct metaphysical substances. It is this idea, that

---

222 John R. Searle, *Mind: A Brief Introduction*, (New York: Oxford University Press, 2004), 11.
223 René Descartes, *The Meditations Concerning First Philosophy* in *Discourse on Method and Meditations*, trans. Laurence J. Lafleur, (1641; repr., USA: The Liberal Arts Press, Inc., 1960), 81.
224 Skrbina's core argument for panpsychism begins: "Mind is real. I know this because I experience it first hand, and I hold it as an indubitable feature of reality," (Skrbina, 254).

mentality and physicality are fundamentally different in an ontological sense that gives rise to the mind-body problem. If such is the case, how can something physical be acted upon by something mental, and vice versa? While Descartes phrased the problem somewhat differently than is done today—questioning how the soul, which was created by God, was able to act upon the body—the question of how the two substances interact still forms the core of the problem which is currently thought of in terms of "how can brain processes produce mental phenomena?"[225] The panpsychist family of philosophies[226] wholly rejects this bifurcation with the position that subjective internality, mentality, is not only a quality that is *incapable* of emerging from pure objective externality, but is common to *all*. Freya Mathews, a prominent contemporary panpsychist, further details panpsychism as "the view that every material object is also a subject," a position that includes "*any* view that reunites mentality with materiality, and thereby dismantles the foundational dualism of Western thought."[227] This monistic approach is wholly in line with the Neoplatonic spirit, yet if mentality *cannot* be seen as an emergent quality, how can this thesis operate within MacLennan's framework?

The answer lies in the pairing of MacLennan's psychology with the pre-psychic ontology of a breed of panpsychists who arose within the early 20th century Anglo-American philosophical tradition: those who took "pure experience" as the unifying link between mentality and physicality.[228] Panexperientialism (lit. "everything experiences") is, like the pansensism (lit. "everything senses") which came before it, a *neutral monist* theory of mind. Under the panexperientialist's metaphysics, this singular substance that neutral monist metaphysics revolve around is the *event*. Also referred to by Whitehead as *actual entities* or *actual occasions*, these "are the final real things of which the world is made. There is no going behind…[them] to find anything more real."[229] What Whitehead has done by putting forth the event as the fundamental constituent of reality is to bring Western metaphysics up to speed with Einstein's special theory of relativity, in which the inseparability of spatiality from temporality results in the space-

---

225 Searle, 12.
226 It is important to note at this point in the discussion that panpsychism is not a single theory of mind, but is a meta-theory that encompasses a number of specific theories which are at odds with one another. "It is a statement *about* theories, not a theory in itself," (Skrbina, 2).
227 Freya Mathews, *For Love of Matter: A Contemporary Panpsychism*, (New York: State University of New York Press, 2003), 4.
228 William James, *A Pluralistic Universe*, (New York: Longmans, Green, and Co., 1920), 348.
229 Alfred North Whitehead, *Process and Reality*, (1927–28; repr., New York: The Free Press, 1985), 18.

time *event* being the elementary unit of analysis.[230] That is to say that, for example, when we speak of John Doe, we are not speaking of John as a spatial object who persists through, but is intrinsically divorced from, time. Rather, the John we are speaking of, of the here and now, is an event—an event which incorporates both spatial extension in the form of his body and temporal extension in the form of his being the present moment's culmination of a *process* that led to the occurrence of the spacetime event that is John at this moment in time. This insistence on the processual nature of reality and in the primacy of becoming over being is what has earned the thought of Whitehead and his students the moniker of *process philosophy*.

But what has the neutral monism of treating the event as ontologically primary have to do with the nature of mind, or with experience? The answer lies in Whitehead's conception of the event as being *dipolar* in nature. Dipolarity has the meaning that every event has both a physical and mental pole of experience.[231] Taking a human being as an example, we are intimately aware of two aspects of ourselves. That we have an internal, subjective, mental pole is—as Descartes' phenomenological investigations shewed—not subject to any doubt. That we are also in possession of an external, objective, physical pole is confirmed by our interactions and relations with the world around us. Where the panexperientialist *differs* from Descartes is in the conclusion that these two modes of perception—the internal experience of being a mind, and the external experience of being a body—are manifestations of two distinct substances at play. Nay, the panexperientialist finds that his experience of himself as a self leads him to the conclusion that "mind, in other words, is sheer interiority, matter sheer externality,"—that the two are experiential modalities of *one* organism, not a house divided.[232] What this thesis then entreats us to consider is that dipolarity is not an attribute particular only to humans, or even to animals, but is a universal feature of *all* actual occasions—thus extending an internal dimension of experience to events. This root-level form of experience is *non-sensory* in nature, being the mind's experience of itself as a mind; this mode of experience is not contingent upon *any* of the five external senses, but is rather a form of pure, unadulterated experience. This non-sensory mode of perception is termed *prehension* by Whitehead, and "is the receptivity…with which every occasion of experience begins."[233]

---

230 Edwin F. Taylor and John Archibald Wheeler, *Spacetime Physics: Introduction to Special Relativity*, 2nd ed., (New York: W.H. Freeman and Company, 1992), 10.
231 C. Robert Mesle, *Process-Relational Philosophy: An Introduction to Alfred North Whitehead*, (West Conshohocken, PA: Templeton Press, 2008), 100.
232 Mathews, 26.
233 David Ray Griffin, "Archetypal Psychology and Process Philosophy," 25.

Panpsychism having been thus defined, the two primary alternatives, humanism and mechanism, ought be briefly explored, as even many Jungians will find themselves questioning a thesis that, on its face, seems as outlandish as panexperientialism. Since the time of Descartes, philosophical humanism has been one of the dominant streams of thought in philosophy of mind, and is thus one of the primary sources of "the incredulity with which panpsychism is usually greeted."[234] The humanist argues that mentality bears three attributes which are exclusively proper to humans: linguistic capacity, reflexive consciousness, and free will.[235] The capability for humans to use language, it is argued, demonstrates that there is a clear distinction between humanity and all other types of life—thus bifurcating nature into two categories: humans and everything else.[236] Similarly do humanists posit that mind is *necessarily* reflexive, that mind is only mind by virtue of being able to be cognizant of its own consciousness. Free will is treated correspondingly, with the humanist proposing that the experience we have of being able to make up our minds and genuinely decide between alternative courses of action is an intrinsic feature of mind, and that this free agency is, again, privy to humankind.[237] The Cartesian humanist believes that "our minds are the source of our freedom, our capacity to choose between alternatives through acts of will that cause our bodily movements. Our bodies, in contrast, are governed by the mechanical laws investigated by the natural sciences."[238] Thus are all entities aside from men wholly determined in their actions. Inanimate objects are ruled by physical and chemical laws, plants and animals by biological instincts which are merely responses to environmental stimuli. Humanity alone is capable of demonstrating externally (via linguistic ability) and knowing internally (via conscious reflexivity) that their behaviors are exempt from these rigidly determined laws.

The panexperientialist "theory of 'prehensions' embodies a protest against the 'bifurcation' of nature."[239] One of the immediate problems that humanistic dualism begets is the sheer improbability of the bifurcation itself. "For humanism, somehow during roughly the past 100,000 years…one species became miraculously endowed with very special features that distinguish it from all that has gone on before."[240] With the specifically Cartesian variety, this presents no major problem, as humanity has been directly endowed with this gift by God with the

---

234 D.S. Clarke, *Panpsychism and the Religious Attitude*, (New York: State University of New York Press, 2003), 55.
235 Ibid.
236 Searle, 17–18.
237 Ibid., 16.
238 Clarke, 56.
239 Whitehead, *Process and Reality*, 289.
240 Clarke, 57.

ensoulment of mankind. However, for those—theists and atheists alike—who are not willing to place a *deus ex machina* kind of explanation at the very core of philosophy of mind, the singular nature of mentality as being distinctly *human* proves a troublesome proposition. Excepting the possibility of divine intervention, how is it *possible* much less *probable* that a wholly divergent substance suddenly came into being and has only done so within a *single* species? And, even *if* such a miraculous event were to occur, the further problem of substantial interaction looms in the distance—the mind-body problem. "All forms of substance dualism inherit Descartes' problem of how to give a coherent account of the causal relations between the soul and body."[241] Descartes attempted to solve this problem of the interaction between the mind and body by theorizing that the pineal gland somehow functioned as a bridge between the two, that "the soul has its principal seat in the little gland."[242] However, as a biological understanding of the pineal gland's function as the producer of melatonin became understood, Descartes' notion of it as being the "seat of the soul" quickly fell out of favor.[243]

How then, is this substance dualism to be explained? How does a brain, which has no consciousness, no mentality of its own interact with a conscious soul which has been grafted to it? It is a theory which, when compounded with advances in modern physics has become less and less tenable. "Substance dualism seems to imply that there is…[a kind of] mental energy or spiritual energy, that is not fixed by physics," that is outside of the purview of the laws of thermodynamics, thus rendering them null and void.[244] This line of reasoning, finding dualism to be more riddled with problems than answers, has led to its rejection not only by panpsychists, but by materialists as well. If dualism fails, "it is natural to suppose that maybe there is only one kind of thing in the universe," which is metaphysical *monism*.[245] However, the materialistic monism that has largely replaced humanism responds to the mind-body problem in a vastly different way than does the neutral monism of panexperientialism. Rather than *integrate* the bifurcated spheres of mentality and physicality, the materialist *eliminates* the former leaving only matter in its place.

This monistic family of philosophies of mind takes three general forms. Identity

---

241 Searle, 29.
242 René Descartes, "The Passion of the Soul," trans. Elizabeth S. Haldane and G.R.T. Ross in *The European Philosophers from Descartes to Nietzsche*, ed. Monroe C. Beardsley, (New York: The Modern Library, 1988), 95.
243 Gert-Jan Lokhorst, "Descartes and the Pineal Gland," *Stanford Encyclopedia of Philosophy*, http://plato.stanford.edu/entries/pineal-gland/ (accessed February 20, 2011).
244 Searle, 30.
245 Ibid., 33.

theory holds that "mental states are real but that these states are identical with brain states."[246] What this does is is to reduce mental activity to neural activity, which deals with both the problem of interaction by accepting only the existence of a single material substance, and with the problem of the mind's emergence by explaining it wholly in terms of the brain's evolution. The second class of materialist theories is functionalism, "which argues that mental states are real and that they are identical with a particular 'process state,' or state of information."[247] Where functionalism differs from identity theory is that it does not rely on specifically *neural* structures in its definition of mind. Indeed, the functionalist theory applies equally to any sufficiently complex physical system, which makes it the preferred position for proponents of strong artificial intelligence. Lastly, there is the family of eliminativism, which is "the view that mind is somehow imaginary or unreal."[248] This radical theory is, in many ways, the logical consequence of behavioralism, which treats mind as a mistakenly labeled category that is naught but a remnant of pre-scientific ways of thinking about the world. The eliminativist would explain everything in purely physical terms, erasing any reference to the very ideas of consciousness or mentality.

Now, taking these counters to panpsychism into the context of MacLennan's work, we draw the following conclusions. In opposition to reductive physicalism, MacLennan acknowledges that his combination of Neoplatonism, Jungian psychology and evolutionary theory may appear to be an attempt "to reduce the archetypes and psychical experience to neuroscience, which runs the risk of diminishing the reality of both."[249] Keeping this in mind, MacLennan ensures that his presentation of the overlap between these fields attempts to *enhance* rather than diminish each sphere. His solution "is to hold fast to the phenomena" themselves, for "the ultimate ground of all our judgments of reality is our lived *experience*," [italics mine].[250] In this way, by advocating the primacy of empirical experience over theory, MacLennan anticipates one of panexperientialism's core arguments. To explain this position further, he states that while evolutionary psychology when applied to the phenomenology of religious experience can certainly glean a certain degree of insight into "the adaptive function of religious behavior," it must remain mute regarding the internality of the experience itself.[251] The answer to Cartesian humanism in light of evolutionary psychology is all but standard nowadays. The notion that an evolutionary trait which we readily observe occurring in lesser degrees in our primate cousins is the exclusive property

---

246 Skrbina, 8.
247 Ibid., 9
248 Ibid.
249 MacLennan, "Evolutionary Jungian Psychology," 6.
250 Ibid., 7.
251 Ibid.

of *humanity* is all but laughable. Thus, while we *may* be able to speak of the emergence of self-reflective consciousness as a function of correspondingly complex neural systems, the idea that *mind* itself is somehow limited to humanity completely runs afoul of the whole nature of the evolutionary process as being a continuum—an idea which yet again anticipates aspects of panexperientialism.

The Core Argument

What follows is a related group of arguments which are incorporated into what David Skrbina calls the "core argument" for adopting panpsychism. The argument assimilates the following lines of reasoning: the argument from indwelling powers, the argument by continuity, and the argument from non-emergence.[252] The first part of the core argument, the indwelling powers section, proposes that "all objects exhibit certain powers or abilities that can plausibly be linked to noetic qualities."[253] The argument from indwelling powers is very similar to Descartes' *cogito* examined previously. This is the argument that the self's prehension *of itself* as a dipolar subject with mental and physical aspects sufficiently demonstrates the reality and and interrelatedness of both mind and body. This argument takes into account our autophenomenological knowledge of our own mental and physical existence as well as our heterophenomenological knowledge of the same reality of external subjects with whom we interact. The indwelling powers argument directly addresses the eliminativist thesis which claims mind is unreal, the idealist thesis of the unreality of the body, as well as dualist theories which posit that there is an ontological separation between the two. Our intimate prehension of our selves is one of holistic unity. We experience ourselves as real, whole centers of subjectivity.

The argument from indwelling powers does not, however, sufficiently demonstrate the *ubiquity* of prehension, and could thus be utilized to prop up a neutral monistic variant of humanism which adhered to the idea of mentality and physicality being polar aspects of one substance but only admitted that dipolarity applied to humanity. Thus, to extend the thesis outwards from ourselves at the center, the argument by continuity is raised. This argument posits that not only are mind and body poles of a common substance, but also that there is an unresolvable problem with attempting to draw a firm line between "enminded and supposedly mindless objects."[254] This argument works in a variety of ways to combat what it views as fallacious dichotomies and mistakenly concretized separations between types. For example, if we accept the indwelling powers argument

---

252 Skrbina, 250–254.
253 Ibid., 250.
254 Ibid.

and agree that humans are enminded, where is the line drawn between mind bearing humans and mindless apes? As Lamarck himself noted, *all* classificatory systems are fictive in nature.[255] *That* there is some type of distinction between a chimpanzee and a man is not doubted, but that there is an intrinsic distinction between these two groups as discrete classes *is*. All such taxonomic systems are purely *artificial* in nature, and thus cement our understandings of differentiations of continua into discontinuous categories. Thus does the argument by continuity impel us to look backwards in our evolutionary history and see the absurdity of attempting to delimit the point at which we made the transition from being mindless animals whose behaviors were determined to enminded humans with free will. For if the humanist thesis is correct, then there had to have been a discrete point at which this monumental shift occurred. Yet, such a distinction between man and his non-human ancestors is admittedly a fiction—an artificial schema used to pragmatically group differentiations within a continuum. That being the case, the same line of reasoning holds true in determining the transition points between *anything*, for there is a smooth evolutionary continuum that leads from non-living matter to 21st century man. Thus does the continuity argument extend mentality of some form to *all*.

The closely related argument from non-emergence rounds out the core argument for panpsychism. This position proposes that "it is inconceivable that mind should emerge from a world in which no mind existed; therefore mind always existed, in even the simplest of structures."[256] The non-emergence argument attempts to seal up the last gap in this line of argumentation. Even if both the preceding arguments were accepted, it would be possible to argue that mind emerged from non-mind in roughly the same way that humans emerged from non-humans, on a continuous path. What the argument from non-emergence does is to acknowledge that mentality is such that its emergence is impossible. There is a radical and complete difference between the conceptions of a mind-bearing subject with free will and an inert object whose actions are absolutely determined. The difference is so great that the humanists erected an ontological wall between the two—so great that the materialists eliminated mind and free agency entirely. In arguments from non-emergence, the mental property of *novelty* or *spontaneity* takes center stage. Novel behavior is behavior that cannot be predicted by physical laws. It "is that which is done from the point of view of the organism," and is the mental attribute that manifests itself as the freedom to make true decisions between courses of action—decisions that are not purely the con-

---

255 Jean-Baptiste Lamarck, *Zoological Philosophy*, trans. Hugh Elliot, (New York: Hafner Publishing Company, 1963), 19.
256 Skrbina, 250.

sequences of genetic and environmental factors.²⁵⁷ We know, internally, that this is an attribute we are in possession of, yet is it sensible to conceive of novelty emerging from its absence? Panpsychists would claim that "it is a contradiction in terms to assume that some explanatory fact can float into the actual world out of nonentity," and that novelty is such a fundamental central *fact* of the human experience that the very notion of its emergence is nonsensical.²⁵⁸

These three arguments come together in an interwoven manner to form the core argument, which we can now articulate as follows.²⁵⁹ Mind is real; we experience it as an inseparable, intrinsic aspect of ourselves. Our bodies are real; we experience them as we experience the mind, as perceiving extensions of the prehending mental cores of our beings. We do not experience any manner of bifurcation between the two, but experience mentality and physicality as singular, unified wholes. We know that some parts of our physicality are unique (e.g. our human forms are particular to humans, our mammalian features are particular to mammals, etc.), but our physical nature itself is universal; *all* that we encounter can be interacted with as physical objects. We also know that some parts of our mentality are unique, as with the body, yet the principle of continuation that holds true for physicality holds true for mentality as well—entreating us to think that a facility for prehension is universal as well. Since our mentality and physicality are intrinsically connected and experienced as dipolar faces of a single entity, so can we assume this is the case for all. Further, complete and total difference between the novelty that we experience as being conterminous with our mentality is so radically different from its absence, determinism, that its emergence is inconceivable. "Therefore, panpsychism must be true. QED."²⁶⁰

Objections to Panpsychism

The case for panpsychism being such, the principle objection to the panpsychist position is its implausibility. As Clarke asks, are we, in adopting panpsychism, going to propose that thermostats have minds in the same we that *we* have minds?²⁶¹ Panpsychist responses to this critique differ wildly, with some stronger forms of animism²⁶² and hylozoism²⁶³ answering in the *affirmative*. However, the

---

257 Clarke, 124.
258 Whitehead, *Process and Reality*, 46.
259 Skrbina, 254.
260 Ibid.
261 Clarke, 4.
262 Animism, from the Latin *anima* (a translation of the Greek *psuchē*), is the belief that the soul is not limited to humans, but is possessed by all kinds of natural objects such as rivers, trees, boulders, etc.
263 Hylozoism, from the Greek *hylē* (ὕλη—"matter" or lit. "wood") and *zōē* (ζωή—"liv-

panexperientialism this paper seeks to defend counters this charge with its very definition of mentality. Panexperientialism is not proposing that the kind of complex consciousness that is manifest in humanity is any more omnipresent than is our particular material configuration. Indeed, this part of the panexperientialist theory is upheld entirely by Jungian psychology. As we remember from Jung, the *conscious* mind is but a single facet of human mentality, with the vaster portions being *unconscious*. The interconnectedness of the material and mental means that the more unified and persistent the physical organization of the entity in question is, then the more complex will the object's mental organization be.[264] The prehension that panexperientialism posits to be universal is the mental equivalent of what a fundamental particle is to matter. It is the primary core from which all mental structures of advanced evolution are built. That all objects prehend no more makes them conscious in the same way that we are than does the fact that all are made of the same fundamental particles make them able to taste or smell the way that we do. Prehension is the internal relatedness of the object to the world around it. It "denotes the bare process of seizing, excluding extraneous notions of...consciousness."[265] However, it is only in what Whitehead calls *compound individuals*—"that is, a sentient individual composed of lower--order individuals such as cells, molecules, atoms, and ultimately 'occasions of experience,'" that we find something relatable to the human mind.[266] We find, again, that this definition of mentality as prehensive largely fits with Jung's notion of the way in which the unconscious responds to external stimuli. The only *real* distinction, then, that we see between the human *psuchē* and that of any other self-organizing system is the internal complexity of the psychic complexes that emerge.

The second objection, which itself emerges from considerations of the first, is namely: what is the distinction between compound individuals like humans or dogs who obviously are self-organized, mind-bearing subjects, and aggregates like a pile of sand or a garage which, although formally complex, are somehow distinct from *true* individuals? This is a serious problem and if not addressed properly threatens to give rise to an ontological dualism between individuals and aggregates that is just as metaphysically damning as is the mind-body dualism of Descartes. It is here, again, that the concept of the continuum comes into play. The difference between an individual and an aggregate is, according to Griffin,

---

ing" or "life"), was embodied in the beliefs of thinkers as disparate as Thales, Anaximenes, and Heraclitus in an *inherently animated* universe whose fundamental substance(s) teemed with life.

264 Clarke, 1.
265 Elizabeth M. Krause, *The Metaphysics of Experience: A Companion to Whitehead's "Process and Reality,"* (New York: Fordham University Press, 1998), 16.
266 Skrbina, 244.

not an *ontological* duality, but "only an *organizational duality*."[267] So, we might say that "the rock has experience *in* it—the primitive animist was this far correct; but the *rock itself*, considered as a whole, has no experience over and above that of its molecular parts."[268] Though a rock and a man are both collections of *actual occasions*, the latter displays a degree of self-regulatory homeostasis and unity that the former does not. Although, as the rock *does* display *some* of these attributes, we can say that the two exist on a continuum of individuality—that, rather than a "true" individual being something wholly different from an aggregate, that there is a fluid boundary between the two. The simpler a system, the simpler and more reactive the mind. The more complex systems carry more internal differentiation and capacity for complex mental behavior.

A third objection arises from the panexperientialist's insistence on the ubiquity not only of prehension but also of novelty and spontaneity. This objection is really the mirror opposite of the objection to mechanism's complete denial of novelty in favor of determinism. The mechanist would counter the panexperientialist's assertion by questioning that if *all* events, excepting the already contested example of humans, are novel in nature then why do physical laws as fixed stabilities appear to govern the world. To this, the panexperientialist would argue that these laws are *not* fixed, that "the laws of nature…are merely transitory stabilities that emerge at one phase of cosmic history only to lapse from creation and give way to variant modes of operation in the fullness of time."[269] And, while "all genuine individuals have at least some iota of freedom…higher-grade, more evolved individuals have more freedom: cells more than molecules, psyches more than cells, human psyches more than chimpanzee psyches."[270] This gradation of capacity for novel behavior must also take into account the nature of conditioning. Prehensions, moments of experience, are conditioned by their past —they are, in their capacity as instances of pure receptivity, uniquely open to the continuingly patterned influences of their past actions upon their future courses.[271] So, while novelty *does* pervade the real in the same way that materiality and prehension does, its manifestational strength is contingent upon the internal complexity and level of self-organization in the organism being considered.

Process Ontology

---

267 Griffin, 24.
268 Ibid.
269 Nicholas Rescher, *Process Metaphysics: An Introduction to Process Philosophy*, (New York: State University of New York Press, 1998), 91.
270 Griffin, 26.
271 Ibid.

If then, we accept the panexperientialist thesis, and apply it to MacLennan's emergent restructuring of Neoplatonism, what are the ramifications? The metaphysical, and specifically ontological, consequences of panexperientialism's truth are embodied in process philosophy's insistence on the primacy of the actual occasion or event as reality's fundamental building block. The large scale outgrowth of this idea is manifest in the supposition that process affords the most effective conceptual tool with which to understand the world—that *all* things are reducible to processes.[272] Thus do the process philosophers present us not with a world *that changes*, but with a world *that is itself change*. Rather than seeing the world as a collection of objects, it is seen as a sea of interrelated processes—all of which seethes with mentality and novelty. While MacLennan's work, as presented thus far, seems completely in accord with this kind of foundational ontology, his treatment of numerical archetypes forms the basis for my third disagreement with him.

After detailing the ways in which the Gods evolve and change, he says: "so we must exclaim πάντα ῥεῖ[273] and agree with Heraclitus that Pythagoras had much learning but little understanding? I think not."[274] Although he indeed does posit that the human genome—and thus the personified Gods—is in a state of evolutionary flux, he further proposes that "behind the Gods are the divine numbers, the more abstract, impersonal archetypal Ideas, which are the psychical aspects of natural law."[275] This higher class of archetypes is not something about whose *existence* I disagree, but I find his downward extrapolation of the fixity of this layer of the hierarchy down to the ontological foundation to be troubling. Certainly, we can agree that numbers and mathematical laws do *not* change, and are the very definitions of eternality and stability. However, is the proper way to deal with this fact to engage in a metaphysical juxtaposition of Aristotelian realism regarding *most* archetypes and Platonic realism regarding a *few* archetypes really the correct path to resolution? I think not. This is a situation in which we must make a choice between one mode of ontological constitution: top-down or bottom up. There is no room for *both*.

With that in mind, how might Aristotle's theory of universals apply to mathematical entities? Similar to all other instances we have examined to this point, it would derive universals, in this case numbers, from particulars. And as mathematics is, as it is often described, the language of nature, we find instantiations of number all around us, at every conceivable level of the hierarchy. Indeed, des-

---

272 Rescher, 28.
273 *Panta rhei*, "everything changes," was the Pre-Socratic philosopher Heraclitus' most famous saying, (Coppleston, *Greece and Rome*, 39).
274 MacLennan, "Evolution, Jung, and Theurgy," 16.
275 Ibid.

cending all the way to the *bottom* of the emanative hierarchy, we find that the foundation of reality is a plenary field of events. For as Whitehead writes, "there is a becoming of continuity, but no continuity of becoming," meaning that the ontologically prime layer of reality is one of quantized differentiation; "thus the ultimate metaphysical truth is atomism."[276] This atomic nature of reality's root hypostasis means that the principles of numeration are found in the ontological beginnings of the world. In this way, just as the archetypes of the collective unconscious are universal abstractions of human instantiations, so are the numerical archetypes abstracted from particulars that are themselves ontologically primary. In this way we may retort that yes, πάντα ῥεῖ indeed! *All* of the events that comprise this primary layer are in process. The event is a fundamentally processual unit. And, as all higher layers which emerge from this root system are ultimately built up from change it is indeed true that, in a way, everything changes. It is, however, just as true to maintain that the numerical archetypes *are* the embodiments of fixity and are—insofar as anything at all exists—eternal and unchanging. The very principles of quantization and differentiation could not *but* cause numerical abstractions to emerge. The fundamentally atomic nature of the world necessitates this.

This adoption of process ontology as a foundation for MacLennan's Aristotelian recasting of Neoplatonism has, however, yet another dramatic ramification. So far we have spoken of the medial layers of the humans and Gods, and of the plenary bottom of the hierarchy that is the event field. What, then of the top? As we discussed earlier, at the top of the Neoplatonic hierarchy sat the One, the divine principle of unity from which all subsequent hypostases emanated. But, as we have just explained, the numerical archetypes, by virtue of their emanative constitution, *cannot* occupy this position. Quite the opposite, in fact, turns out to be the case, with "oneness" being an emergent attribute of each and every of the *lowest* constituents of the hierarchy. This being the case, what is the *ultimate* emergent layer? In this instance we shall, as in the reshaping of panpsychism to suit our current needs, do the same for the panentheistic top entity in Neoplatonism's emanative chain.

There are, however, several tremendous differences between the Classical conception of a panentheistic deity and the picture that emergentism presents. The first, and most dramatic, of these is that within such a model this God is *not* ontologically primary. This is a gigantic leap away from the category of the ultimate in emanative theologies, where the One was seen as both ontologically prime *and* metaphysically greatest. Emergentism necessitates that these two attributes *cannot* be shared by one entity, as the occupy polar opposite ends of the hierarch-

---

276 Whitehead, *Process and Reality*, 35.

ical continuum. While this type of theology does result in a model which is largely incompatible with strict monotheism—and is likely why subsequent panentheistic theologians, nearly all of whom have been Christian, have not espoused it—it does *not* intrinsically clash with polytheism, making it the natural expression of the ultimate for a polytheistic theology which seeks to express itself in concert with the emanative and evolutionary processes of the middle realms.

This being the case, let us flesh out this final layer somewhat. As mentioned previously, panentheism is distinguished from both Classical theism and pantheism by the way in which it treats the ultimate deity as both immanent *and* transcendent. This unity of seeming opposites is achieved, in our emanative system, by the fact that this God is the subject who ultimately emerges from the complete totality of *all*. Indeed, "panentheism affirms that although God and the world are ontologically distinct and God transcends the world, the world is 'in' God ontologically."[277] This is radically different from the Classical theistic position that achieves distinctness and transcendence by erecting an ontological wall of separation between God and the world. It is just as different from the pantheistic view that God is *not* transcendent, but, by virtue of being *identical* with the world, is wholly immanent. The key difference between these theologies and panentheism is that *both* Classical theism and pantheism treat God as *non-emergent*. In this way, the kind of bottom-up panentheism is really the only kind of ultimate theological principle that *can* spring forth from an emergentist philosophy. So, if we think of a cell as emerging from atomic systems, human bodies emerging from cellular systems, and the planet Earth as emerging from combinations of geological and biotic systems, we can extrapolate this process upwards to conceive of the panentheistic deity as the individual who emerges from the totality of galactic processes. For this being, the whole fabric of the cosmos would be her body, and the mentality which would emerge would necessarily incorporate levels of such emergent complexity that it would bear as much similarity to what *we* think of as mind as our own consciousness does to the internality of a lepton. So great would the gulf of complexification be between she and us that to speak of her as ineffable even seems inadequate. This complete and total degree of abstraction goes *far* beyond Paul's adjuration of the "Unknown God,"[278] and places at the world's pinnacle a deity who is all but *unknowable*.

Yet for all this transcendent greatness, panentheism brings the deity just as close to us as it is far. The emergent nature of this relationship, however, calls for a reversal of several key attributes commonly applied to metaphysically ultimate

---

277 Cooper, 18.
278 Acts 17:23.

deities. First, the idea that God made the world; the emergent position would completely reverse this, treating God as being constituted *by* the world. Just as man cannot without his body exist, neither can the panentheistic deity *be* without the universe as her external form. Second, the notion that pervades both Classical theism and Plotinian Neoplatonism, that the ultimate can be immediately prehended by the soul without first traversing the myriad of intermediary emergences does not seem to be compatible with this type of deity. Rather, the Iamblichean notion of the levels of the hierarchy being akin to steps on a staircase that one must climb *one at a time* rings true. Third, the conception of the ultimate as being *singular* needs a theological readjustment. In this way rather than there existing a sole deity who is at once ontologically primary and metaphysically ultimate, we find ourselves with a dyadic system. This dipolar model which leaves us with a base level ultimate category of pure fluxating becoming and a top level category of emergent totality bears far more similarity to the pre-Platonic conception of the world's beginning being rooted in the interplay between Nyx (Νύξ —"night") and Chaos (Χάος—"the first state of the universe"). Reaching back to Hesiod's *Theogony*,[279] we find that in the beginning there was only Chaos, the God of pure fluxating novelty, and from Chaos emerged Nyx, the Goddess whose body is the night sky. With a bit of poetic license it is not *too* hard to see this as a mythological expression whose application is quite appropriate to the cosmology painted by this interpretation of process philosophy. At the root level of reality seethes Chaos, the plenary God of indeterminate novelty and becoming—the God whose very form is a myriad of atomic microprocesses all in a constant state of flux. And, at the top level sits Nyx, the Goddess of the night sky, whose body encompasses the cosmos—she whose being contains the intergalactic whole. In such a system it is *He* of whom we are made, and *She* within whom "we live, and move, and have our being."[280]

Theurgic Ramifications

The model being such, what implications does this Aristotelian reversal of the vector of ontological dependency have on the theory behind and the practice of theurgy? As the shift from emanation to emergence leaves the psychic layers more or less in tact, changing only the ways in which they are constituted, much of the accompanying lower theurgy also requires no theoretical change. Praxical changes among contemporary psychonauts and theurgists are generally less geared around the theory behind what one is doing and much more around the efficacy of the practice itself. That is to say that, although the practice of constructing the *augoeides ochēma* was thought, by the ancient Greeks, to literally

---

279 Hesiod, 87.
280 Acts 17:28 (KJV).

allow the theurgist's soul to leave his body and traverse the higher worlds, contemporary practitioners tend towards far less literal interpretations, treating the out of body experience as a subspecies of lucid dream.[281] So, in this instance, the practices used to induce such an experience would, owing to the near identical nature of human psychology between the ancients and ourselves, be all but identical, but the theoretical explanation of the experience's phenomenology would differ somewhat. In other words, the *how* does not change, but our understanding of the *what* does. A prime example of this is in the aforementioned Neoplatonic practice, where the ancient theurgists believed themselves to have left their physical bodies behind and traveled into the higher levels of the hierarchy by means of the subtle body. This idea, leaving behind of the physical, *does* stem from the emanative notion of the physical as being the lowest emanation. However, for one working within the emergent paradigm, it is understood that the physical body and world can never be disregarded, and that higher spiritual experiences are themselves *contingent* upon the presence of the body. If the higher is birthed by the lower, and is constituted by it, to "leave" the lower would make the prehension of the higher impossible. So, in this way, the contemporary theurgist who operates within the intellectual backdrop of evolutionary Jungian psychology would likely see such experiences of lucidity as intrinsically tied to neural activity, not as something that can be divorced from bodily processes as did the ancients.

Keeping in mind this ontological primacy of the body over the higher forms of mentality, it would seem to follow that the modern theurgist would see physical health and well-being not as incidental to, but as an imperative aspect of the higher modes of theurgy. This is in *stark* contradistinction to the ascetic practices that evolved in concert with the world's emanation theologies. Even today, it is not uncommon for a Hindu *sādhu*, holy man, to perform all manner of bodily mortifications that result in the permanent loss of fitness and health.[282] Ascetics of the Shaiva denomination are particularly well known for performing the *urdhvabahu* mortification which involves holding up one arm for years at a time—a process which is believed to aid in spiritual ascent but inevitably results in the atrophying and eventual loss of the arm.[283] This, then, would be an instance where our Aristotelian perspective results in a change in practice *and* theory, as an emanative theurgy must be built upon a physical foundation. This leads us to agree fully with Teilhard's statement that in regards to spiritual practice, "what is involved firstly, is the care and improvement of the human body, the health and

---

281 A lucid dream is where the dreamer becomes conscious of the fact that he is dreaming while maintaining the dream state.
282 Dolf Hartsuiker, *Sadhus:India's Mystic Holy Men*, (Rochester, VT: Inner Traditions, 1993), 11.
283 *The Illustrated Encyclopedia of Hinduism*, c.v. "urdhvabahu"

strength of the organism," for "thought can only be built up on this material basis."[284] Under this model, then, the *psuchē* could not be treated as detached and separate from the body, but rather must be seen as something which emerges from it, thus resulting in some sort of comprehensive fitness regimen being a necessary precursor to any higher theurgic work.

Certain aspects of other lower theurgic practices such as *telestikē* and *katochē* would require theoretical adjustments as well. In both cases, what the theurgist was, in the Classical world, thought to be dealing with was the descent of a God or daimon into the physical world via the temporary habitation of a statue, child, etc. In contemporary terms, we would not speak of such an event as happening wholly *without* but nearly entirely *within*. In other words, when the theurgist prepares the statue for the *telestikē* operation and succeeds in calling down the God or daimon to the physical, this is not a case of an entity who exists in complete ontological separation from the theurgist literally inhabiting a statue and entering into conversation with him. Rather, we would make use of Jung's understanding of the processes of archetypal possession and projection. In such an event, the theurgist would be possessed by the entity he has invoked, but in order for his ego complex to converse with this higher complex or archetype, he would *project* this possession onto an object external to him—thus allowing these two compartments of his *psuchē* to engage in a dialogue with one another as mutually autonomous entities. Jung considered this type of practice to be an integral aspect of the individuation process, terming it *active imagination*.[285]

Regarding the *higher* theurgy, we see that the theoretical changes become even more pronounced. As mentioned in the preceding section, our presently examined model presents the ultimate in *duotheistic* rather than monotheistic terms, with the ontologically primary forming the hierarchy's base and the metaphysically greatest occupying the top position. Correspondingly, to describe the highest levels of theurgic *henōsis*, we will need to refer to *two* modes of prehension, not one. As discussed before, the Neoplatonic One was at once both ontologically prime and metaphysically supreme. Beginning at the bottom, we can attempt to provide a rough sketch of the methodology and phenomenology of the prehension of the atomic plenum at the hierarchy's base. Panexperientialism tells us that "consciousness is a later emergent phenomenon of experience which highlights certain aspects of it but cannot in any way be exhaustive of it."[286] To understand what an experience of this pre-conscious root level would entail, we

---

284 Teilhard, 282.
285 MacLennan, "Individual Soul and World Soul," 15.
286 Ernest L. Simmons Jr., "Mystical Consciousness in a Process Perspective," in *Process Studies* 14, no. 1 (Spring 1984), http://www.religion-online.org/showarticle.asp?title=2585 (accessed June 18, 2011).

must take into account the two modes of perception that Whitehead's panexperientialism proposes: presentational immediacy and causal efficacy.

> Presentational immediacy is clear and distinct and presents to our awareness the immediate "buzzing" confusion of the world around us. It is the "there" and "now" element in human perception. Causal efficacy, on the other hand, while being more massive as the conformation of our experience to the reality of the past as it impinges upon the present, is also vague and a fairly undiscriminating mode of perception. Causal efficacy is the more fundamental mode, however, for it is the perception through which the interconnectedness and causal influence of one actuality upon another is experienced.[287]

In other words, perception in the mode of causal efficacy takes into account the causal webs of dependency and emergence that present us with the coherent and "finished" picture of reality that is the hallmark of everyday consciousness. Presentational immediacy is quite different, disregarding such logical connectors and being more of a direct prehension of an event *qua* event. What this means for theurgy is that since our ontologically primary deity is *not* the being *qua* being of the Neoplatonists, but the Whiteheadian *event*, the corresponding prehension would be a downwardly directed process of phenomenological reduction in which the mode of causal efficacy is, by means of various methodologies proper to meditation, gradually shaken off. Indeed, the method of *Rāja yoga* presented by Patañjali (2nd century BC) is the model of perfection for the theurgist attempting to reduce his prehensive mode to that of pure experience.[288] This yogic method begins with the practice of a particular posture (*āsana*) and breath control (*prāṇāyāma*) designed to allow the mind to focus on the act of prehension, and to not be bothered by agitations of the body. The resulting physical state resembles the kind of complete unawareness of one's physical presence that accompanies sleep. This physical practice is paired with mental training which begins by teaching the student to examine in impassive detail one's mental contents (*pratyahara*), to fully concentrate upon an object (*dhāraṇā*), to concentrate so fully that the ego is eclipsed by the experience of the object of one's concentration (*dhyāna*), and finally to penetrate into the truly ontologically primary mode of prehending experience itself as such, in its pure state (*samādhi*).[289]

---

287 Ibid.
288 Swāmi Vivekananda, *Rāja Yoga*, (London: Kegan Paul, Trench, Trubner, & Co., Ldt.), 17.
289 Ibid.

On the completely opposite end of the hierarchy, the praxical methods leading towards the metaphysically highest would necessarily be completely different, as such an experience would *not* be one of presentational immediacy, but rather of the causal efficacy of the *whole*. In other words, whereas the kind of *henōsis* proper to the hierarchy's bottom would, by virtue of our recasting of the Neoplatonic hierarchy, be one in which consciousness is focused and contracted to the point of it being eclipsed by the experience of the object of concentration, the *henōsis* of the uppermost layer would be attained in the exact opposite fashion, via the *expansion* of one's consciousness. In this way, the traditional practices of theurgic ascent comport quite nicely, beginning with the assimilation into one causal picture the daimonic contents of one's own *psuchē*, following with the complete assimilation of the theistic archetypal field, resulting in the identification of the theurgist with the *Anthrōpos*, or higher self. This, then, if the process of prehensive expansion and integration were continued would keep building in upon itself by assimilating higher and vaster levels of the metaphysical hierarchy into a singular causal picture, the end result of which would be the prehension of the Great Goddess herself: Our Lady of Infinite Spacetime—the greatest of all Goddesses of whom we catch but a fleeting glimpse when we lose ourselves in transfixed wonder while gazing upwards at the night sky.

Recapitulation

And so ends this paper's journey. We began with the purpose of fully exploring the ramifications of MacLennan's Aristotelian recasting of the emanative vector of ontological dependency on the doxa and praxes of Classical Neoplatonism. After first detailing the Neoplatonic metaphysics of Plotinus and the theology and theurgy of Iamblichus, we compared this with the psychology and psychiatry of Carl Jung, finding the two systems to be, excepting lexical differences, largely descriptions of the same set of phenomena. Following this, Jung's psychology was examined in light of contemporary advances in evolutionary psychology. The paper's focal point, MacLennan's work, synthesizes all of this, resulting in an Aristotelian inversion of the Neoplatonic vector of ontological dependency, resulting in a shift from metaphysical emanationism to emergentism. Finding MacLennan's model to be deficient in certain areas, this work was supplemented with excursions into Whiteheadian process philosophy. The resultant picture which emerged from this synthetic process was one of a hierarchical cosmos whose layers are ordered in a bottom-up fashion which is driven by the twin processes of emergence and evolution. At the hierarchy's ontologically primary root system is the plenary field of events, which provides the system with an overarching *process* orientation. From these atomic microprocesses emerge further layers of ever increasing complexity and internal homeostasis, eventually reaching the medial layer which *we* occupy. This layer begins with the physical foundation of our bodies, from whose neural systems emerge the complex form of mentality that is humanity's hallmark. However, we also, via the infusion of Whitehead's process ontology, have discovered that the emergence of such mental systems is *not* synonymous with the emergence of mentality, for the event-oriented metaphysics are by necessity panexperientialist. This medial layer of *psuchē* is populated by strictly ordered hierarchies of several types of daimons and Gods, the constellation of whom forms the mindscapes of individual humans, families, ethnicities and humanity as a whole. Continuing upwards from this point, the hierarchical system culminates with the logical conclusion of emergent panentheism. Taken as a whole, it is my hope that the model presented provides a system which is capable of encompassing our everyday experience of the world, our heterophenomenological scientific understandings of the world's physical and biological processes, as well as our autophenomenological experiences of pluralistic religious truth into a holistic, consistent account. It is in this way, by applying a rigorously multi-disciplinary analysis to phenomena of polytheistic religiosity, that I believe an overarching idea of such can "be so formulated as to preserve, perhaps even increase, its religious value, while yet avoiding the contradictions which seem inseparable from the idea as customarily defined."[290]

Epistle to the Heathen

The Heathen, after reading this far, may still find himself questioning not only the *relevance* but also the *applicability* of such a study to the beliefs and practice of Heathenry in the modern world. First among these concerns is likely to be the sneaking suspicion that this paper is advocating the establishment of a kind of Heathen orthodoxy. It has long been my experience that a significant portion of Heathendom is possessed by a *strong* libertarian streak and reacts with extraordinary vigor against ideas which are seen as embodying the same kind of rigid intellectual dogmatism that was perceived to have been in place in the religions which they either belonged to or within whose community they grew up prior to converting to Heathenry.[291] This is not, however, a fear I intend to pla-

---

[290] Charles Hartshorne, *The Divine Relativity: A Social Conception of God*, (New Haven, CT: Yale University Press, 1967), 1.

[291] A perfect example of this kind of knee-jerk reaction to the very *idea* of a Heathen dogma can be found in Mark Stinson's collection of essays, *Heathen Gods* (Liberty, MO: Jotun's Bane Kindred, 2009). In "Reasons I'm Heathen," he states that one of the attractive features of Heathenry (versus Christianity) is that "there is no central authority or codified dogma used to control believers," (20). The same sentiment is repeated in "Differing Views Within Heathenry," where Stinson states that "there is no central authority, no all-encompassing dogma to follow," within Heathenry (31). In the same essay he expands on this with the statement that "there is no real benefit

cate. This paper *does* present a theological position that I am more than comfortable to characterize as having the potential to be orthodoxic. Now, before you turn away in disgust, let us explore exactly what orthodoxy means and why it is not only *already* present in the sapling that is Heathen theology, but why it must become a *more pronounced* feature of our thought if Heathenry is to actualize its potentiality and grow once more to be a mighty oak.

The term itself stems from the Greek roots, *orthos* (ὀρθός—"true," "right," or "straight") and *doxa* (δόξᾰ—"an opinion," "judgment," or "belief"). These two roots come together to create an impression of a set of beliefs, generally that pertain to religious matters, that are correct or *true*. There is a common misconception that an orthodoxy *must* rest upon some sort of religious authority, but, in actuality, that could not be further from the truth. While there are indeed a number of religious organizations whose orthodoxic precepts make, when questioned, an appeal to either a textual or clerical authority, it should be understood that this mode of justification is a particular type of fallacy of defective induction.[292] Known as the *argumentum ad verecundiam* (lit. "argument to authority"), this fallacy is one of the most commonly encountered, yet most obviously fallacious forms of argumentation. Its form can be explained as such:

1. A claims that B is true.
2. A is an authority.
3. Therefore, B is true.

While this argumentative structure certainly does not *preclude* the possibility of B being true, it is fundamentally false to claim B's truth based solely on A's authority. To concretize the example, we can flesh it out:

1. Stephen Hawking claims that black holes exist.
2. Stephen Hawking is an authority on theoretical physics.
3. Therefore, black holes exist.

---

to suppressing local tribal beliefs, traditions, and practices in favor of an over-arching unifying dogma," (32). This aversion to religious orthodoxy is not unique to Stinson, but seems to be representative of *many* who have converted to Heathenry from religions with strong orthodoxic precepts (e.g. Roman Catholicism). However, this seems to be more of a species of cognitive bias, where new Heathens are quick to distinguish their new faith from the old in as many ways as possible, with no regard as to the broader theological ramifications or internal consistency of these reactionary beliefs.

292 "Argumentum Ad Verecundiam," *Introduction to Logic*,
http://philosophy.lander.edu/logic/authority.html (accessed July 19, 2011).

While propositions one and two are indeed true, nothing about them *necessitates* that the conclusion is true, making the argument—regardless of the truth or falsity of the conclusion—formally false. What the fallacy comes down to is that an authoritative *doxa* is only as true as the *evidence* upon which it is founded. In theology's case—particularly in the United States—far too often are so-called "revealed" or "inspired" texts taken to be, in and of themselves, authoritative. Philosophically, this is an irrevocably flawed process of thought, as the doxic points in any given religious text cannot cogently be argued to be true unless those points can themselves be argued in favor of by means of argumentation other than "God says it's true." While Heathens are *generally* not in the habit of claiming theological propositions to be true or false on the sole basis of "Óðinn said so," there *is* a particular variation on the appeal to authority that is not uncommon: the argument from *historical* authority.[293] This variant's form may be demonstrated thusly:

1. Pre-Christian Heathens believed A to be true.
2. The historicity of A is authoritative.
3. Therefore, A is true.

While the second proposition is generally implied rather than explicitly stated, the argument's form is the very definition of a classic *argumentum ad verecundiam*. In this way, it would be irreparably flawed for a Heathen theologian to argue, for instance, that Óðinn exists simply because of the historical fact that Heathens in ancient times believed it to be so. Arguments must be rooted in one or both of the two following epistemological categories:

1. Empirical Data[294]
2. Rational Thought[295]

In respect to theological arguments, St. Anselm's (1033–1109) ontological argu-

---

293 An example of this can be found in Bil Linzie's essay, "Reconstructionism's Role in Modern Heathenry," (http://www.angelfire.com/nm/seidhman/reconstruction-c.pdf [accessed July 1, 2011]) where he states that he began promoting reconstructionism versus the (largely unacknowledged) syncretism that was the hallmark of 20th century Heathenry because he believed that Heathenry "should be rebuilt on historical fact and that by encouraging this we were stepping forward to support its validity in the modern world," (2).

294 *A prosteriori* knowledge is gathered from experience and the collection of empirical evidence (e.g. there are two apples on the table).

295 *A priori* knowledge is epistemologically primary, meaning that its knowing is thought to be independent of experience (e.g. one apple plus another apple equals two apples).

ment[296] is *the* exemplar of rational theology, while Thomas Aquinas' cosmological argument[297] fills a similar position in that it is among the most established of all empirical theological arguments. At this point, the second question against the paper might be raised: why resort to these mental gymnastics *at all*? After all, if our ancestors had no formal philosophy or theology, why should we import these anachronistic patterns of thought into what is supposed to be a *reconstructed* religion? The answer again lies in the necessity of orthodoxy—of *true* belief. It does us no good as a religion to hold beliefs which are either inconsistent with scientific consensus or that are internally inconsistent. For a belief to be *correct*, it ought correspond to reality—to the way things are. This mode of orthodoxic theology simply cannot be reached by solely relying on the phase of religious development that simply happens to be the source of Heathen textual and archaeological documentation. In adopting these beliefs at face value, not only is one committing the grave error of making an argument from authority, but it is also the case that the specific beliefs being adopted were developed prior to the emergence of true rationality among the peoples of Northern and Western Europe,

---

296 Anselm's ontological argument for the existence of God is composed of the following chain of propositions:
 1. We can conceive of something which has the property of maximal greatness.
 2. When this conception (1) is conveyed, it is understood.
 3. Thus (1 and 2), this conception (1) exists in our understanding.
 4. Maximal greatness cannot be conceived of in understanding alone.
 5. That which can be conceived of in our understanding can also be conceived of as existing in reality.
 6. Reality is greater than understanding.
 7. Thus (4, 5 and 6), maximal greatness conceived of *as existent* is greater than the same being conceived of in understanding alone.
 8. Thus (3 and 7), maximal greatness is, by definition, existent.
 9. That being having the property of maximal greatness is God.
 10. Therefore, God exists (Anselm of Canterbury, *Proslogion*, trans. William Mann, from Graham Oppy's "Ontological Arguments," *Stanford Encyclopedia of Philosophy*, http://plato.stanford.edu/entries/ontological-arguments/ [accessed June 19, 2011]).

297 The Thomist version of the cosmological argument can be broken down into the following form:
 1. Things in the world are in motion.
 2. All things in motion were put in motion by an ontologically antecedent mover.
 3. The mover which put the thing in question into motion must itself have been moved by a similarly prior mover.
 4. This sequential causation cannot proceed indefinitely.
 5. Therefore, there must exist an ontologically primary unmoved mover, understood to be God (Scott David Foutz, "An Examination of Thomas Aquinas' Cosmological Argument as Found in the Five Ways," in *Quodlibet Journal*, http://www.quodlibet.net/aqu5ways.shtml [accessed June 19, 2011]).

making such beliefs hardly worth adopting as literal truths. The Christian conversions occurred while our ancestors were still in the pre-philosophical phases of their intellectual development. They had not yet reached the levels that the Greeks or Indians had, and so did the conversions contort this eventual development into a kind of pseudomorphosis—forcing European thought to develop within an imported Christian framework.

As Stephen McNallen[298] and Collin Cleary[299] have both pointed out, none of this is to say that much of this cannot be *reclaimed* and applied to Heathen theology with great effect. Indeed, quite the opposite is true; Heathen theology is at such an infantile state of development at present that the ways in which this development can be guided by established philosophical schools are all but innumerable. At some point in the future we may be able to speak of existential, process-relational, or even eco-feminist *schools* of Heathen theology in the same way that other major religions do. Yet, without the intentional development of the seed-ideas that the faith of our ancestors presents us, we will remain locked into either a primitivist understanding of Heathenry as a static, historical relic, incapable of doxic development, *or* continue down the path of libertarian fragmentation where everyone believes what they want to believe and deal with the contradictory beliefs of others not by attempting to determine *which* theology is true, but by resorting to an epistemologically relativistic theological framework in which it is socially unacceptable for a theologian to publicly claim his position to be correct for fear that others may find his "dogmatism" unacceptable. If Heathenry is *true*, it is our duty as rational practitioners to uncover *how* it is true; for if its truth lies not in literalism, it must lie in a philosophically grounded theology.

So, having met these initial concerns, the third that is likely to rear its head revolves around the paper's panentheism. Is it not, the polytheist may ask, simply monotheism in disguise? After all, if panentheism is *true*, why would we deal with the Gods at all; why not directly worship *God* as the Christians do? My response to this comes in the form of an analogy. The cosmic picture that my theological model presents is one of an ordered hierarchy. In social terms a similarly structured hierarchy can be found in a military unit. Let us, for the purposes of this argument identify ourselves—the Heathen population—with an Army's privates. Let us further identify the daimones with the noncommissioned officers of our company, the Gods with the officers of our battalion, and the metaphysically ultimate Goddess with the commander in chief of the armed forces. Now, as

---

[298] Stephen A. McNallen, "Three Decades of the Ásatrú Revival in America," *TYR: Myth—Cuture—Tradition* 2 (2003–2004): 217.
[299] Collin Cleary, "Paganism Without Gods," *TYR: Myth—Cuture—Tradition* 3 (2007–2008): 429.

a soldier, around whom do the *vast* majority of your duties and military interactions surround: the NCOs and officers of your unit, or the President of the United States? True, all soldiers are sworn to obey the orders of the President, just as *all* organisms in the cosmos are under the dominion of the Cosmic Goddess' downward causation. However, ninety-nine percent of the time, the President is the furthest thing from a soldier's mind. It is the NCOs who nurture, support and train soldiers. It is the officers who command, guide and lead them. These mid-level tiers of the organizational hierarchy are, due to the simple fact of their ontological *closeness*, incredibly more important to the experience of the individual being considered. In this way, just as the soldier's immediate levels of leadership are not only more important, but also more closely involved in his military life, so are the wights and Gods to the Heathen. Under the emergent model it is not as if the Gods are hypostatic façades of the uppermost Goddess and are utterly contingent upon her. Indeed, quite the opposite is true; the panentheistic deity is herself wholly contingent upon the Gods—a fact which ought alleviate any concerns that this paper's theology slips into the soft polytheism and resultant existence monism of Wicca, Theosophy or Advaita Vedānta.

Fourthly, having mentioned the wights, as this theology somewhat psychologizes the daimones and Gods (by treating them as denizens of the emergent *psuchē* of the individual or group unconscious), where does this leave the *land* wights and the benevolent Jötnar such as Jörð and Sunna without whose interaction our lives would be impossible? Surely *they* cannot be treated as emergent qualities of the human race in the same way the more anthropomorphic Gods can, right? To this concern I would answer with a qualified "yes." The evolutionary Jungian model presented previously applies strictly to entities who exist *within* the hierarchical continuum that we, ourselves, are a part of. While those beings which exist *without* are parts of branches that we do not participate in. In Heathen terms, this difference is illustrated in the Norse bifurcation between the *innangarð* and the *útangarð*. That is to say that the anthropic continuum, or *innangarð*, is the ring of troth and relatedness that constitutes the various classes of Æsir, Vanir and Jötnar *qua* Gods, while the extra-anthropic continua, or *útangarð*, are the Jötnar, Risar, and Þursar who were never joined in troth with the Gods.

In this way, not only would a *purely* Jungian approach to the telluric and stellar deities of the *útangarð* rob them of their numinosity, it would also be incongruous with the panexperientialist framework within which MacLennan's neurotheology can be seen to rest. We must remember that panexperientialism is a *panpsychist* philosophy of mind, which grants a degree of mentality and interiority to *all*. That being the case, as mentality and physicality form an organizaitonal duality with the former being a function of the latter's structural complexity, highly organized natural systems such as plants in one's garden, forests, mountain ranges and up to the Earth herself could not *not* display corresponding mental dimensions. While their completely non-human constitution would necessarily make communication as we think of it as occurring between persons impossible, Whitehead's ontology *would* permit the prehension of this internality by one who specifically sought to do so. Moreover, as the numinous experiencing of the mentality of nature would likely transport the experience to a *religious* frame of reference, it is quite probable that the Jungian projection mechanism would kick in and *overlay* the experience in a mythic symbology proper to the holistic *Weltanschauung* of the Heathen doing the prehending. In this way the gardener who treats his craft as a spiritual practice might literally experience himself working in concert with both the wights of the land and Jörð herself.

Finally, on the *applicability* of this model to the Heathen pantheon, the best answer would be to provide a tentative exploration of how MacLennan's Neoplatonic hierarchy applies to the various denizens of the Heathen cosmos. At the base level, the seething Chaos of the Greeks perhaps finds its best analog with the Norse Ginnungagap: "the primeval void that existed before the creation of the cosmos."[300] Skipping forward to the medial layers, we find the lower egoic complexes of the individual unconscious, Iamblichus' archons, to be cognates to the Norse *hugr*, *minni* and *ek*—the mind, memory and ego respectively.[301] These lower complexes whose primary function is to bind the self to its material base might find themselves best described as the constellation of material wights which comprise Miðgarðr. The higher, superegoic complexes are best represented in the Norse mythos by the personal tutelary spirit: the *fylgja*. The next few layers, those of the complexes of the family and tribal unconscious are likely best paired with the dísir, matrones and various household godlings that formed the plenary continuum between the individual and the Gods. This uppermost medial layer, the archetypes of the ethnic unconscious, that of the Gods would of course be filled by the Æsir, Vanir and select Jötnar (with many of these being excluded due to their occupation of extra-human natural hierarchies). Being super-ethnic, the archetypes of the *human* unconscious would, of course have no direct cognates as they are beyond the grasp of a single people's mythology. Skipping upwards once more, the final panentheistic layer is an extremely close fit with the Greek Nyx being a near exact cognate to the Norse Nótt. As the *primary* purpose of this paper was not to specifically map out these cross connections, but rather to develop the framework within which such a thing could be done the above sketch is rather rough around the edges, leaving much room for future clarifica-

---

300 John Lindow, *Norse Mythology: A Guide to the Gods, Heroes, Rituals and Beliefs*, (New York: Oxford University Press, 2001), 141.
301 Edred Thorsson, *Runelore: A Handbook of Esoteric Runology*, (York Beach, ME: Red Wheel/Weiser, LLC, 1987), 169–171.

tion and expansion. However, a tentative table of correspondences is presented, detailing the connections between the different layers of the emergent hierarchy this essay presents and Heathen theology:

Emergent Neoplatonism	Heathen Theology
The One, as the Panentheistic Pleroma	Nótt
[Ascending Levels of Solar Systemic, Galactic and Universal Hierarchies]	—
The Earth	Jörð
Anthropic Archetypes	—
Ethnic Archetypes	Æsir, Vanir, and (Some) Jötnar
Ethnic Complexes	Einherjar and Valkyrjar
Family Complexes	Dísir, Matrones and (Family) Hamingja
Individual Higher Complexes	Vörðr, Fylgja and (Individual) Hamingja
Individual Lower Complexes	Hugr, Minni and Ek
Human Body	Lik
[Ascending Levels of Physical (Sub-Atomic → Atomic → Molecular) and Biotic (Cellular → Organic) Hierarchies]	—
The Many, as the Panexperientialist Prima Materia	Ginnungagap

As this table presents a sketch of the hierarchy within which *we* exist, it necessarily excludes certain categories of wights and Gods which are, nonetheless, of great import in Heathen theology. Some of the *landvættir*, like the rock-dwelling *bergbúi* would find their place between the hierarchical continuum that stretches from the molecular level to Jörð. Others, like the *álfar*, with their connections to the forests and crop fertility would likely emerge from the biotic layer and, again, contribute towards the emanation of Jörð. Certain Jötnar who dwell *outside* of Miðgarðr find themselves part of extraterrestrial emergent hierarchies that diverge from our particular hierarchy at the physical level and only intersect at the level of the solar system (e.g. Sunna and Máni). Others, yet, embody principles which are far closer to the root level of Ginnungagap than they are to us; the entropic Hrímþursar of Niflheim and energetic Surtr of Múspell seem to be mythic projections of the kinds of primal processes that affect *all* levels of the hierarchy not by virtue of being metaphysically great, but by means of ontological priority. If, for a moment, we imagine the cosmic hierarchy as Yggdrasil, we can see the ontologically primitive entropic forces curled around the roots in the form of Niðhöggr and the extraordinarily emergent processes of *awareness* and conscious mentality in Veðrfölnir and the unnamed eagle who sit atop the tree.

In closing, it is my great hope that this paper will, above all else, be found to be *useful* by my Heathen brethren. I have done my best to present those of us who are progressively minded in matters of theology with a working platform upon which more in-depth work can be done. Whether you agree or disagree with the thesis put forth, it is my aspiration that your reaction will spur you towards the kind of systematic thought and analysis that went into this paper's construction. After all, as I have said before, Heathendom would be an *awfully* boring place if we all agreed about *everything*. While we will invariably concur on certain *doxa* (e.g. the existence of a plurality of Gods, that among these Gods exist those of the Germanic pantheon, etc.), it is amidst our philosophical disagreements that we, as a community, will find the greatest opportunities for growth and development. May this work serve as a starting point from which further theological debates spring forth. The greatest innovations occur amidst strife, so let me implore you to, in the spirit of dialectic philosophy, "as brothers fight ye!"[302]

---

[302] Aleister Crowley, *The Book of the Law: Liber AL vel Legis*, centennial ed., (York Beach, ME: Red Wheel/Weiser, LLC, 2004), III:59.

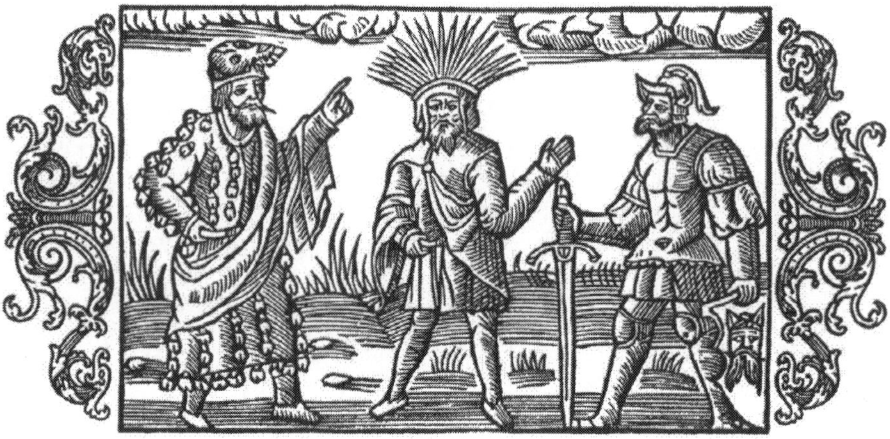

Hero, Anti-Hero, Villain

Kris Stevenson

One might ponder the contrast between the legends of the torture of Prometheus and of Loki: the one for assisting men, the other for assisting the powers of darkness.[1]
—J.R.R. Tolkien

The above quote was written by J.R.R Tolkien in 1936 as a footnote to his seminal essay *Beowulf: The Monsters and the Critics*. It forms the topic of this present essay. Both Loki and Prometheus hold fascination for me, and being primarily Odinist[2] I cannot but be interested in Loki, whose relationship with Óðinn is complex to say the very least. Whilst Prometheus' defiance of Zeus in his aid (and defence of) humanity has (for me) the very spirit of indigenous northern belief written within it despite the tale being rooted in the warmer climes of the Aegean. I was asked if I would extend my study to one other figure, namely Lucifer. The idea of including Lucifer in a Heathen journal may seem odd but as someone who personally both enjoys Christian mythology[3] and who sees merit in researching and comparing (though not too strictly) different mythological traditions it would seem a natural progression, particularly since I am going to focus on the character of Lucifer as he is portrayed in Milton's *Paradise Lost*. Milton's epic is a synthesis of Christian and Pagan themes. It is also to be noted that I am far from the first to see similarities between Lucifer and one of my other studies, Prometheus. Percy Bysshe Shelley's work *Prometheus Unbound* has come under scrutiny for his Satan-like Prometheus figure, which Shelley himself compared to Prometheus, albeit a far more heroic one free of the flaws of Satan. It is also to be recalled that Percy Shelley's wife was Mary Shelly, author of *Frankenstein* with the often forgotten subtitle *Or the Modern Prometheus*.

Tolkien believed all myths were primarily about a fall. I am not expert enough in the field to argue for or against his assertion but a fall does certainly link our trio. The fall of Satan and the consequent fall of man are familiar enough. Prometh-

---

[1] J.R.R. Tolkien, "Beowulf: The Monsters and the Critics," in *Interpretations of Beowulf: A Critical Anthology*, ed. R.D. Fulk, (USA: Indiana University Press, 1991), 28.
[2] In this context, I use the word for one, such as myself, who is primarily a follower of Óðinn.
[3] It is indeed mythology. It would be bizarre to suggest there are no similarities between some aspects of Christian and Heathen lore.

eus' fall comes about through his defiance of Zeus over infant mankind. Finally Loki who engineers the fall of many of the Gods and of the established order at Ragnarök.

Along with the theme of a fall we have another common theme: binding. All three of our protagonists find themselves bound at some point in their tale. H.R. Ellis Davidson points out that the binding of a giant figure is a common theme in pre-Christian European mythology.[4] Such a theme may well have passed into Christian lore with the conversion. The Old English poem *Genesis A* has Satan bound, and while it is unlikely that this was the source of the more Classical influenced *Paradise Lost,* it is interesting that Milton begins his story with Satan bound in adamantine chains upon the burning lake.

Finally, why "Hero, Anti-Hero, Villain" and who do I guise in which role? It occurred to me that the three figures I have chosen could well fit such a scheme. Both Prometheus and Lucifer display characteristics of the hero. Indeed, one of the reasons I chose to include Lucifer on advice is because he displays the indomitable will that is, for me, characteristic of our native lore. Both he and Prometheus are matched against impossible odds, neither Prometheus nor Lucifer have it in their power to directly harm the source of their enmity, Lucifer can no more harm God than Prometheus can harm Zeus. Indeed, Lucifer is doubly damned in that he plays a part ordained for him by God and thus is pretty much a puppet, the instrument of God to test his creation. Yet Lucifer falls more into the role of anti-hero. Where Prometheus is motivated by unselfish love of humanity, Lucifer is full of jealousy, disappointment and an urge to self-aggrandisement. The benefit that man derives from Lucifer's action, freedom of conscience, is an indirect one born of Lucifer's hatred for God's creation and a will to corrupt it. This leaves us with Loki as the villain. This was, paradoxically, both an easy and a hard choice. In my philosophical outlook, heavily influenced as I am by men such as Nietzsche, one accepts that destruction and the darker aspects of human nature are as vital as their opposites. To ignore this is, in essence, to follow on the path of philosophers such as Plato and religions like Christianity, hankering after a type of man that does not exist. In my estimation, man himself is not flawed, though he may well see creation as flawed, which is an entirely different matter and, to a degree, lies behind myths such as Prometheus and Lucifer. In a sense, then, it was hard to cast Loki as a villain given his necessary place in any philosophy that sees destruction as necessary for creation and the continuance of becoming. Yet it was also this point that undeniably cast Loki in the role of villain. Whilst Loki cannot be accused of not creating, without him Óðinn would

---

4 H.R. Ellis Davidson, *Gods and Myths of Northern Europe*, (London: Penguin Books, 1964), 179.

not have Sleipnir, and he was responsible for many of the gifts the Gods enjoyed, he is also, ultimately, key to the destruction of the world the Gods sought to protect. Nor can his betrayal of the Æsir, who took him as one of their own, be overlooked in any strict reading of the myths.

Hero

> *After he had fashioned men from water and earth, Prometheus also gave them fire, which he had hidden in a fennel stalk in secret from Zeus. But when Zeus learned of it, he ordered Hephaistos to nail his body to Mount Caucasos. So Prometheus was nailed to it and held there for a good many years; and each day an eagle swooped down to feed on the lobes of his liver, which grew again by night.*[5]
>
> —Apollodorus

Prometheus as the benefactor of mankind is familiar enough, however Apollodorus also claims that he created man, which differs from Hesiod's account. Whatever the provenance of Apollodorus' account, what is not in doubt is the suffering of Prometheus for his aiding of humanity.

> So, here's the whole truth in one word: All human skill and science was Prometheus' gift.[6]

Prometheus' binding is the culmination of a long battle to thwart the plans that Zeus has for the human race. We learn from Hesiod that the climax came after Prometheus defied Zeus' injunction to deny man knowledge of fire. This itself was punishment for the trick Prometheus had played on Zeus when it came to establishing the relationship between Gods and men as regards sacrifice. At a place called Mekone, Prometheus was given the task of dividing up an ox into two portions, one for mortals and one for Gods. One portion Prometheus dressed up as an unappealing ox's stomach, which contained within succulent meats, the other portion was a pile of bones dressed up in appetising fat. Zeus was to choose which portion the Gods were to have, he chose the latter. Angered by this trick, Zeus denied man the gift of fire, so Prometheus stole it hidden in a hollowed out fennel stalk. In Aeschylus' play, Strength urges of a reluctant Hephaestus in his task of binding the Rebel Titan;

---

5 Apollodorus, *The Library of Greek Mythology*, trans. Robin Hard, Oxford World's Classics, (Oxford: Oxford University Press, 1997), 36.
6 Aeschylus, *Prometheus Bound: The Suppliants; Seven Against Thebes; The Persians*, trans. Philip Vellacott, (London: Penguin Classics, 1979), 35.

> It was your treasure that he stole, the flowery splendour of all-fashioning fire, and gave to men an offence intolerable to the gods, for which he now must suffer, till he be taught to accept the sovereignty of Zeus, and cease acting as champion of the human race.[7]

Prometheus, however, remains anything but repentant, and certainly has no intention of acknowledging Zeus' authority. This is important since something of a blemish on Prometheus' character may be said to exist in his role in bringing Zeus to power. Prometheus is, by birth, not one of the Olympians, he is a Titan, son of Iapetos and Klymene (or Themis), brother to Epimetheus, Atlas, and Menoitios. During the *Titanomachia* (the "War of the Titans") the Olympians battle with the Titans in Thessaly for mastery, and after ten years of conflict the Titans were defeated and cast into the depths of Tartaros. We learn that Prometheus' father, Iapetos, resides there comforted by his son Menoitios, whilst Atlas is forced to hold up the sky for eternity. Prometheus is conspicuously absent, the reason being he aided Zeus in his war against his father's people.

> At that time I, offering the best of all advice, tried to convince the Titans of Heaven and Earth, and failed. They despised cunning; in their pride of strength they foresaw easy victory and the rule of might...my mother Themis, or earth, had many times foretold me, that not brute strength, not violence, but cunning must give victory to the ruler of the future.[8]

Cunning is a virtue we find extolled elsewhere in Greek myth, Odysseus' ability to lie and outwit is praised by Athena (a goddess linked intimately with Prometheus who is, according to Apollodorus, one of two possible Gods, the other being Hephaistos, responsible for striking Zeus skull and allowing Athena to be born).

> Anyone who met you, even a god, would have to be a consummate trickster to surpass you in subterfuge. You were always an obstinate, cunning and irrepressible intriguer.[9]

Here, then, we have our reason for Prometheus' abandonment of his own family and, also, his future defiance of Zeus. It was a revolt of principle and a sacrifice made for the future. Prometheus, a son of the earth, was the first of the Titans

---

7 Ibid., 20.
8 Ibid., 27.
9 Homer, *The Odyssey*, trans. E.V. Rieu, (London: Penguin Classics, 1991), 201.

born to see rationality, morality, technology as the way forward. The Titans were interested solely in brute power, the Olympians understood more, they were a better prospect. Yet to Zeus, mankind was wretched, a failure, of little account or worth compared to earlier creations.

> Of wretched human he took no account, resolved to annihilate them and create another race. This purpose there was no one to oppose but I; I dared. I saved the human race from being ground to dust.[10]

Yet does not Prometheus here condemn himself and, thus, justify Zeus' wrath? Humanity is a creature capable of the greatest nobility and the worst savagery, we all understand this. Zeus could hold his hands up and say, "well, I wanted better, I knew you folks were flawed and no good, I intended to make something superior, do not blame me, blame Prometheus, if it was not for his pride and interference you would all be living in paradise." This seems a reasonable argument on the face of it, and would certainly be reasonable from a Christian perspective, but it would miss the point of Greek mythology entirely. The race that Zeus despised was, for Prometheus, full of infinite potential, maybe that servile people huddled in the cold was what Zeus feared most, a people capable of change, capable of becoming more than they are, while the Olympians are not, they are immutable immortals largely infantile in many ways and interested only in the status quo:

> I know of nothing poorer under the sun than you gods! Wretchedly you feed your majesty on the tithes of sacrifice and the breath of prayer, and would famish, if children and beggars were not optimistic fools.[11]

Pandora was the first woman, a beautiful creature sent by Zeus to beguile Prometheus' gullible brother, Epimetheus, and with her she brought a jar (often described as a box). Prometheus warned his brother not to accept gifts from Zeus but to no avail. Pandora opened her jar and out poured all human suffering into the world, all that was left in the jar was one thing, hope:

> Yes: I caused men no longer to foresee their death…I planted firmly in their hearts blind hopefulness.[12]

---

10 Aeschylus, 27.
11 Johann Wolfgang von Goethe, "Prometheus," in John Reed's *The Schubert Song Companion*, (Manchester: Manchester University Press, 1997), 357.
12 Aeschylus, 28.

The daughters of Oceanus (the chorus in Aeschylus' play) lament Prometheus' actions that such a creature as man who lives "but for a day" possesses hope and fire…little wonder the Gods were angry-what could man achieve with such gifts, could he bring down Olympus itself?

In the Greek eye, man was not fallen (at least not in early Greek lore-we have to wait until Plato before we see a more life-denying attitude to the state of humanity). It is, surely, no accident of history that the first people to begin to see the world as something ultimately understandable and capable of being controlled arose in the Aegean world some time in the Sixth Century BC. The indifference (and downright hostility at times) of the Gods to men in Greek mythology has been commented on before; for Tolkien, the Greek Gods were only interested in men as far as they were useful to their own schemes. He went further to say that as Greek knowledge of the world advanced the Gods could only survive in philosophy. Perhaps this indifference was the break man needed? Greek man accepted joy and sorrow as the lot of the world. Moreover, he had hope, his knowledge of death did not cripple him and he came to believe that world was understandable and with fire, the technology to develop and advance, the gifts of Prometheus, he did not need to live at the whim of capricious Gods. The Prometheus myth represents more than indomitable will in the face of overwhelming power, it represents the emancipation of man. For this, Prometheus found himself bound to his rock but he willed it so, he would change nothing of his fate.

Anti-Hero

> *Here I sit, forming men in my own image, a race that shall suffer, weep, enjoy, and be happy, as I am, and that shall take no notice of you, as I do!*[13]
>
> —Goethe

Lucifer is a stereotypical anti-hero. His rebellion against God is entirely motivated by jealousy and self-interest. The promotion of Jesus above the arch-angels is bad enough for him. Even worse, God intends to create a new race of almost angelic bearing that will usurp the place of the angels in his affections. To Lucifer this is intolerable, but out of his intent to harm God's plan he also (from a certain non-Christian perspective) does some good for humanity, he also has remorse within him, which many anti-heroes do but no true villain ever has.

Milton's Satan was deliberately given a classical heroic bearing in the first two books of *Paradise Lost*. At the beginning he is a giant but increasingly shrinks as

---

13 Goethe, 358.

the work progresses to the point where he becomes a lowly serpent. It is to be stressed that Milton had no deliberate intention of making us sympathetic to Satan; his work is Christian throughout and the Pagan deities that are named are considered devils. Nonetheless, this piece is not a literary criticism of *Paradise Lost* but rather a study of Satan in my own theme.

As has been mentioned, Lucifer does display qualities that are similar to Prometheus, not least his defiant attitude (initially at least):

> From what highth fall'n, so much the stronger prov'd he with his thunder: and till then who knew the force of those dire arms? Yet not for those, nor what the potent victor in his rage can else inflict, do I repent or change.[14]

Lucifer's fall to the "thunder" of God has clear parallels to Prometheus' fall at the hands of Zeus, lightning wielder of the Olympians. Also of note is that Lucifer is rebuked in his folly just as the Chorus in Aeschylus' play condemns Prometheus' actions. Here Abdiel, initially a supporter of Satan's rebellion turns against him:

> Fool not to think how vain against th' omnipotent to rise in arms; who out of the smallest things could without end have rais'd incessant armies to defeat thy folly; or with solitary hand reaching beyond limit, at one blow unaided could have finished thee.[15]

Lucifer is as out of his depth against God as Prometheus is against Zeus, neither can hope to overthrow their opponent, indeed Lucifer is more a pawn in God's plan than anything else as we learn at the start of Book III:

> If him by force he can destroy, or worse, by some guile pervert: and shall pervert: for man will heark'n to his glozing lies, and easily transgress the sole command, sole pledge of his obedience.[16]

God sees what will be as well as what has become, Satan is the original author of disobedience to the will of God, yet this was known to God for he would have man free to choose to love or reject him, Satan can rebel only because God wills it to be. Even so, one can still see Satan as a pawn moved by a hand and mind

---

14 John Milton, *Paradise Lost: A Poem in Twelve Books,* (Indianapolis, IN: Hackett Publishing Company Inc., 1997), 8.
15 Ibid., 142.
16 Ibid., 65.

greater than his, which makes his will to defy more sympathetic. Even Prometheus has a vision that he can threaten Zeus with,[17] but Satan has, effectively, nothing, he is an actor, but his disobedience has consequences (happy from our perspective):

> Others apart sat on a hill retir'd, in thoughts more elevate, and reason'd high of providence, foreknowledge, will, and fate. Fixt fate, free will, foreknowledge absolute, and found no end, in wand'ring mazes lost. Of good and evil much they argu'd then.[18]

Belial, in an almost Nietzschean passage, argues against an immediate assault on Heaven:

> For who would lose, though full of pain, this intellectual being, those thoughts that wander through eternity.[19]

Intellectual freedom bought at the price of ignoring God's plan-not for nothing does the name Lucifer derive from the Latin *lux* (light) and *ferre* (bring). Just as Prometheus brought the flame of technology to man to allow him to impose his will so does Lucifer (light bringer) give man the intellectual freedom to think past God. Of course, for Milton, this was folly of Satan to believe that his knowledge was greater than God's will, but for those who have no belief in the Abrahamic God…

Satans' child "Sin" is of interest to us. Sin is the lover/child of Satan, here she explains her birth:

> All on a sudden miserable pain surpris'd thee, dim thine eyes, and dizzy swum in darkness, while thy head I sprung.[20]

The birth of Sin here is startlingly similar to the birth of Athene from Zeus' skull. Milton describes Sin as being of a serpent from the waist down, the obvious parallel is to Satan's serpent form in Eden, a less obvious but, I believe, equally telling a connection to Athene. Early representations of the goddess show her wearing a cloak of snakes and holding serpents in both hands. We have already seen above that Satan's rebellion leads to an intellectual freedom, and it is note-

---

17 This is the prophecy that Zeus in turn will be overthrown by the progeny of his union with the nymph Thetis. As it turns out, Thetis instead marries Peleus, King of the Myrmidons, whose son is Achilles.
18 Ibid., 45.
19 Ibid., 34.
20 Ibid., 51.

worthy that Athene is herself the goddess of wisdom in Greek mythology. Naturally, Pagan thought would have been abhorrent to the pious Milton but to us Heathens the connection between Sin and Athene opens delicious possibilities to explore. Sin has connections to Eve and also Pandora. In Christian myth particularly it is common to paint woman as the bringer of man's doom, Eve brought about Adam's fall, Satan's incestuous relation with Sin births Death, the same consequence that befell man for eating from the Tree of Knowledge. In Greek lore, Pandora is also given a bad press. However, are we not looking at this wrong? Does Belial not have the right of it? Suffering is a necessary part of freedom (particularly intellectual). Personally, I prefer to see in mythological figures like Sin, Eve and Pandora aspects of the Earth herself calling man (her child of greatest potential) forth from innocence into understanding, and testing him along the way.

Yet it is in the very act of creating sin/wisdom that Lucifer feels remorse for his actions, the scene in the Garden of Eden provides the backdrop to this conflict within Satan:

> Upon himself; horror and doubt distract his troubl'd thoughts, and from the bottom stir the hell within him, for within him hell he brings, and round about him, nor from hell one step no more than from himself can fly by change of place: now conscience wakes despair that slumber'd, wakes the bitter memory of what he was, what is, and what must be.[21]

Satan long debates himself over his path, his urge to strike back at God is tempered by the sight of the angelic beings Adam and Eve in their innocence, an innocence he himself gave up. He regards Eden as it might have been if he could have freely walked in its gardens. This remorse is purposefully woven by Milton (it bears no relation to the Biblical Satan). For Milton, Satan's greatest sin was not his original transgression of God's will it was simply that Satan felt he could not ask for forgiveness, he felt pressed to continue along his path. So we arrive at the point of no return and the tempting of Eve, the "Queen of the Universe." We know the tale well enough but see a pertinent quote from the serpent as he overhears the innocent couple's conversation:

> From thir own mouths: all is not theirs it seems: one fatal tree there stands of knowledge call'd, forbidden them to taste: knowledge forbidd'n? Suspicious, reasonless. Why should thir lord envy them that? Can it be sin to know, can it be death? And do

---

21 Ibid., 84.

they only stand by ignorance, is that thir happy state, the proof of thir obediance and thir faith?[22]

Lucifer's reasoning for the corruption of the young couple rests on freeing them from slavish obedience and to make them "Gods" in their own right. We understand this as self-delusion on Satan's part; by this point, Satan is thoroughly embittered and full of malice, he is destroyer rather than creator and can only corrupt the work of God not create things himself, yet not intentionally at least. From a Heathen perspective, the reading of Milton is one of unintended consequence. Prometheus wilfully empowered man at the expense of his own freedom, Lucifer did so by accident in an attempt at his own aggrandisement and hunger for revenge. We could, of course, argue that the end result negates the motives in Lucifer's actions-without his rebellion and his wish for revenge we would still be working in God's garden. Happier, perhaps, but of the same account as man before Prometheus brought him fire, scrabbling in the dirt and avoiding the tread of the Gods. Milton's Lucifer is a complex character, worthy of consideration from a Heathen perspective.

Villain

> *Then the Æsir took his guts and bound Loki with them across three stones...and these bonds turned to iron. Then Skadi got a poisonous snake and fixed it over him so that the poison would drip from the snake onto his face. But his wife Sigyn stands next to him holding a basin under the drops of poison. And when the basin is full she goes and pours away the poison, but in the meantime the poison drips into his face. Then he jerks away so hard that the whole earth shakes...There he will lie in bonds until Ragnarok.*[23]
>
> —Snorri Sturluson

Out of any mythological figure I am aware of, Loki Laufeyson is the most enigmatic, trying to pin him down is like trying to grab water, no matter how much you get more always slips through. I have no doubt I will fail, like most, to truly understand this character but, perhaps, in the context of his ultimate fate as described above something can be said. Snorri's description has obvious similarities to the binding of Prometheus, indeed this connection pointed out by Tolkien was the genesis of this essay, the circumstances, though, could not be more dif-

---

22 Ibid., 99.
23 Snorri Sturluson, *Gylfaginning* in *Edda*, trans. and ed. Anthony Faulkes, (London: Everyman, 1995), 52.

ferent.

Loki's role in the Norse myth seems to evolve over time, we have on the one hand a trickster figure and on the other a giant/demon. Loki seems to have a role in the creation of man. This is pretty standard fair for many trickster Gods who take on the role of culture hero, particularly in African and North American mythology.

> Breath they had not, spirit they had not, character nor vital spark
> nor fresh complexion; breath gave Odin, spirit gave Hoenir, vital
> spark gave Lodur and fresh complexion.[24]

"Vital spark" and "fresh complexion" can be read as a sort of child-like mischief breathed into the nascent human. In North American myth, Coyote often opposes Earthmaker and the dull, orderly world he creates, Coyote stands for a world where men can laugh and take pleasure in their senses. Davidson expands on this theme explaining Óðinn as a solid, impressive, serious figure in comparison to Loki as a comical mischief maker essentially making fun of the more serious Gods.[25] It is interesting to note that in some African cultures, a figure playing the role of a laughing god will mock the serious ceremonies of the priests, during their processions. How far we can take such a role for Loki is open to question but I believe there is some profit in the comparison. Of course, Prometheus also plays the role of a culture hero in defying Zeus, we may even have some cause to regard him as a trickster if we consider his conning the Gods out of their due sacrifice at Mekone. Loki and Óðinn, like Coyote and Earthmaker, are bound together so far that one wonders whether we are dealing with aspects of a similar figure. Coyote is often seen as a figure responsible for bringing sexuality into the world, John Lindow marks the connection between Loki and Óðinn regarding sexual ambiguity.[26] In *Lokasenna*, Loki accuses Óðinn of being a pervert:

> But you once practised seid on Samsey, and you beat on the drum
> as witches do, in the likeness of a wizard you journey among
> mankind, and that I thought the hallmark of a pervert.[27]

Both Loki and Óðinn travel the nine worlds in disguise and both question other

---

24 *The Poetic Edda*, trans. Carolyne Larrington, Oxford World's Classics, (Oxford: Oxford University Press, 1996), 18.
25 H.R. Ellis Davidson, *Gods and Myths of Northern Europe*, (London: Penguin Books, 1964), 181.
26 John Lindow, *Norse Mythology: A Guide to Gods, Heroes, Rituals, and Beliefs*, (Oxford: Oxford University Press, 2002), 219.
27 Larrington, 89.

supernatural beings for information. Óðinn and Loki are sworn blood brothers, Lindow believes that Óðinn swore to this in order to prevent conflict with Loki in the future, perhaps this is so. Equally, though, we could see that whilst Óðinn and Loki display similar traits they are put to differing purposes, as I expanded on in my previous essay in this journal. Óðinn prepares for Ragnarök and the coming of Fenris the cosmic destroyer. Loki's role using similar methods is to bring about this very episode of destruction. Loki's parentage is interesting. Whilst Snorri points out that Loki was counted amongst the Æsir his father seems to have been of giant stock, the unusual point, though, is that his mother may have been of the Æsir. If so, this would be a turn around from the more usual taking of a giantess as a mate by an Æsir (as Óðinn does on several occasions). Whether this was deemed an unnatural or perverse state of affairs is unknown but its uniqueness is surely not without meaning. Davidson has suggested that Loki may have evolved from an underworld figure, a giant of trickery who comes to the Æsir in guise of a trickster before reverting to the role of giant after the events of Baldr's death.[28] This would make sense given his siding with the giants at Ragnarök. Taking this possibility, I began to wonder at Loki's overall role (both trickster and demon in the myths). If we accept that myth is multi-layered and open to more than one meaning, is it possible to see the myths in the guise of some strange sport at play? Consider that whilst Loki plays the key part in the destruction of the Æsir and Vanir he also helps them on numerous occasions. He is father of Fenris, the killer of Óðinn, but he is also mother of Sleipnir, without which Óðinn would not be able to travel the nine worlds. He is responsible for Þórr acquiring Mjölnir, the very weapon employed to keep the giants out of Ásgarðr and presumably annihilating the Æsir long before Ragnarök. What to make of this? To me, it can read as some bizarre test; Loki placing the Æsir in tricky situations and providing them tools in order to develop and make better opponents at Ragnarök. The Æsir foresee their end as Loki says in *Lokasenna*:

> The son of Earth (Thor) has come in, why are you raging Thor?
> But you won't be so daring to fight against the wolf, when he swallows up Odin.[28]

Whatever play is at work here the Gods know of it, in a sense one sees Óðinn and the Æsir locked into a game orchestrated by the giants with Loki as a sort of puppet master. It would certainly chime with the overall fatalism of Norse mythology, one can almost see the connection of the laughing god in Loki: Laugh, what else can you do but play my game?

---

28 Davidson, 182.
28 Larrington, 94.

Whatever the possibility behind this in *Lokasenna* we come directly to the reversal from trickster to demon:

> Ale you brewed, Ægir, and you will never again hold a feast; all your possessions which are here inside may flame play over them, and may your back be burnt![29]

This is Loki's parting shot, his aim in *Lokasenna* is to sow discord amongst the Gods and to poison the mead of inspiration. This is where we head inexorably towards Ragnarök. Loki mocks Frigg over the death of Baldr:

> Frigg, do you want me to say still more about my wicked deeds; for I brought it about that you will never again see Baldr ride to the halls.[30]

Gone is the laughing god, the trickster to test the Gods, now we have Loki as pure evil, the sense of betrayal strong in Ægir's Hall as one can imagine the figure of Loki becoming more menacing, more giant-like in the fire of the hall as his true purpose is revealed.

After Þórr enters, Loki escapes but is eventually hunted down and bound. I assume that Loki's murder of Baldr is well known enough to readers of this journal, yet it forms the main reason why Loki is eventually bound by the Gods. Baldr himself remains something of an enigmatic figure, a god that seems out of place in the ethically dubious world of the Æsir. Can this really be the son of Óðinn, a god whose guile would put Odysseus to shame? Interpretations of Baldr ranges from his being an outright copy of Christ to the Loki-Baldr story being a heavily interpolated version of those Christ and Satan conflict stories doing the rounds in early medieval Europe. I think it reasonable to suppose that some Christian influence is at work in the story but the tale is too central to Norse mythology to be wholly Christian. Apparent Christian influence could be interpreted in the very nature of Baldr and Loki, which reads as a good versus evil tale in a way that is somewhat alien to what we would expect to find in pre-Christian myth. Perhaps it is plausible to suppose that by the time Snorri wrote the *Prose Edda* and the collection of poems erroneously called *Poetic Edda* were gathered together, that Loki, a mischievous trickster spirit of autochthonous tradition, had become equated with the Christian Satan and his evilness greatly expanded. We may go too far with this analysis, after all Loki is a genuine threat to the Gods, the reason that many of Óðinn's plans are turned astray and, finally, the reason Óðinn is

---

29 Larrington, 95.
30 Ibid., 89.

killed. Satan, by contrast, poses no such threat to God's will. Perhaps an alternative interpretation can be found in the very nature of reality (politically and socially). The Æsir may be unethical by modern standards but Óðinn is very much a figure who does what is needed to ensure the Gods are ready for Ragnarök. Perhaps Baldr represents the innocent ideal of one who can remain pure because others are willing to step into the dirt.

However we look at it, Loki comes out as an embodiment of evil in the later stages of the myth, not just an external threat such as the giants pose but one that is internal, lying within the home of the Æsir waiting for the right moment to strike at them. In this sense, Loki is very much the villain; he is stylish, he has the carefree cowboy manner that appeals to all of us to a great extent, but this is a gloss on something far more perverse and wicked, for ultimately Loki brings Ásgarðr and the world of men down. Prometheus was bound because he empowered humanity because he gave them a chance. Loki suffered the same fate because he would destroy the world of men and of the Gods who aid them. Perhaps a summary can be found in the symbol of the eagle and the serpent. Prometheus suffered the eagle to eat his liver each day for it to grow again at night, Loki had a serpent drip poison on his face. The eagle (a symbol of Zeus) has often been taken as higher/divine consciousness, the serpent as a more base level of being. Perhaps this tells us as much as we need to know about the nature of these two beings. And Lucifer, who started out as a giant to end up crawling on his belly as a snake, well, whether you see him as a fallen character or free is a choice the reader must make for himself.

Entropy Personified

Zacrey Monte Hansen

Entropy

Entropy as the scientific world knows it, the measured disorder of a system, is not the topic of this paper. This paper explores that entropy which resides in the philosophical realm of symbolism. Symbolic Entropy and its personifications lie on the far side of a continuum in opposition to the forces of Creation. Imagine that this continuum, with Entropy on one side and Creation on the other, acts as the board of a teeter-totter, with the status quo existing when the two forces are at equilibrium. As the strength of either faction grows the board leans in its favor, throwing the status quo out of balance, and in reaction the continuum attempts to regulate itself back to the status quo, which brings the other side of the continuum into power.

This interaction, termed the Archetypal Dialectic,[1] can be mapped out through the use of the thesis/antithesis equation. The empowered side of the continuum presents the thesis and the opposing side presents the antithesis, resulting in synthesis or the new status quo, and leading to a new thesis and so forth.

Because of the dualist nature of the dialectic, assumptions about the morality of either Creation or Entropy might develop. In Christianity Jesus conserves and creates, while Satan destroys. The parallels are obvious, but these assumptions are fundamentally one-dimensional attributions as Jesus will come as a great destroyer during Armageddon, acting as an agent of Entropy, and the term "spawn of Satan" stems from the idea that Satan procreates, acting as an agent of Creation. While someone might favor one end of the continuum, they are still on a continuum and have the ability to move back and forth as it suits them. Creation may be seen as more good than evil, and Entropy more evil than good, but they have no intelligence and therefore no moral compass.

However, this does not remove the burden of morality from those living along

---

1 Archetypal Dialectic was a term generated by the author bounding around the Utah Valley University Integrated Studies department offices in search of a proper way of encapsulating the teeter-totter effect mentioned in the paper. He would like to thank the faculty and staff of the department in surmounting that intellectual hurdle. The author later discovered that Richard Tarnas PhD had previously used the term, in a separate context, in his book *Cosmos and Psyche* (New York: Plume, 2007).

the continuum. Culpability lies in each individual person for their actions. An axe does not go to jail when the man using that axe busts open a window, the man does. Creation and Entropy are merely tools.

Of course, humans have the tendency to give faces to things they do not understand, in an effort for better comprehension. In doing so, mankind has created mythical figures that, while not pure translations of these primal forces, personify Creation and Entropy. Here we will leave Creation to its own devices and delve into the personifications of Entropy. Of primary concern are three figures that share surprising similarities and personify Entropy to the fullest extent possible.

The first and most potent of the personifications is the dragon Níðhögg from Norse mythology. The second is Hastur, the King in Yellow, an invention of American-Gothic writer Robert W. Chambers. The Man in the Yellow Suit from Natalie Babbitt's *Tuck Everlasting* brings up the rear. Each personification will be inspected separately, accompanied with a running comparison of how the symbolism of each bleeds into the others.

The examination of these figures should uncover some of the long held opinions of mankind as to the nature of the universe. Understanding the Archetypal Dialectic and how it influences every facet of life might give a broader perspective on the human experience, and lessen the structural violence that generates from not properly comprehending the nature of existence.

Níðhögg

Níðhögg represents the most primal and undiluted of the personifications, and in determining the attributes of Níðhögg a template manifests by which the other personifications might be compared. As told in the *Prose Edda*, one of the few great works concerning the mythology of the ancient Norse, "The ash Yggdrasil suffers hardships more than people realize...Nidhogg eats away at it below."[2] While there are many others intent on undermining the World Tree's foundations, Níðhögg commands considerable destructive force and depictions represent him as the World Tree's most formidable assailant.[3] The dragon gnaws at one of Yggdrasil's three primary roots, and brings to bear its voracious hunger with a wicked cunning.

The Prose Edda further explores the nature of Níðhögg's character through its communication with an eagle that nests in the top of the World Tree, by way of a

---

2 Snorri Sturluson, *Edda*, trans. Anthony Faulkes, (London: Everyman, 1995), 19.
3 Ibid.

messenger squirrel which travels frequently between them. This squirrel relays an ongoing correspondence that takes the form of vicious threats that the eagle and the dragon frequently exchange.[4] As a being of free will, instead of one driven by pure instinct, Níðhögg cannot just be written off as a creature that merely works within its natural boundaries. It gnaws at the foundation of the cosmos not because it needs to, but because it wants to. Níðhögg also heralds the beginning of the Ragnarok, flying forth from his underworld domain to rend the corpses of those who fall in that final battle on the great field below Ásgarðr.[5] The appearance of the dragon foretells the direst of omens, the end of life as we know it, and Níðhögg only appears where he might easily satisfy his appetite for destruction, when the world is ripe for harvesting.

The Norns

In opposition to this great beast are the Norns, three sisters who also dwell among the roots of the World Tree at the Well of Urðr, from which spring the fates of all things. The Norns are responsible for two tasks, the first to engage the power of the well to weave and manipulate fate, the second task requires them to take water from the Well of Urðr and spill it out onto the roots of Yggdrasil to undo the damage the dragon and his kind have wrought upon it.[6] The World Tree depends on the interaction of Níðhögg and the Norns to indefinitely sustain itself, as the waters from the well infuse its ancient bark with new life, seeping down through the wounds and into the very core of it, healing and sustaining the foundation and pillar of the cosmos.

Entropy Template

Willful destructive tendencies lead the list of attributes that describe any of Entropy's personifications, the defining feature. Níðhögg shows this very clearly in reference to his single-minded pursuit of destruction, for which the creature bears an insatiable hunger. In each proceeding personification then, a similar defining characteristic should surface that connects strongly to the desire for destruction, and not just wanton destruction, but destruction guided in a willful manner.

Following that is the power to inflict destruction in the pursuit of these entropic tendencies. The dragon couples the need for destruction with the ability to bring it down upon his quarry. Yggdrasil holds up the entire cosmos, and theoretically

---

4 Ibid., 18-19.
5 "The Prophecy of the Seeress: Vǫluspá," in *The Poetic Edda*, trans. Lee M. Hollander, (Austin, TX: University of Texas Press, 2008), 13.
6 Sturluson, 17-19.

would consist of such a height and width that Níðhögg would need to be of an enormous size and strength to threaten it in the manner ascribed.

However, size and strength are not the only venues of control available to those who wield power. The malicious intelligence of the dragon cannot be stressed enough. The dragon's power would not be so well-known if not for its ability to use it to the full advantage, and textual evidence suggests that Níðhögg's status as a bad omen comes not because of any evil riding in his wake, but rather from his cunning, enabling him to discern the most opportune moment for his arrival. Níðhögg, just like the other personifications, has being in the wrong place at the right time down to a science.

The final attribute that Níðhögg provides concerns opposition: a personification of Entropy lives in opposition. A dialectic relationship between the personification and an opposing force must exist; otherwise the conflict and progression of life is rendered moot. If opposition does not exist to oppose the forces of Entropy, the destruction of the dialectic and all life is inevitable. Within the framework of an opposing relationship, the dragon feasts as it pleases for as long as it pleases. Níðhögg's overarching goal consists of hedonistic indulgence, not oblivion.

Hastur, the King in Yellow

In 1895, Neely's Prismatic Library published a collection of short stories by an artist-cum-writer by the name of Robert W. Chambers called *The King in Yellow*. While Chambers keeps the title character obscure and mostly in the background, enough material exists in the text to construct Hastur's persona and compare him to the above template. The first and least obscured piece of this puzzle lies in *In the Court of the Dragon* where the protagonist of that short story has the misfortune of actually encountering the King in Yellow:

> I raised my seared eyes to the fathomless glare, and I saw the black stars hanging in the heavens: and the wet winds from the Lake of Hali chilled my face.
>
> And now, far away, over leagues of tossing cloud-waves, I saw the moon dripping with spray; and beyond, the towers of Carcosa rose behind the moon.
>
> Death and the awful abode of lost souls, whither my weakness long ago had sent him, had changed him for every other eye but mine. And now I heard his voice, rising, swelling, thundering

> through the flaring light, and as I fell, the radiance increasing, increasing, poured over me in waves of flame. Then I sank into the depths, and I heard the King in Yellow whispering to my soul: "It is a fearful thing to fall into the hands of the living God!"[7]

The last line Hastur mockingly quotes from the Bible,[8] as the unnamed protagonist styles himself as a regular churchgoer, the remark appears intentionally ironic. Even in a church, a bastion against evil, the King in Yellow seeks out his prey, enabled because the protagonist "had been reading *The King in Yellow*."[9] The protagonist further confides in the reader that he "had recognized him almost from the first; I had never doubted what he was come to do; and now I knew that while my body sat safe in the cheerful little church, he had been hunting my soul in the Court of the Dragon."[10] Hastur, intent on claiming his prize, leaves the other patrons within the church unaware and unharmed; specifically going after the narrator.

In the Court of the Dragon describes the King in Yellow as having "a look of hate, intense and deadly" when observing the protagonist, and since the King did not attack the narrator immediately after he read the play, but waited until he had entered the church, this could indicate strong feelings of jealousy.[11] The narrator states, "I was worn out by three nights of physical suffering and mental trouble: the last had been the worst, and it was an exhausted body, and a mind benumbed and yet acutely sensitive, which I had brought to my favorite church for healing."[12] Here the narrator admits his trespass against Hastur, as those who read the play come under his influence and the narrator unwisely tries to rid himself of it.

The King in Yellow takes his place amongst the old pagan deities as an adversary of God and his church, as well as governmental bodies and the press:

> When the French Government seized the translated copies which had just arrived in Paris, London, of course, became eager to read it. It is well known how the book spread like an infectious disease, from city to city, from continent to continent, barred out here, confiscated there, denounced by press and pulpit, censured

---

7 Robert W. Chambers, *The King in Yellow*, (NY: Neely's Prismatic Library, 1895), 96.
8 Hebrews 10:13.
9 Chambers, 87.
10 Ibid., 96.
11 Ibid., 88.
12 Ibid., 85.

> even by the most advanced of literary anarchists.[13]

Hastur acts as a free agent, enforcing his will as he pleases, infecting the world with madness, seemingly to spite church, state and humanity as a whole.

The Dragon Personified

In the Court of the Dragon offers more on the nature of Hastur, specifically in the residence of the narrator, the titular Court of the Dragon. A passage from Jack Tresidder's *Dictionary of Symbols*, sheds some light on the subject: "in pagan legends the dragon [may be] an unflattering image of a powerful ruler whose possessions have been seized by force."[14] Hastur, instead of dragon's gold, sets out to possess the souls of men. Chasing the narrator back to the Court of the Dragon evokes the reclamation of that which was temporarily lost, corralling his prey back into the proverbial "dragon's den." The narrator blindly assumes that he will find some sort of safe haven from Hastur in the Court of the Dragon, however, once he arrives the way is barred and he finally realizes the extent of Hastur's power: "the deep vaults, the huge closed doors, their cold iron clamps were all on his side."[15]

Entropy Template II

Where Níðhögg utilizes his cunning in conjunction with his strength, Hastur runs a cerebral game of domination. In much of *The King in Yellow* he does not even show up in person, instead he simply leaves a convenient copy of the dread play within the reach of the people he wishes to destroy, and they take it up and read the contents with only token resistance. *In the Court of the Dragon* Hastur has little trouble dispatching his quarry, he simply needed to glare menacingly and the prey ran right into his trap.

Aside from differing methods, Hastur and Níðhögg share many similarities. Hastur shares close association with the draconic as well as with the underworld. In the short story *The Yellow Sign*, he sends a grotesque zombie to do his bidding for him.[16] His realm Carcosa is patterned after the long ago ruined city described by Ambrose Bierce from his story *An Inhabitant of Carcosa*[17] and *In the Court of*

---

13 Ibid., 13.
14 Jack Tresidder, *Dictionary of Symbols*, (San Francisco, CA: Chronicle Books, 1995), 68.
15 Chambers, 95.
16 Ibid., 118; 125-127.
17 Ambrose Bierce, "An Inhabitant of Carcosa," in *The Hastur Cycle*, ed. Robert M. Price, (Hayward, CA: Chaosium, Inc., 2006), 10.

the Dragon it appears as if it will be the narrator's residence in the afterlife. Even though Níðhögg and Hastur are separated by nearly a thousand years of literary tradition, they are certainly cut from the same thematic cloth.

Man in the Yellow Suit

The final of the three personifications was introduced to the world in 1975 as the antagonist of Natalie Babbitt's *Tuck Everlasting*. "His tall body moved continuously; a foot tapped, a shoulder twitched. And it moved in angles, rather jerkily. But at the same time he had a kind of grace, like a well-handled marionette. Indeed, he seemed almost to hang suspended there in the twilight."[18] The Man in the Yellow Suit's all consuming passion amounts to finding the whereabouts of the Tuck family and then finding the source of their immorality. He spent most of his life in search of the fabled Tuck family, finally finding them in a wood on the outskirts of a small town called Treegap, a town that comes to quickly distrust the sly and corrupting stranger.

The Least of Three

Of the three personifications, the Man in the Yellow Suit only has his wits to use against those he encounters, in addition to the flaw of mortality. He is also the least successful. While Níðhögg assaults the World Tree and Hastur breaks the minds of those foolish enough to read the dread play, the Man in the Yellow suit winds up in the dirt with a gunshot wound to the back of his head. "His eyes were closed now, but except for that, he looked more than ever like a marionette, a marionette flung carelessly into a corner, arms and legs every which way midst tangled strings."[19] Ma Tuck, fearing for the safety of her family, pulls the trigger and prematurely ends the quest.

In spite of the circumstances, some small victory goes to the Man in the Yellow Suit. The Tucks, after encountering this stranger, are pushed out into the world, ending their long stasis. From a certain perspective the Man in the Yellow Suit found his immortality in the memories of the Tuck family and especially in the conscience of Ma Tuck, who will probably remember him for the rest of time, not having the benefit of death to save her.

Entropy Template III

Like Hastur, the Man in the Yellow Suit shares many similarities with the great

---

18 Natalie Babbit, *Tuck Everlasting*, (New York: Square Fish, 1975), 18.
19 Ibid., 102.

dragon Níðhögg. He seeks to possess the power of the Tucks, and the source of that power springs forth from the roots of a tree in the forest, just as the Well of Urðr at the base of Yggdrasil. The Tucks symbolically represent the World Tree, and the Man in the Yellow Suit preys upon them. In opposition to the Man in the Yellow Suit are the novel's protagonists, Winnie and Ma Tuck, who are analogs for the Norns that watch over the Well of Urðr, and when the Tucks are threatened it is the feminine creative force that rises to counter the machinations of Entropy.

The recurrence of the dragon motif in the texts might connect with Entropy's unfeeling destructive nature. Entropy and its personifications push forward in selfish abandon, striking out and manipulating whom they please to meet their ends. The ends would justify the means for these figures, but the ends and the means are generally the same anyway.

Final Thoughts

Níðhögg, Hastur and the Man in the Yellow Suit all share common bonds; bonds that any person of decent moral fiber would shirk away from, for they are cruel, vicious, conniving, jealous and selfish creatures; epitomizing the very worst that the world has to offer. However, the forces of Creation and Entropy must work in concert for life to continue forward; the one does not exist without the other. These three figures are the undiluted essence of Entropy's power given form and thought so that mankind might easily recognize and understand the dread power that afflicts them at every moment.

The Horned Man

Stephen Pollington

In northern European art, a figure of a male with horns projecting from his head is found from the Bronze Age onwards, beginning with the Swedish rock art.[1] The Bronze Age figure probably reflects an early divinity, and 'unites human and animal attributes.' This figure can be traced throughout the Iron Age, and reaches a particular florescence in the heathen art of Anglo-Saxon England and Scandinavia.

Whether the horns emerge from the man's head or form part of his headgear is not always easy to determine, although the majority of examples show some form of helmet. Bronze head-coverings with sinuous 'handlebar' attachments have been recovered from Danish Bronze Age sites, but the projections on the 'horned man' figures are more often adjacent or joined above the crown of the head. The horned man is often naked but for a belt, and he sports both helmet and spears.

Horned figures recur in Germanic art, especially of the Migration and Vendel Periods—notably turbulent ages which may have looked to traditional imagery as a stabilizing factor in religious observance. Often the horns on the figure's helm terminate in bird-heads; due to limitations in the casting process, these bird-heads often meet so that the beaks are touching above the man's head.

The horned and helmeted figure recurs on the Vendel Period helmet plates—for example, that from Grave 8 at Valsgärde, Sweden. He is depicted behind an armoured rider, and is leaping onto the horse's rump and grasping the rider's upraised spear with one hand and his own spear with the other.[2] His helmet's horns do not appear to end in birds' heads, but the scale of the piece is such that this detail may have been too difficult to incorporate. A belt is again his only garment. The figure's small size relative to the rider has suggested to some observers that he is a supernatural character, but it may be due to nothing more

---

[1] Terry Gunnell, *The Origins of Drama in Scandinavia*, (Woodbridge: D.S. Brewer, 1995); Stephen O. Glosecki, "Movable Beasts: The Manifold Implications of Early Germanic Animal Imagery," in *Animals in the Middle Ages*, ed. Nora C. Flores (London: Routledge, 2000), 16; Aleks Pluskowski, "Animal Magic," in *Signals of Belief in Early England: Anglo-Saxon Paganism Revisited*, eds. Carver, Sanmark & Semple, (Oxford: Oxbow Books, 2010), 116.

[2] Wilhelm Holmqvist, *Vår Tidiga Konst*, (Stockholm: Lts Förlag, 1977), 132-5.

The Horned Man

Figure 1: A speardancer figure on a gilt-bronze mount from Cambridgeshire (Image: Lindsay Kerr).

than the mediaeval convention that less important figures are shown smaller and less obtrusive than the main ones. This figure finds a parallel at Sutton Hoo where the rider also has a smaller figure behind him grasping his spear.[3]

Clearly the figure with the horned headgear was important; possibly he was a cult-leader (priest) or a devotee of the god(s). He may have been a man transformed into a god within the mythic enactment, or he may be the shape of a god as it appeared to his human worshipper.

The helmet with the curved horns is an enigma. It is consistently represented in

---

3 At least two more "horned man" figures await publication at the time of writing.

Anglo-Saxon and Scandinavian heathen design. And it appears to be commonplace of the religious or ritual art of these peoples but no archaeological examples are known to survive. Scandinavian examples from the Bronze Age feature graceful, curving antenna, but they do not feature the birds' head terminals for the horns which are such a prominent feature of the 6th and 7th c. designs.[4]

Representations of horned helmets are found in religious art—on the Gallehus horns and the Gundestrup cauldron, for example—but they appear to be traditional symbols rather than depictions of current war-gear; their environment in both cases is mythic rather than military.[5] It seems likely, then, that the design is not showing something literally present; rather, like a Christian saint's halo, the birds' heads denote a sacred quality—which in the nature of the case must be possession by Woden.[6]

Horned headgear is not uncommon among some shamanic traditions, but it is

---

4   Stephen Pollington, Lindsay Kerr & Brett Hammond, *Wayland's Work: Anglo-Saxon Art, Myth & Material Culture From the 4th to the 7th Century*, (Swaffham: Anglo-Saxon Books, 2010), 434-8, 443.

5   Gunnell; Peter Vang Petersen, "Warrior Art, Religion and Symbolism," in *The Spoils of Victory: The North in the Shadow of the Roman Empire*, ed. Jørensen, Storgaard & Thomsen, (Copenhagen: The National Museum, 2003); Kris Kershaw, *The One-eyed God: Odin and the (Indo-) Germanic Männerbünde*, Journal of Indo-European Studies Monograph no. 36, (Washington: Institute for the Study of Man, 2000), 85; notes the impractical nature of the headgear as depicted. It is worth noting that one of the traditional attributes of the circumpolar shaman is a hat or cap sporting two horns. While this item is not closely similar to the Germanic horned headgear, its presence in ritual contexts may point to an inherited tradition.

6   Some would rather see the "horns" terminating in birds' heads as symbolic dragons and the ear-flaps of the helmets as the dragons' tails. It remains a possibility that the "helmets" were some form of ritual headgear, possibly made from textiles or leather, which would not survive archaeologically. The horned headgear worn at Abbots Bromley horn-dance would be of this kind. According to Speidel (122ff) the curved horns may be a representation of "dragon power" and the wearer would then be a king or warlord; the duality of the horns may represent the dual gods, the *Alcis*. It is also tempting to connect the personal names *Anselm* and *Oshelm* (**ansuhalmiz* "helmet of God") with this phenomenon (S.C. Hawkes cited in Sonja Marzinzik *Early Anglo-Saxon Belt Buckles [Late 5th to Eraly 8th Centuries AD]: Their Classification and Context*, [Oxford: British Archaeological Reports, 2003], 52; Helen Geake, *The Use of Grave-Goods in Conversion-Period England, c.600-c.850*, B.A.R. British Series, no. 261, [Oxford: British Archaeological Reports, 1997], 100; Samantha Glasswell, *The Earliest English: Living and Dying in Early Anglo-Saxon England*, [Stroud: NPI Media Group, 2002], 141; Michael P. Speidel, *Ancient Germanic Warriors: Warrior Styles From Trajan's Column to Icelandic Sagas*, [London: Routledge, 2004], 30-1).

Figure 2: A helmeted head from Yorkshire, found as part of a Viking period cache among several pieces of Anglo-Saxon metalwork (Copyright Timeline Originals).

invariably worn with a special coat or cloak, which seems to be generally absent in the Germanic examples unless the strangely amorphous figures (e.g. on the

The Horned Man

Oseberg tapestry) are meant to be shown enveloped in a large cloak.[7] The association with horns is also a means of showing that the wearer has access to the feral power of the animal, to the strength and speed and special knowledge of beasts.[8]

Gaimster suggested that the horned men are the war-god's devoted followers, the Einherjar, and that their marching and dancing forms are intended to portray some of the traditional rites associated with Óðinn.[9] This idea was also developed by Gunnell to imply that the figures shown in horned headgear are not warriors advancing to battle, but rather cult devotees—who may be warriors also —taking part in the rites of their gods.[10] The immediate source of these rites probably lies within the Roman army, among the horned-helmeted warriors known as Cornuti. Likewise, Wickham-Crowley suggested that the horned headgear is a representation of the *woþ*, the divine inspiration of Woden, and that the figures wearing this ritual garb are initiands into the god's cult, pubescent males becoming men.[11]

On the Viking period tapestry from Oseberg (Norway), a small figure in a horned helmet leads a procession of humans, animals and waggons; he is armed with a spear, and bears a strong resemblance to the diminutive figure behind the rider on the Sutton Hoo helmet plate. Miniature figures of horn-helmeted warriors brandishing weapons are known from Swedish contexts: one from Ekhammar (Uppland) holds two spears in his left hand and a sword in his right; another from Birka has a sheathed sword in his left hand and a rod, wand or spear in his right.[12]

---

7   Lotte Motz, *The King, The Champion and the Sorcerer: A Study in Germanic Myth*, Studia Medievalia Septentrionalia, no. 1, (Vienna: Fassbaender, 1995), 83.
8   Hilda Roderick Ellis Davidson, *Myth and Symbols in Pagan Europe: Early Scandinavian and Celtic Religions*, (New York: Syracuse University Press, 1988), 209.
9   Marit Gaimster, *Vendel Period Bracteates on Gotland: On the Significance of Germanic Art*, Acta Archaeologica Lundensia, Series in 8° no. 27, (Lund: Coronet Books, 1998), 214.
10 Likewise the bird's heads and boar-masks, which he believes would not have been worn in war. However, it is not beyond possibility that such apparel might have been worn in the rituals which took place before fighting began (Gunnell, 63).
11 Kelley Wickham-Crowley, "The Birds on the Sutton Hoo Instrument," in *Sutton Hoo: Fifty Years After*, eds. Farrell & Neuman de Vegvar (Oxford: American Early Medieval Studies, 1992), 50-1; Kershaw.
12 Ellis Davidson, "The Finglesham Man: The Significance of the Man in the Horned Helmet," in *Antiquity*, vol 34 (1969): 36; Rupert Bruce-Mitford, *The Sutton Hoo Ship-Burian: Arms and Armour and Regalia*, vol. 2, (London: British Museum Publica-

Figure 3: A much abraded helmeted head mount from Saxlingham Nethergate, Norfolk, with banded horns which appear to extend behind the head and emerge at the lower jaw (Copyright Norwich Castle Museum and Art Gallery, item ref. NMS-F90626 MOUNT).

The absence from archaeological finds of any such horned headgear may be due to their having been made from perishable materials, specifically leather.[13] The Pressbleche of the Vendel, Valsgärde and Sutton Hoo helmets were all formed by

---

tions, 1978), Ch. III; Gunnell, 60-6; Neil S. Price, *The Viking Way: Religion and War in the Late Iron Age of Scandinavia*, (Oxford: Oxbow Books, 2003), 112, 385-6, 177-9; refers to staves as ritual implements.

13 Herbert Schutz, *Tools, Weapons and Ornaments: Germanic Material Culture in Pre-Carolingian Central Europe, 400-750*, (Leiden: Brill Academic Publishing, 2001), 165; notes the find of a leather and horn helm in a prince's grave beneath Cologne cathedral. Price (174) notes the suggestion that some of the curious faces on Viking Age runestones may represent leather face-masks.

beating a metal foil over a die. Examples of such dies were found at Torslunda, Öland, and it was noted that two of the four were re-cast from clay moulds formed from foils with their backing, which is believed to have been leather. Alkemade accepted that that the early Pressbleche were attached to leather headgear, and only later were they re-used on metal war-helms; Arrhenius and Freij reached similar conclusions, citing parallels from the Avar tradition, and the leather headgear found with the young prince at Cologne.[14] An intriguing find from a (possibly) Tokharian burial at Zaghunluq, central Asia, is a white felt hat with a chin-strap and a roll of felt attached to the front, its stiff, crescent profile resembling horns; the Tokharian culture has many astonishing parallels with those of Central and Northern Europe, and Tokharian priests and soothsayers were highly respected in antiquity for their learning.[15]

Gunnell saw the horned figures in representational art (e.g. the Oseberg tapestry fragments and the helmet plates) as either idols of the gods, or as priestly figures whose donning of the horned headgear made them symbolically equivalent to the god himself within the ritual drama to be enacted.[16] In other words, they are human beings acting out the roles of the gods. Given the association between Woden, the spear and the bird of prey, there is little reason to doubt that the figure behind the rider on the helmet plates (Sutton Hoo, Pliezhausen, Valsgärde) is either drawn from myth or shown in the act of re-enacting myth, as in a ritual or ceremony. He may be, as Ellis Davidson suggested 'a power from the Otherworld intervening on the battlefield.'[17] His strong association with the warrior in the wolfskin points to cult or ritual, so that the figure physically present is symbolic of—indeed, the embodiment of—a figure in myth. Gunnell maintained that the evidence of the Torslunda dies suggests that helmet plates conventionally showed either myths or rituals in action—observable human behaviour rather than spirit-world beings.[18] If so, this implies that the Dancing Warrior figure in his horned helmet must be one of three things:

---

14 Monica Alkemade, "A History of Vendel Period Archaeology: Observation on the Relationship Between Written Sources and Archaeological Interpretation," in *Images of the Past: Studies on Ancient Societies in Northwestern Europe*, eds. Roymans & Theuws, (Amsterdam: I.B.D. Limited, 1991), 291-2; B. Arrhenius & H. Freij, "Pressbleck Fragments from the East Mound in Old Uppsala Analyzed With a Laser Scanner," in *Lab Ark*, vol. 6 (1992): 109; Price, 171-4.
15 J.P. Mallory & Victor H. Mair, *The Tarim Mummies: Ancient China and the Mystery of the Earliest Peoples from the West*, (London: Thames and Hudson, 2000), 214, 326.
16 Gunnell, 63-76 and figs. 39-43.
17 Ellis Davidson, "The Finglesham Man," 25; Gaimster, 66 likewise associate the horned figures with the dancing warrior motif and connects this to the *Alcis*.
18 Gunnell, 66-76; Alexandra Sanmark, "Living On: Ancestors and the Soul," *Signals of Belief: Anglo-Saxon Paganism Revisited*, 164-5.

The Horned Man

Figure 4: The rider motif from the Sutton Hoo helmet. The mounted warrior attacks with his raised spear, while a smaller figure with a shield guides his spear. A fallen warrior in mail gallantly stabs the rider's horse (Image: Lindsay Kerr).

1. In the secular world, a possessed warrior, a berserk or some other devotee of the god.[19] His nakedness would then be a typical act of devotion as noted by Tacitus of the Germanic warriors of his day (*Germania*, ch.6).[20]
2. In the mythic world, a member of Woden's retinue involved in some activity, such as dancing, especially associated with that group.

---

19 Gunnell, 60-6; Kershaw, 2000, 61-2; Ustinova, "Lycanthropy in Sarmatian Warrior Societies," in *Ancient West and East*, vol. 1 (2002): 114-5.

20 Tacitus, *Germania*, trans. J.B. Rives, (Oxford: Oxford University Press, 1999); Price, 361; There may be a parallel in the rite of the naked man lighting the funeral pyre, as witnessed by Ibn Fadlan among the Rus on the Volga.

Figure 5: Bronze die from Torslunda, Sweden, showing a warrior in horned headgear advancing with two spears followed by a wolf-warrior with spear and sword (Image: Lindsay Kerr).

3. In the world of ritual, a cult member enacting some rite or ceremony.[21] Again, Tacitus mentions (Germania, ch. 24,1) the custom of Germanic male youths to dance naked among unsheathed swords and standing spears—a close parallel to the actions depicted, including male nudity, weapons and dancing. Historically, Germanic warriors danced to the rhythm of the barritus war-chant and swung their shields—the Goths, Batavi, Sugambri and Bastarnae are all recorded as having danced and sung before battle.

Another English example of the horned man was found by metal-detecting in 2007, near the River Derwent in Yorkshire. The metal mount is in the form of an elongated male face with a neat beard and full moustache, surmounted by a cap bearing two horned projections which meet above the apex; some slight surface

---

21 Tacitus, 87, 216; Speidel, 115ff.

The Horned Man

detailing appears to be the familiar bird-head imagery.[22] A fitting with similar imagery was found at Rempstone (Nottinghamshire)—a flat cast mount showing a moustached and bearded male above whose head is a pair of horns with bird-head terminals; parallels have been found at Soberton (Hampshire), Blakeney (Norfolk), Letheringsett (Norfolk) and Attleborough (Norfolk) and elsewhere.[23]

The horned man probably has to be seen as a figure from the world of myth, given expression in the warrior-rituals of the Anglo-Saxons and Scandinavian peoples.

---

22 Reported in *Treasure Hunting* magazine, Nov 2007, 39ff.
23 Keith Raynor, *The Rempstone Mount: Anglo-Saxon and Viking Horned Man Images and Artifacts*, (East Leake: Privately Printed, 2010).

Against the Primitivists

Stephen M. Borthwick

Ἀπολογία Πολεμικου

I have, in recent months and days, beheld a particularly malign school of thought playing a prominent role in the community of faith to which we belong, which has occasioned me so much concern that I feel deeply compelled to bear witness to its undeniable falsehood and pernicious nature. A community of believers united by common spirit communicated through the ages by ancestral inheritance must stand united in strength; on this, I fervently hope, all readers can agree. Further, any community of faith must acknowledge that it inevitably must exist within and make dealings with a broader, preexisting social reality. This is especially true of young faiths, as ours must be regarded, for when it was violently uprooted so many centuries ago, it had not developed the philosophical maturity of its conqueror or foreign counterparts, leaving the task to subsequent generations to strengthen the faith in this way. Indeed, the strength lent to any school or faith through philosophical and intellectual pursuit is incomparable to all other sources of strength for its permanency and the deep spiritual grounding it lends to a faith combined with the continual elevation and improvement of the faith. Thus should the faithful—or at least those among the faithful so inclined that they may take leadership in the enterprise—dedicate themselves to so elevating the faith. In the case of young faiths, it is especially necessary to look to predecessors and existing bearers of knowledge to undertake this task. Like the child born into the world of his parents, the young faith must forge its identity within the cultural milieu of its authors—otherwise it becomes isolated, and twisted in its isolation, it becomes unable to nourish itself on the fruit of knowledge and wisdom that flows from the very nature of human exchange of ideas, for as Aristotle rightly declared, we are singular and unique among all born things in our nature as the *zōon politikon* (ζῷον πολιτικόν—"political animal").[1]

Finding and acknowledging the truth of this, it becomes blatantly apparent how dangerous and yet how natural the school of anti-intellectual primitivism is. If we set before us an image of a modern child, the adolescent or "teenager" as an independent entity—a concept alien to the ancients—it is plain that this school of thought is something we have seen before. The child, growing and developing, no longer accepts the authority or knowledge of his parents, but feels compelled

---

[1] Aristotle, *Politics*, 1253ᵃ1-3: "ὁ ἄνθρωπος φύσει πολιτικὸν ζῷον," (man is by nature a political animal).

to reject them in order to forge his own identity. It is an experience shared by our contemporaries—but likewise shared by the intellectually and emotionally mature is the knowledge that before a child becomes a functioning, integrated adult, he must cast off this youthful rebelliousness and self-insistence and take up the task of learning. Indeed, it would be reasonable to say that any mature adult would say that anyone who prevents maturity does irreparable harm to such a child—and herein resides the great danger of this school of primitivism. This school of thought that has so vexed my mind of late, as it must vex the minds of all the learned of our faith, is a childish and self-insistent rebellion and primitivism. It is the child who declares that he can survive without the nourishment and care of his parents—those who believe that a young, immature faith can survive without the benefit of learning and angrily reject the world of their authors—the Christian world—purely for the sake of this rebelliousness, with no effort exerted to take hold of and establish a firm grasp and understanding of those universal tenets of wisdom and knowledge present in established theology and learning.

In order that our young faith not succumb to this puerile rebelliousness and this school of primitivism, and instead that it might flourish, fed on the rich nectar of the wisdom of experience and acquired knowledge available to all the faithful through intellectual and philosophical pursuit, I have taken up this task of laying bare the falsehood of primitivism and refuting and rejecting primitivist thinking and providing an alternative in the rich philosophical tradition of our Civilization heretofore unfortunately cradled against the bosom of the false religion of Christianity. It will become apparent in the course of this refutation and this polemic that this dangerous primitivism is not a new phenomenon—rather it is an ancient error refuted before, and by the very means and by the very people that contemporary primitivists so violently rebel against. It is to the great boon of our community that the theology and methodology of those who preceded us inform our own theological ventures, since it is irrefutable that the core of true religion is deep, thought-out philosophy, and a religion without theological or philosophical basis is either a cult or escapist fantasy.

Basis of Primitivism

Though the learned find themselves rightly outraged and appalled at the anti-intellectual, anti-philosophical nature of primitivism and the primitivists, none of this number should pretend themselves surprised by it—for, indeed, as said above it is not without precedent. In the first place, it is a natural reaction of the newly converted to be drawn to this sort of youthful rebelliousness and, I dare venture, *purism* because of the simplicity of it, which contrasts heavily with the often complex systems from which the converted have apostatized. It is the very height of naiveté to imagine that many converts to any given faith, especially a new faith, are not merely this very type of adolescent, dissatisfied rebels, with very little real devotion to the faith outside of its ability to provide them with the satisfaction of having rebelled. As the ancients—indeed, our own ancestors—readily recognized, there are always divisions of ability within any group, religious or otherwise, from the smallest club to broad society itself, with the learned and able populating the highest level and the most material-minded spiritual adolescents and *thralls* populating the lowest portion. We find this declaration of natural inequality among men, be it spiritual or social, spelled out plainly in our own holy books:

> Mother bore a son and clothed him in silk.
> She sprinkled him with water and called him Earl.[2]
>
> Then Rig came walking from the grove.
> Walking Rig came, taught him the runes
> and granted his own name.[3]

"Mother bore a son"—that *Jarl* ("Lord") was the chosen son ofRíg (Heimdall, the guardian of the Gods) and the sign of his being chosen was the learning of the Runes, representative in all cases of knowledge and wisdom, not inherent but *learned*—even by the Alfather Óðinn himself.

In the *Rígsþula*, it is apparent that there is a definite hierarchy established with *learning* placed at the top of the hierarchy and *ignorance* at the bottom; it is not so unlike the famous statement of Socrates in Diogenes Laërtius that: "but by my reckoning there is a single good, which is knowledge, and a single evil, which is ignorance."[4] There are, however, many interpretations as to this meaning; a more modernist and liberal interpretation points to the fact that Ríg has three sons in succession each to successively younger parents, meaning that the tale describes the development of a man from immature to mature thought, supporting the supposed inherent equality of men. Alternatively, an interpretation truer to the pre-liberal Western vision, sees the fact that the three classes are born with inherent traits to point to the natural hierarchy and natural inequality of individuals,

---

2 "Svein ol Moðir silki vafði, iosu vatni, Iarl letu heita," (*Rígsþula* in *The Eddas: The Keys to the Mysteries of the North*, trans. James Allen Chisholm, http://www.woodharrow.com/images/ChisholmEdda.pdf [accessed July 15, 2011], 33).
3 "Kom þar or runni Rigr gangandi, Rigr gangandi, runar kendi; sitt gaf heiti, son kveðz eiga," (Ibid., 35).
4 Diogenes Laërtius, Βίοι και γνώμαι των εν φιλοσοφία ευδοκιμησάντων, Book 2, 31: "ἔλεγε δὲ καὶ ἓν μόνον ἀγαθὸν εἶναι, τὴν ἐπιστήμην, καὶ ἓν μόνον κακόν, τὴν ἀμαθίαν."

ranked from the greatest (those with knowledge, learning, and wisdom) from the lowest (those with only the simplest understanding). This latter interpretation subsequently can point to the fact that the lower two castes, the warriors and *thralls*, have many more children than the greatest child ofRíg, showing that the most inferior are always in the greatest numbers, a notion that was common among the ancients but has been discarded by the children of the post-Enlightenment age.[5] In either interpretation, however, it is clear that the truth of there being many kinds of men in various stages or states of intelligence and development only emphasizes the inevitability of angry reactions by the inferior against the superior, and the rise of rebellious and immature schools such as primitivism.

Nor is this the only reason that the learned should withhold their surprise at the prevalence of primitivism, for it is certainly not a phenomenon unique to our number. It pervades all peoples and all religions, organic and reformed. Indeed, among our immediate predecessors, the argument was put forward by prominent thinkers including Fathers of the Church. Among these writers and Church Fathers, foremost is Quintus Septimius Florens Tertullianus, better known in our tongue as Tertullian. Born the son of a Berber centurion in Carthage, Tertullian is representative of the most dangerous breed of primitivist. Heretofore, primitivism has been described as the realm of the plebeian and the uneducated; if only it were so, such a polemic as this need not be written, for the inferior are easy enough to shrug off, and require no well-reasoned argument against them. There are, however, many kinds and many levels of primitivist, from the childish, plebeian follower to the half-educated, proud demagogue, to the learned but wilfully ignorant. Tertullian resides somewhere between these latter two—for he was a man educated in grammar, rhetoric, and the law before his conversion to Christianity, three of the most important and highly reputed skills of his day. Tertullian began his career as a theological writer (presumably as a presbyter of the Church in Carthage) in the middle of his life, around 197 CE, initially writing a series of apologetic works for the young faith and exhortations to martyrdom. These writings were followed by a series of polemical works against Gnostic Christian teachers and heresy in general, focusing especially on attacks against

---

5 Indeed, one interpretation need not preclude the other. The Medieval Church held that there are in fact four levels of interpretation of Christian scripture: the literal, the moral, the allegorical, and the eschatological. The word "Jerusalem," for example, could mean the literal city itself, the human soul, the person of Christ, or the Heavenly Jerusalem of the End Times. This was itself borrowed from Hebrew hermeneutics, which held likewise there were four "phases" of interpretation: *pshat, remez, d'rash,* and *sud,* meaning respectively, "simple," or plain meaning, "hinted," or alluded meaning, "homiletic," or ethical and moral meaning, and "secret," or occult meaning (this last is typically reserved for *Qabalah* interpreters). Greater exposition on such hermeneutics is necessary, but unfortunately not appropriate here.

Pagan learning and the use of philosophy to defend and prove Christianity. Ultimately, however, Tertullian would spend his final days writing apologetics for a heresy he himself converted to—Montanism, rooted almost exclusively in the cult of martyrs and mystical revelation.[6]

Tertullian's faith, therefore, was already marked by a primitivist bent of mind long before his ultimate abandonment of the Christian orthodoxy in favour of the Montanist heresy. One of his earlier polemics, *De praescriptionibus Haereticorum* displays the best example of the anti-intellectualism and extremist purism that prevails among contemporary primitivists in our own ranks. The work was written in the style of a legal prescription, very common in Roman law and essentially the equivalent of a plea suit in American law (which, despite its trappings, is itself more heavily indebted to English Common Law than Roman law). The central issue he addresses, in legal terms, is the property rights of Christians over scripture against the heretics, who likewise claim rights to the texts. He argues that because scripture belongs solely to Christians, heretics have no right to make property claims over the texts, since while a heretic claims to be Christian, he perverts the truth inherent to Christianity and therefore has no right to the title of "Christian." The concept is one almost entirely foreign to our neo-liberal age marked by economic socialism and universal suffrage; it might be better understood in the context of two centuries ago, when legally only certain persons could own property. It might be understood, therefore, as the equivalent of an eighteenth century property case in which a single woman who has never married, lays claim to a house which legally she cannot possess being a woman and having not come into the property through any late husband. Another, simpler example would be the Dred Scott case.[7]

Nor, however, should Tertullian find himself refuted for this purism alone—indeed, a desire to see only right doctrine taught and heresies condemned is laud-

---

6 All information on Tertullian's life is derived from *The Library of Christian Classics*, Edited by John Baillie, John T. McNeill, and Henry P. Van Dusen, editors, Vol. 5: *Early Latin Theology*, translated and edited by S.L. Greenslade (Philadelphia: Westminster Press, 1956), 21-30.

7 *Dred Scott v. Sandford*, 60 U.S. 393 (1857), was a case of a slave named Dred Scott who was brought out of slave-owning territories into free territories by his owner, one John Emerson and subsequently his owner's widow, Eliza Irene Sanford, whose brother, F.A. Sanford, was executor of Emerson's will. Scott attempted three times to sue his owners, who were not financially in a position to sell him (in fact they were forced to rent out his services to make ends meet). His third attempt was the most publicised and famous, going before the Supreme Court, which ruled that because Scott was a slave he was not a citizen and therefore had no right to claim property rights over himself, and likewise no right to bring a suit to an American courtroom.

able of any true believer, and those without true faith, Tertullian is right, do not deserve the title "believer" among Ásatruar any more than among Christians, for the unbeliever, the atheist, the plague-ridden relativist is an infection which knows no religious or cultural preference, and contaminates the ranks of all religions and all communities of faith. In this, Tertullian is right in his polemic, and it is not the inherent flaw of Tertullian that demands to be addressed, since such an individual polemic would reveal nothing of the danger of primitivism, but would serve to isolate and target positive and negative traits of the faithful to the benefit of none but our enemies. Rather, it is Tertullian's own weakness of faith, his narrowness imposed on a young faith which aids its destruction and isolation that needs to be addressed, for so often is it true that the most zealous purists who silence debate, reason, and acquired knowledge (who are called anti-intellectuals) in favor of dubious revelation and occultic ritual imitation are the weakest in faith, the least wise in the truths inherent to the faith, and the greatest danger to the community they purport to defend.

It is to this category that the anti-intellectuals, the primitivists, belong. It is not the purist of our faith who seeks to maintain cultural integrity through the refutation of universalism, modernism, and those poisonous idealisms of the Liberal "Enlightenment" such as the brotherhood of man and the rule of irreligious reason, but rather quite the opposite—the extremist fixation on any number of idealisms, that can only be refuted philosophically; the obsession with ritual over content and morality is exemplary of this type. For indeed, true faith must be grounded in intuited, eternal wisdom as well as observed, acquired knowledge; it is neither pure revelation, which is occult, nor pure rationality, which is atheist. The primitivists represent a combination of the worst of these extremes: unwilling to surrender the superficial attachment to the imitation of purported ancestral practices (despite most "ancient rituals" being of fairly recent vintage) or the notion that primitive lack of understanding is superior to the quest for truth—which is the central purpose for which religion and philosophy came into being among men after the first revelation of the existence of the Eternal and Divine to our ancestors.

The attachment to scripture and revelation is one of the defining features of Tertullian's treatise and prescription: "indeed, the rash interpretation of the purpose and substance of the divine is the core of worldly 'wisdom.' In the end, heresy is equipped by philosophy herself."[8] Thus does Tertullian declare the relationship between Christianity and philosophy, so too do the primitivists declare the rela-

---

8 "Ea est enim materia sapientiae saecularis, temeraria interpres divinae naturae et dispositionis. Ipsae denique haereses a philosophia subornantur," (*De praescriptionibus Haereticorum* 7:2-3).

tionship of philosophy and theology to Ásatrú. He continues along this line of thinking for the duration of Ch. VII in *De praescriptionibus Haereticorum*. The chapter is devoted to this very same attack of philosophy, which ought to be rejected because of all its errors and defiance of the truths of existence that need no questioning, since they are contained entirely in the Holy Writ. In support of his polemic he offers two distinct but nevertheless related forms of argument; the first is an explicit appeal to scripture—the Letter to the Colossians specifically— and the second is both culturally and also scripturally based.

He writes: "Our tradition is from the portico of Solomon, who himself had related that the Lord ought to be sought in simplicity of heart."[9] Indeed, this firm grounding in the teaching of Solomon is both religious and cultural, in its clear loyalty to the people of Solomon, who are the children of Abraham, as promised him in Genesis 17. This basis in the history of the Israelites is accompanied with a direct appeal to Paul of Tarsus, who wrote, "beware lest any man spoil you through philosophy and vain deceit, after the tradition of men, after the rudiments of the world, and not after Christ."[10] While this is his only extensive quote, he makes other references to the Epistles to Timothy in the same section; he makes it clear that he is well familiar with the scripture, but likewise displays that within the words of the Apostle, who in I Timothy 1:4-8 says:

> Neither give heed to fables and endless genealogies, which minister questions, rather than godly edifying which is in faith: so do. Now the end of the commandment is charity out of a pure heart, and of a good conscience, and of faith unfeigned: From which some having swerved have turned aside unto vain jangling; Desiring to be teachers of the law; understanding neither what they say, nor whereof they affirm. But we know that the law is good, if a man use it lawfully.

Tertullian references the first line, I Timothy 1:4, when he says, "from here [come] those fables and endless genealogies and fruitless questions."[11] Likewise

---

9 "Nostra institutio de porticu Solomonis est qui et ipse tradiderat Dominum in simplicitate cordis esse quaerendum," (*DpH* 7:10).
10 The Passage itself is derived from Colossians 2:8, "videte ne qui sit circumveniens vos per philosophiam et inanem seductionem, secundum traditionem hominum." Tertullian paraphrases the last portion of the passage after "traditions of men," into "praeter providentiam Spiritus sancti," or "against the providence of the Holy Spirit," (*DpH* 7:7).
11 "Hinc illae fabulae et genealogiae interminabiles et quaestioness infructuosae," (*DpH* 7:7).

does he reference II Timothy when he says, "speech that creeps just as a canker."[12] The passage he references, II Timothy 2, speaks of the dangers of, "the profane and meaningless speech" in the Vulgate; for "that speech which creeps like a canker."[13] The entire passage is more precise in its command from Paul to Timothy:

> Of these things put them in remembrance, charging them before the Lord that they strive not about words to no profit, but to the subverting of the hearers. Study to shew thyself approved unto God, a workman that needeth not to be ashamed, rightly dividing the word of truth. But shun profane and vain babblings: for they will increase unto more ungodliness. And their word will eat as doth a canker: of whom is Hymenaeus and Philetus; Who concerning the truth have erred, saying that the resurrection is past already; and overthrow the faith of some.[14]

Paul is fairly clear here in what exactly it is he expects of Timothy, and outlines the dangers posed by persons who have much to say and about things of which they know very little. Paul would have recognised the danger of false teachers or foolish teachers who misinterpret scripture, as Hymenaeus and Philetus did, saying that the resurrection had already occurred, confusing the resurrection of the dead (as foretold in Isaiah 27:19 and Daniel 12) with the resurrection of Jesus himself, which had indeed already occurred.[15] Tertullian himself makes an adaptation of the scripture, therefore, himself interpreting the command given to Timothy in regards to the philosophers, who, since they are not divinely inspired, cannot but write "profane" words. Thus, "for us there is no need of research after Christ Jesus, nor need of questioning after the Gospels."[16]

---

12 "Sermones serpentes velut cancer," (Ibid).
13 "Profana...inaniloquia" and "sermo eorum ut cancer serpit," (II Timothy 2:16-17). *N.B.: inaniloquia* is a word that is in fact unique to Vulgate Latin; it is a Latin neologism created to translate the Greek *kenophōnia* (κενοφωνία), meaning literally "discussion of vain and useless matters." We might roughly translate it as "gossip," though here it clearly refers to foolish talk.
14 II Timothy 2:14-18.
15 It is, of course, repeated throughout the New Testament as well, such as in Matt 22:23-32, Mk 12:18-27, Lk 14:14 Lk 20:27-40, Jn 11:24-25 Acts 4:2, 17:31-32, 23:6-8, 24:15, 21, as well as numerous Pauline Epistles; these are not listed in the main text because with the exception of the Epistles themselves, the New Testament was written after the deaths of Peter and Paul, and therefore Paul's only sources for the prophecy would have been the Old Testament books and what he had heard from the other Apostles, not what was written in the New Testament.
16 "Nobis curiositate opus non est post Christum Iesum nec inquisitione post evangelium," (*DpH* 7:12).

Against the Primitivists

It is necessary to discuss at length how beholden the argument of Tertullian's prescription is to the scripture, that it might be understood precisely how he used the Bible and also to highlight his experience and learning in the study of scripture. For the struggle between revelation and deduction is what yields Tertullian's famous question, "what, therefore, has Athens to do with Jerusalem? What the Academy with the Church? What the heretic with the Christian?"[17] This is, after all, the central question posed by the primitivists in regards to the relationship of Christianity and Heathenry. For those purists of revelation, the question is phrased, what has reason to do with faith? Or, for the purists fixated on ritual, what has theology to do with religion? Or, those obsessed with freeing themselves of the "Christian corruption," what has Christianity to do with our ancestors? There is a central error in all of this lack of questioning, lack of interest in understanding; it is a narrowness all primitivists share with Tertullian, and it is this common flaw, rather than each question individually, which poses the greatest danger and which most cries out for refutation.

Basis of Refutation

Tertullian was, of course, met with disapproval in some circles. Chief among these was his far more widely read counterpart Augustine of Hippo as well as the latter's mentor, Ambrose of Milan. Both Augustine and Ambrose became extremely influential Church fathers; both are, in fact, counted as Doctors of the Church, alongside Pope Gregory the Great and Jerome of Stridonium, the former an important interpreter of the latter's highly influential translation of the Bible into Latin. It should therefore go without saying that Tertullian's anti-intellectual model was never accepted as canon to Christianity, since, while Tertullian remains an important Father of the Church, his teaching in general, even before his fall into heresy, is taken into the Church with some reservation and much commentary.

The chief refutation of Tertullian's anti-philosophical doctrine can be found in Augustine's *De Doctrina Christiana*, though the work addresses concerns of pagan influence on Christianity throughout. Augustine, too, finds outrage in the primitivism of Tertullian and the Tertullianists; however, he expresses this outrage in subdued rhetoric rather than polemical language.[18] He parallels rules of speech and knowledge found in Christian Scripture with those found in pre-Christian authors of both Gentile and Jewish provenance, establishing firmly the

---

17 "Quid ergo Athenis et Hierosolymis? Quid academiae et ecclesiae? Quid haereticis et christianis?"

18 The refutation is found chiefly in Book II, specifically in 2:18.28 and 2:27.41-2:28.42.

necessity of the Christian faith to examine and, indeed, draw from, the established wisdom and acquired knowledge of its predecessors.

There exists in Augustine several appeals to previous teachings, but we need concern ourselves with but a fraction of the whole here. It would nevertheless behoove all who read this to find an edition of *De Doctrina Christiana* and examine its usefulness to the faith of our ancestors, just as Augustine himself examined Cicero for the benefit of young Christendom. The first, and most important, refutation is found in 2:18:28, where Augustine examines the rejection of Pagan ideas and practices and the reasoning thereof. He writes, "For example, neither should we neglect to learn literature because it is said to be of Mercury, nor ought we to shun virtue and justice because temples are dedicated to them, and what ought to be borne in the heart is adored in stone."[19] For these things do not belong to paganism, but to that universal truth that may be found in all things; thus he continues, "no indeed, any good and true Christian, wherever he will have come upon truth, should know it to be of the Lord Himself."[20] The reader should note well the great chasm that exists here between Augustine's quest to find God's Truth in all things from Tertullian's insistence that all things conceived of man are inherently divorced of God.

Here, too, does Augustine appeal to scripture, specifically the Pauline epistles, when he cites Romans, in which Paul declares:

> Because that, when they knew God, they glorified him not as God, neither were thankful; but became vain in their imaginations, and their foolish heart was darkened. Professing themselves to be wise, they became fools, And changed the glory of the uncorruptible God into an image made like to corruptible man, and to birds, and fourfooted beasts, and creeping things.[21]

Indeed, by this accusation, Tertullian finds that he has fallen to the same blindness of the philosopher he so despises, in that he refuses to recognize the glory of God in the acquired knowledge of philosophy. A very serious accusation to level indeed against a proclamation made to condemn the Godless and heretical. Indeed, though, this citation of Paul is reflective of his writing elsewhere: of man's

---

19 "Neque enim et litteras discere non debuimus, quia earum deum dicunt esse Mercurium, aut quia iustitia uirtutique templa dedicarunt et, quae corde gestanda sunt, in lapidibus adorare maluerunt, propterea nobis iustitia uirtusque fugienda est," (*De Doctrina Christiana* 2:18.28:6-10).
20 "Immo uero quisquis bonus uerusque christianus est, domini sui esse intellegat, ubicumque inuenerit ueritatem," (*Doct. Chr.* 2:18.28:10-12).
21 Romans 1:21-23.

Against the Primitivists

inability to recognize and understand God where he finds God's glory, and to speak much about that of which he knows little.[22]

Augustine has addressed a central problem of primitivism hitherto unspoken of, since it does not constitute our focus. In the passages above, addressing the eternal nature of Truth and moral good, Augustine highlights one of the other problems of the over-zealous purism of the primitivists. For it is indeed a problem that is found amongst the primitivists claiming to be Ásatrú to reject all Christian morality simply because it is Christian, blind to the eternal nature of such "Christian" notions as charity, virtue, and self-restraint. What it is replaced with speaks again to the central problem of anti-intellectualism, for the pseudo-Nietzschean understanding of Christian morality reflects an adolescent reading of the modern philosopher, useful though he is to all anti-Christians regardless of their religion or lack thereof. Indeed, just as Augustine might speak of the eternal truths attested in Paul, might not also the Ásatruar resort to those famous lines which are the foundation of our entire faith? Is this not the meaning of the passage:

> I know that I hung, on a wind swept tree
> for all of nine nights,
> wounded by spear, and given to Odin,
> myself to myself,
> on that tree of which no man knows
> from what root it rises.
>
> They dealt me no bread, nor drinking horn.
> I looked down, I drew up the runes,
> screaming I took them up,
> and fell back from there.[23]

---

22 See II Tim. 2:14-18.
23 *Hávamál* 138-139 (in Chisholm's *Edda*):
"Veit ek at ek hekk vindga meiði a
netr allar nío,
geiri vndaþr ok gefinn Oðni,
sialfr sialfom mer,
a þeim meiþi, er mangi veit, hvers hann af rótom renn.

Við hleifi mik seldo ne viþ hornigi,
nysta ek niþr,
nam ek vp rvnar,
opandi nam,
fell ek aptr þaðan."

Is it mere mistake or coincidence that the highest God of our ancestors was a God of wisdom and knowledge, or that to gain his knowledge he sacrificed himself on the tree "of which no man knows whence its roots run"?

Nor does Augustine neglect this anti-intellectualism of the Christian primitivists. Indeed, he devoted more space to this even, just as it justifies a greater examination on our part. Augustine's dealing with anti-intellectualism can be found in 2:27.41 and 2:28.42 of *De Doctrina Christiana*. His principle refutation follows from the above, in the peculiar usefulness of empirical study and philosophy to understanding of the world, such that it would be error to call these things corrupted or purely human institutions. Thus he writes, "Now, we should not consider those things human that were not established by men but that Truth revealed either through time or divine revelation to human investigation, wherever it is learned."[24] As he declares above that all knowledge and all truth flows from God regardless of who finds it or how it is found, so too must those institutions solely dedicated to the discovery of truth be regarded as divine institutions in the hands of men; he speaks of the very same *philosophia* that Tertullian so vehemently condemns.

Nor does Augustine terminate his refutation after only so brief a statement. Following the declaration of all truth flowing from a common source, thus essentially ending the debate, he goes a step further. "Whatsoever therefore reveals the order of times past—that which is called history—greatly animates our understanding of the sacred texts."[25] This is something of especial relevance in the on-going battle with primitivism. As Augustine writes, the understanding of the scriptures can only be enhanced by learning things like history, geography, and other sciences, which in those days were dominated by heathen sensibilities, and which today are dominated by Christian sensibilities. Where, for example, is the source of the contemporary categories of BCE and CE, but in the Christian BC and AD? What is the so-called "Common Era", if not the Christian Era? So Christendom is unavoidable in scholastic undertakings of even this most basic nature. More important, however, is the importance of learning the history of our specific religion. The Jews had no history but that which was recorded as semi-myth in their scriptures, therefore it was necessary to resort to pagan histories and time-lines and genealogies to corroborate what was found in the scriptures. Is it not the same today? Snorri Sturlusson, for example, was undoubtedly a Christi-

---

24 "Iam uero illa quae non institudendo, sed aut transacta temporibus aut diuintus institute inuestigando hominess prodiderunt, ubicumque discantur, non sunt hominum institute existimanda," (*Doct. Chr.* 2:27.41:1-4).

25 "Quicquid igitur de ordine temporum transactorum indicat ea quae appellatur historia, plurimum nos adiuuat ad libros sanctos intellegendos," (*Doct. Chr.* 2:28.42:1-3).

an; yet we must depend upon him for our own scripture, to say nothing of history to corroborate that scripture. Here resides the principle argument posed by Augustine against Tertullian's *genealogiae interminabiles.*

Primitivism Today

It must be recognised that there are several principle consequences of primitivism in addition to the drives mentioned above. In the first place, primitivism stunts the growth of a religion; whether it is the anti-intellectualism of the narrow-minded occultist or that of the childish rebel, primitivism does not allow for the new discovery of holiness in living and experiencing, that being the very heart and soul of a living faith. This is the principle argument posed by Augustine against Tertullian's primitivism, and, indeed, it remains true of the eternal primitivist. It is from our past alone that we may learn those things by which our future is necessarily shaped; like Paganism for Augustine and Ambrose, Christianity is a defining feature of our past and our present, a feature that defies our efforts to reject it utterly or ignore it.

Likewise of the second consequence of primitivism, if the faith cannot grow within itself, it cannot grow numerically. It is often written that ours is not a faith of conversion, of mission, of preaching, and as it is written and said, it is justly so. This does not preclude, though, those of our Folk not yet of our Faith. The principle fault of the primitivist is the weakness of his religion. The primitivist's religion is like the over-pruned plant; it is made to look better than the other hedges and bushes, but when winter falls, it has been so weakened that it shrivels and succumbs to the extremes of the weather, it has none of the natural hardiness of those plants that are properly pruned or untouched. Rather than growing forth and blooming into a rebirth of our ancient faith, the primitivist in his zealotry would stagnate and even shrink those numbers that have already answered the call of the ancestors.

It is important that the primitivists of today not remain some theoretical mass. There are real reasons for their existence, both interior and exterior, and they are a definable group within our community. Those exterior causes for their existence come from true believers in the Christian community who survive in many Protestant sects, and work fiercely to re-convert those who are apostates from their religion. There is a great drive among the weaker to cast out all "that is not of us" because of the persecution suffered for our faith. Here, especially, is there much to be learned from the Christian experience. For the Christians thrived in persecution, each drop of martyr's blood feeding the millions and bringing that faith into a position of civilization-shaping dominance the likes of which had never been seen before.

Mark Stinson, a contemporary leader in the Ásatrú community, formerly of the Ásatrú Folk Assembly, might qualify as a contemporary Tertullian, though to create such an attachment creates inequity for both men. Nevertheless, there is a seed of primitivism in his writing and his "Temple of Our Heathen Gods." In an essay written titled "A Final Note on Christianity," Stinson contributes the following:

> These Christian teachings encourage people to disown their own family members that aren't Christian. It encourages job discrimination. It encourages harassment. It encourages abuse and bullying at school. It encourages fear-mongering. It encourages a lot of behaviors on the part of its followers that are absolutely harmful to non-Christians.[26]

What this passage contains is a distinctly primitivist understanding of the relationship of Christians and Christian teaching. It was, after all, Christians who developed the notion of contemporary "tolerance," a notion rooted strongly in the adaptive approach to proselytising first found in Augustine himself. The word "tolerance" itself derives from medical terminology; it refers to the body's ability to withstand toxins. Anything that seeks to damage or destroy Christianity is without doubt a toxin to the faith; this is as true of Christianity as with any faith.

Alain de Benoist touches upon the nature of the situation Stinson finds himself in. His essay, "Intolerance and Religion," highlights the reasoning behind the Roman rejection of Christianity; Christians, he writes, "were condemned…for being bad citizens."[27] The point here is that the Romans condemned and rejected Christianity not for religious reasons, but for moral and social reasons. This may strike the mind with a distinct sense of oddity, this notion that there can be a sense of moral outrage without a sense of religious outrage. The reason for this is not, as many atheists or secularists might suggest, because morality exists independently of religion, but because Roman society had its own social *mores*, in the way contemporary Christian society has its own *mores* independent of the religion itself.

The primitivist will feel persecution; he will see his rejection by society as a distinctly Christian phenomenon, a religious phenomenon. This is clearly declared

---

26 Mark Stinson, "A Final Note on Christianity", Temple of Our Heathen Gods Facebook page, http://www.facebook.com/notes/temple-of-our-heathen-gods/a-final-note-on-christianity/390560808955 (accessed July 14, 2011).
27 Alain de Benoist, "Intolerance and Religion," trans. Jennifer Roberge-Toll, in *The Journal of Contemporary Heathen Thought* 1, (2010): 129-135.

in Stinson's writing. What Stinson does not realise, or what he ignores (it is not the place of this writer to speculate), is that the experience of persecution is not religious; it is purely social. The social mores of the world Heathens dwell in are informed by Christianity. This is inescapable, as inescapable as the Pagan influence on education in the days of Augustine. Stinson, in fact, hints in another work that he understands and accepts this as true, but still does not seem to grasp the irrevocability of it. One should not see these examples from one man's writing as a levelled attack against that one man—rather, it is fortunate that Stinson has seen fit to publish his writings, as he is exemplary of the type which we are discussing here, and it is that type—the primitivist—not Stinson himself, which is worthy of the scorn heretofore prescribed.

However, Stinson has shown elsewhere that he actively endorses a primitivist strain, and another illustration of contemporary primitivism would not be remiss here. He writes in his article "Beating the Christian Addiction":

> Christianity is something many of us were indoctrinated with from birth. This makes it difficult to shed all of our Christian thought processes and habits. I do not see Christianity as an addiction, as much as a bad pattern of thought and behavior well worth breaking. Christianity is a crutch or weakness we need to grow beyond. "Isn't Heathenry rich enough and complete enough that we can transition to it without having to borrow beliefs and practices from Christianity?" To this question I answer strongly, "Yes," as before.[28]

There is self-satisfaction here, echoing almost exactly the phrases of Tertullian when he proclaims, "our tradition is from the portico of Solomon."[29] It is a wilful ignorance, as illustrated above, which bears this poison fruit. Just as Augustine illustrated, Christianity in its youth, relying only on the Jewish lore and the "portico of Solomon," would perish without looking to those things which are eternal beyond the portico of Solomon, which all who have read know was not established by God, but by men appealing to their ancestors' God. The primitivist's question "isn't Heathenry complete enough?" is Tertullian's question: "what has Athens to do with Jerusalem?" Our response must be Augustine's response; for no young faith is at all "complete," it is not "rich enough" to ignore what can enrich it from the wiser, the more experienced. Further, what Augustine saw that Tertullian either wilfully ignored or was himself blind to, namely that the philo-

---

28 Mark Stinson, "Beating the Christian Addiction," in *Heathen Gods* (Liberty, MO: Jotuns Bane Kindred, 2009), 23.
29 "Nostra institutio de porticu Solomonis est," (*DpH* 7:10).

sophy and knowledge that the pagans mastered before the coming of Christianity were not "a bad pattern of thought and behavior well worth breaking"—rather, they were for the benefit of pagan and Christian alike. Likewise the wisdom, the philosophy, the theology, and the knowledge mastered by the Christians over the last millennium are to the benefit of Christianity and Heathenry alike.

Just as Christians made efforts to adapt themselves into the pagan world in which they lived, from eating the meat of animals sacrificed in the Pagan temples, to abandoning the ancient practice of circumcision, to Augustine's own teachings, the Christians, despite their tales of martyrdom and defiance, made every effort possible to become part of the world into which Christianity was born, and as such brought themselves closer each century to the position eventually achieved when Fortune blessed them with Constantine the Great.

The exterior causes for primitivism are most certainly born in misunderstanding of the nature of the persecution of our faith. This is by far the more difficult form of primitivism to overcome, because all believers can fall into this trap and harm themselves and our faith. It takes tremendous strength, willpower, and patience to work to appeal to the social *mores* of a Christian society, to use Christian methods to further our faith. To merely mimic Augustine when he writes of the use of history to inform the scriptures or pre-Christian rhetoric to preach the young faith would be a tremendous failure of understanding. It is the very Christian society in which we live that demands our adaptability; we must use Christian stones to sharpen our swords.

Far easier to combat is the primitivism born of the interior efforts of our leaders. Chief among the dangers created by religious leaders of Ásatrú is to destroy the faith by bringing to its bosom the lowest ranks of society, the least intelligent, the most deficient of understanding. This is a danger that is presented by those who would use actual Christian religious doctrine to further our faith. Indeed, one can use the social *mores* of Christian civilisation to further the position of Ásatru in society, but so often do these social mores directly defy religious doctrine—and there is special danger for the Ásatruar that does not exist for the Christian that would preach this doctrine.

The Ásatrú prison ministry is chief among efforts by leaders in the Ásatrú community to increase our numbers. There is specific danger in this because those who are imprisoned, those who are poor, those who are sick, those who are weak, all those to whom the devout Christian is ordered to preach, come from a portion of our people that is not only unsavory, but inferior.

The prisoner is in prison for an offense he has committed, so grave that society has seen fit to separate him from them, to cast him out, to banish and ostracise him. This practice originates in our most ancient of ancestors, who saw a holy caste system handed down by the Gods themselves. Thus our language has even a word for these: outcasts. Necessarily, these lowest of the ancient and sacred hierarchy are those with the smallest spiritual and intellectual capacity. They are given, therefore, to the least intelligent and least wise group that our religion can possibly incorporate. Why, then, is the greatest effort for proselytizing our faith reserved for these lowest of our people? The result is inevitably that those of little thought, and little capability for thought, are brought in the greatest numbers to the highest ranks of the faith swiftest. More dangerous seeds could not have been sown.

The greatest concern created by prison ministries is the society that is created within the prisons themselves. Far from merely housing criminals, the prison is itself a den of vice, where crime incubates and grows and is fed upon fear, hatred, and all of the basest qualities of its inhabitants. Among these is the hatred of Christianity as a "Semitic religion" specifically. For indeed, Christianity is a foreign faith, and it is shunned for this reason: not where it is from but merely that it is not from our own. Germanic culture, the pride of our ancestors, is exploited and perverted in a prison setting, a breeding ground for anti-Semitism, racism, and primitivist rejection of those who could be our allies, the only surviving Folkish Faith in the Western World, the Hebrews.

The Calling to the True Faith

It is the ability to find the Truth of the Gods in ourselves and the world surrounding us that brings us to understanding and love of that which is Holy. It is this that Augustine imparted to the Christians, that the pursuit of Truth has many methods and many tools, and that these methods and tools have been better used by those who have come before us. This truth itself is bound up in our own love for our ancestors, and our worship of their accomplishments, our heroes and teachers. For thousands of years, though, our ancestors were Christian, and though the mystery of the Folk was alive within them, they did not see it. But nevertheless they did seek Truth and sought after the Divine using methods and tools that are ours yet to use. In seeking a universal God, the Christians have succeeded in preparing the way for those who seek a particular God, for when one seeks after a universal God, one inevitably finds the court of many Gods.

It is for this reason that the primitivists in all their forms must be corrected or shunned. It is our boon that they be taught and corrected, since it increases the numbers of those of understanding and brings balance to the faith. Nevertheless, if they refuse to be taught and are stubborn in their ways, we are left with no choice but to bring them to light and shun them from our numbers. It is our boon to learn from the Christians, who have far greater experience than we in matters of understanding Truth and the relationship of the Divine to our own. It is of great boon to learn from scholars of our ancestors, to discover our Folk as it was rather than as we wish it to have been, and to accept those things that historians have found rather than stubbornly grounding ourselves in late mystics and the occult of this day. For the Tertullians of our number will continue their accusations, "what hath Aquinas to do with Sigurð? What the Church Fathers to do with the Alföðr? What the Christian to do with the Ásatruar?" It is our calling to answer them, as Augustine answered Tertullian, our calling to answer in pursuit of Truth and Wisdom: "Everything."

Interviews and Book Reviews

We are the playground of a veritable theater full of Gods and Goddesses. What do the Gods and Goddesses want with us? Our task is to incarnate them, become aware of their presence, acknowledge and celebrate their forms, so that we may better be able to account for our polytheism.
—David L. Miller, *The New Polytheism*

On Heathen Clergy:
An Interview with Stefn Thorsman and Ed LeBouthillier[1]

Thank you both for participating in this interview. If you would, please begin by introducing yourselves and giving our readers a bit of background on your involvement in Heathenry.

Stefn Thorsman:[2] I am chieftain/*goði*[3] of The Hammer Of Thor Kindred located in Northern California. I am also the clergy coordinator for the Ásatrú Folk Assembly, commonly referred to as the AFA. After searching for years for a spiritual path, I finally came home to Ásatrú/Heathenry in late 1994. I had found a book on runes and this led me to Edred Thorsson's *A Book Of Troth*. After reading that book, I never looked back. I knew I had found my *trú* spiritual home. I formed The Hammer Of Thor Kindred in 1995 and our Kindred began hosting two yearly gatherings each year. Ostara and Ægir's Feast. I met our Alsherjargoði,[4] Steve McNallen, five years ago and was impressed by his years of dedication and devotion to our folkway and I joined the AFA. It has been an exciting journey and a thrill to watch modern Heathenry grow and see other Ásatrú groups come together over the last seventeen years.

Ed LeBouthillier: I work as the curriculum supervisor for Stefn. I have been involved in Ásatrú for about eleven years now. I find it to be a highly spiritual way to bond with my Gods and ancestors. I was attracted to Ásatrú by the spirituality of its rituals and the depth and richness of its lore. Alsherjargoði Steve McNallen was instrumental in bringing me to our religion with his ability to communicate the vitality of Ásatrú as a living way to know our Gods and Goddesses, our ancestors and our place in Miðgarðr. I currently belong to a local practitioner group, called a kindred, where I live. I work as the *goði* for that group. I have been working as a *goði* for our local practitioner groups almost since the beginning of my involvement with Ásatrú.

What led to the decision to formulate a systematized clergy program?

---

1 This interview was conducted by Christopher A. Plaisance (with questions written by he and Stephen M. Borthwick) via email between March and July of 2011.
2 Answers to the first question and final remarks were answered separately by Messrs. Thorsman and LeBouthillier, while all subsequent answers were collaborative.
3 The terms used by the interviewees are the Old Norse terms *goði* (pl. *goðar*) and *gyðja* (pl. *gyðjur*) to refer to male and female clerics respectively.
4 A term literally meaning "*public* priest," but, since Sveinbjörn Beinteinsson's revival of Icelandic Ásatrú, used in the sense of "high priest."

We believe that if Ásatrú, or Heathenry in general, is ever going to be recognized as a "legitimate" religion in the eyes of the modern world we would need ordained clergy—clergy that can legally perform weddings, funerals, and other ceremonies where a member of the clergy is required. Heathen clergy is not a modern invention. There are historical sources describing the roles of Heathen clergy as well as temples and *hoven*.[5] The famous temple at Uppsala, Sweden is a good example. We did not always gather in the forest!

A formal clergy program provides a means to accredit Ásatrú religious leaders as is required for Ásatrúar to receive state recognition for marriages and other important ceremonies in some states. Additionally, although all who lead our religious rituals are *goðar* or *gyðjur*, we think that there is some benefit in providing a standardized set of knowledge and skills for conducting our rituals and representing our religious beliefs. The clergy program facilitates the goal of "practicing and promoting Ásatrú" by providing basic training for our *goðar* and *gyðjur* who want to conduct public ritual.

Has the AFA examined any seminary curricula presently run by established religions as guides for the clergy program's development?

We did have available information on the programs of various religions. Of course, we used them to inform us of what similar kinds of programs contained. However, we had limited resources and we knew that our fellow *goðar* and *gyðjur* had limited time (for example, we couldn't do a four year college program at this time) so we lowered our ambitions and crafted a very practical and manageable program given the resources that we and our fellow practitioners had. In many ways, our current program is a "trade school"[6] approach to clergy training. We hope to be able to improve it in the future, but we've tried to be practical and address the expedient need to provide standardized, recognized training that many people want.

What are the qualifications necessary for an aspirant who wishes to enter into the program—both the preliminary requirements and the course of study involved in the program itself?

They must be a member of the AFA for one year, they must apply to the program, pay a minimal processing fee, they must be willing to take the oath we give them and they must be willing to perform a certain amount of service in return for their

---

5 *Hof* (pl. *hoven*) being the Old Norse term meaning "temple."
6 A vocational apprenticeship scheme operating in the USA.

training. This Service Principle generally means that they agree to mentor a clergy student for one year following their ordination. We also currently want people who want to be doing public rituals. Although our religion can be practiced by solitary individuals, at this point in time, we think we need to concentrate on giving opportunities for our folk to be involved in group rituals. We know that there are many people who, because of where they live, are unable to be involved in public rituals and we think that we would like to improve the opportunity for more people to experience our public rituals.

What sort of disciplinary or ascetic rules, if any, are imposed upon clergymen? How are these behavioral regulations similar or different to clerical regulations found in other religions?

Although we do not have any set rules on personal conduct we expect our clergy members to hold themselves to a higher ideal. To take a deeper, more personal, more responsible approach to Heathenry. We must remember that we represent Ásatrú not only to the Heathen community, but to the outside community as well.

But, at this time, we have just started the program and we feel that we are unable to impose disciplinary or ascetic rules. We also feel that, because of various approaches to ritual and religious expression, it is not practical to impose those kinds of demands. Our program is very practical, reviewing what we feel our religious leaders need to know so that they can get out and do their jobs of conducting ritual and representing our religion. We don't feel that most people can afford to have disciplinary or ascetic rules imposed on their already busy lives.

You might understand this as part of a progression. We feel that we have a program to help people be better *goðar* and *gyðjur*, or at least establish some standards that allow them to work more cohesively with the needs of the AFA at this time. In some ways, it is a trade school or associate's degree level program. We would love to be able to offer a four year bachelor's degree program or a masters or doctoral level program but it is just not practical yet. We hope we can grow in that direction.

However, if you want to say that we do have some rules, our rule would be to live up to their oath which requires that they live their lives honorably in service to the AFA, their Folk and their Gods and Goddesses.

What is the social function of the clergy? How does this compare to, say, the role of a Catholic priest?

Figure 1: Stefn Thorsman, clergy coordinator for the AFA.

Currently, our primary duty is to conduct public rituals; as we say it: to practice and promote Ásatrú. We want to help *goðar* and *gyðjur* go back to their community and feel confident about performing public rituals, helping others experience the spirituality of our religion and getting to know our Gods and Goddesses better. The AFA Clergy are instructed in our basic rituals: *blót, sumbl* as well as what we call life rituals. Life rituals include baby namings, marriages, land takings, man or woman-making ceremonies and wake/burial ceremonies. For an additional part of our instruction in life rituals, we've put out our *AFA Book of Blotar and Ritual*, which originated from the AFA Clergy. In that book, one will find examples of rituals and some of the theory behind them. Hopefully, in the future, we'll be able to offer add-on extension classes for specific rituals other than *blót* and *sumbl*.

Role-wise, I think that an AFA clergy member *can* play many of the same roles as, say, a Christian priest. Of course, we lead *blót* and other rituals, but we may also do many rituals unique to Ásatrú such as the life rituals that are not found in, for example, the Christian religions. But, in contrast to, say, a Catholic priest, the AFA's *goði* and *gyðja* ranks are not as centrally directed. We make an attempt to inform our clergy members of the basic beliefs, attitudes and practices of our religion and the AFA, but we leave a lot more room for personal interpretation and implementation. Our position is that we will formally inform the clergy of the religion's and the AFA's beliefs and attitudes regarding various issues, we will oath the members to represent our religion and the AFA honorably, but they may use their own judgment and preferences in how they realize those ideas. Additionally, since the AFA only has single individual membership, and does not have designated kindreds or local practice groups, the individual clergy represent their own individual, local religious group. We believe, however, that when a *goði* or *gyðja* explicitly represents the AFA (such as at AFA gatherings), that they should attempt to conform in the representation of the rituals and symbolism. This would mean, for example, using specific names for our Gods and Goddesses, having certain elements and processes in the public rituals, but we expect that there will be individual initiative and preferences in how these things are represented. By stating what we expect regarding some of the basic religious representation, we are able to maintain a minimum commonality of ideas about our Gods and Goddesses and rituals. However, we don't expect explicit conformance on all of these elements when someone is not explicitly representing the AFA (i.e. in their own local practices).

Is there any particular moral code or general ethical framework within which members of the AFA clergy are expected to operate?

There is the oath, which demands behaving honorably and for the good of the AFA, the folk and the Gods and Goddesses and incurs a few other obligations (e.g. the service obligation). There are also ethical standards already in place in the AFA which we expect our religious leader to understand and adhere to. To expand on this, the clergy group met and asked ourselves what we believed our ethical ideals and standards were. As a group, we originated the "AFA Statement of Ethics" and it has been adopted by the AFA. This ethical standard is broken down into nine areas:

1. The Æsir and Vanir Principle: identifies who our Gods and Goddesses are.

2. The Folk Community Principle: a statement that we hold our unique community with high value.
3. The Ancestry Principle: a statement that we hold our unique ancestry with high value.
4. The Family Principle: a statement that we value the family as a key social institution.
5. The Organization Principle: a statement that from folk unity comes folk strength.
6. The Personal Excellence Principle: a statement that individuals should seek to better themselves.
7. The Honor Your Oaths Principle: a statement of the unique importance of oaths in our religion.
8. The Warrior Principle: a statement that at times we must face great challenges with honor and bravery.
9. The Life is Good Principle: a statement that we think life is worth living, is good in itself, and is to be enjoyed.

The "Statement of Ethics" was a collaborative effort from most of the clergy. You can find the full statement on the AFA website.[7]

What kind of didactic role is envisioned for clergy in the Heathen community? Is it to be an active missionary role (i.e. sponsoring programs for the education of the populace about Heathenry) or passive and guiding (i.e. waiting for Heathens to come to the clergyman with questions)?

Again, the term is "practice and promote Ásatrú;" our clergy are expected to be practitioners and promoters of Ásatrú and to help others to practice Ásatrú through our holy rituals, and by being authoritative representatives of Ásatrú, its rituals and beliefs. However, we have a different idea of what our authority is, than from Catholicism for example. Our authority comes from our understanding of our heritage and our agreements among ourselves about why we are here together. Those agreements, understandings, customs and folkways define who we are. We have worked to establish some consensus among ourselves about what they are, and we work to live up to our agreements for the good of our community.

So, an authority of consensus arises from these understandings. We inform our clergy members of why we are together, we have them take an oath to those ideals and that means that they can feel confident that they understand and rep-

---

[7] "AFA Statement of Ethics," http://www.runestone.org/about-the-afa/afa-statement-of-ethics.html (accessed July 6, 2011).

resent the ideals, culture and folkway of our religion.

Primarily for practical reasons, though, in the AFA's Clergy Program, we do expect that our *goðar* and *gyðjur* train another *goði* and *gyðja* (or take on some other commensurate service). We have explicitly made the service obligation a condition for *goði* and *gyðja* training. Usually, this means the training of another *goði* or *gyðja* following their own training but we're willing to work with or accommodate our students. This is primarily for practical purposes because we're not formally compensated for our efforts. Once a *goði* or *gyðja* has completed their service obligation, though, they are free to practice without explicit obligations other than those they get from their oath. However, most of the trained *goðar* and *gyðjur* keep in friendly contact with each other. We share ideas and practices with each other.

So, once they've completed their service obligation, the didactic role of clergy isn't as formal. *Goðar* and *gyðjur* educate and train by being examples of the ideals and lifestyle. Our *goðar* and *gyðjur*, though, are excited about their religion and that helps other people also become excited about it too. *Goðar* and *gyðjur* meet people who are curious and they inform them about its ideas and practices, new people are attracted, but it is not an explicit proselytizing activity. Clergy are expected to try to give an opportunity for people to learn about and practice the religion, but we don't expect explicit proselytizing. Proselytizing is not forbidden either, but we prefer that it not be done. World domination is not Ásatrú's ideal—a good community is.

But, *goðar* and *gyðjur* are people who enjoy and accept the responsibility to lead public ritual. That means that they not only do it when the situation arises, but that they make the situation arise. They likely conduct study and classes with those with whom they practice their religion. AFA clergy were *goðar* and *gyðjur* before they entered our training program. They already lead rituals and are leaders in their community. Formal training helps them do that better and more confidently.

Other Heathen organizations have devoted much energy towards prison outreach, yet this is something that the AFA seems to eschew—focusing more on building relations with the US military. Why is this the case?

It is the AFA's policy to not allow prisoners to be members of the organization. That was already in place. We just feel that there are so many other organizations concentrating on prisons that a balanced effort demands focusing on other places, like the military or non-prison community.

Figure 2: Johnny Hulsey, AFA clergyman.

Are clergy members trained to counsel members of their community in matters of life experience, doubts and cases of moral quandaries—particularly in regards to teenagers, but also in cases of adults undergoing major life changes?

At this time, no, not explicitly. They may do that activity in the conduct of their role as a religious and community leader, but we don't feel we're currently qualified or able to train for counseling properly.

Do clergymen receive any bereavement training for dealing with the eventuality of deaths within their communities?

Not currently. We do hope, however, that as they better understand their role in conducting ritual and in helping their folk community, they understand their significant role in helping people through trying times in their lives.

What sort of theology does the AFA seek to impart to the clergy? Is it rooted more primarily in the theophantic results of ritual or in textual hermeneutics?

Our theology is the AFA's Ásatrú based in the Eddas and Sagas. Using your terminology, we are more based on the theophantic results of ritual than on a particular textual hermeneutics. We actually try to use academic sources giving common current understanding of our ancestors views but we leave a lot of flexibility to the *goðar* and *gyðjur* to integrate that into their own practices, beliefs and rituals.

What are the bases of the theological approaches utilized by the clergy program? Is there any use of sources with are not explicitly Heathen in nature, such as classical or contemporary philosophy, Catholic or Hindu theology, etc.?

Much of it is not explicitly Heathen in nature. We expect the students to already be well-read in much of the lore and we try to "round out" that knowledge by adding a little bit of breadth into other topics that might not otherwise be focused on. We add some historical literature to give perspective that may have not been considered, we give some basic philosophy concepts and ideas (such as general ideas of ethics), and a little bit of folk sociology. There is a strong emphasis on the runes, fully one quarter of the curriculum is dedicated to rune knowledge and runic meditations are performed throughout the program. We discuss ideas related to *blót* and *sumbl* and their performance, roles of the *goði* and *gyðja* in society. We also have a section on general principles of leadership to provide understanding of their role as community leaders.

Is any effort being made by the AFA towards systematizing the mythos or towards the establishment of a Heathen canon?

Not really. The AFA utilizes many of the primary sources as its theology: the Eddas and Sagas. If we try to systematize things, it's in an emphasis on Scandanavian/Icelandic lore, terminology and viewpoint, but that's primarily because those are the surviving sources. But we leave it to the *goðar* and *gyðjur* to utilize their judgment about other things to include.

Does the clerical program endorse any specific hermeneutic of the Heathen

mythos (e.g. Dumezil's trifunctional hypothesis, Rydberg's synthetic mythography, etc.)?

No, not really. We may mention them in our discussions, but we don't emphasize them. Personally, I think it's important to understand the difference between "the lore" and extensions to it. There must be extensions to the lore to adapt it to our modern world, but the adaptations need to be made with a larger understanding of the lore.

What is the clergy's stance on the relationship between orthopraxy and orthodoxy? Is there a primacy of standardized ritual over standardized belief, or *vice versa*?

Definitely standardization of ritual over standardized beliefs. We believe that a certain consistency arises from the surviving lore of the Eddas and Sagas and as long as one is aware of where one diverges from them, that is all that we expect. Know your lore, know where you're diverging from the lore. Know what is your UPG[8] and what's in the lore. We don't discount or invalidate UPG but we expect people to understand the difference between what's in the lore and what isn't.

Regarding the role of institutionalized praxis, how does the clergy reconcile the dynamic tension between the desire for strict historical recreation with the perceived need for contemporary innovation? Is one side taken, or does the clergy attempt to find a middle ground somewhere?

Our view is that Ásatrú is a modern religion. We are not merely a reconstructionist society. We are a living, breathing, adapting, spiritual community that is inspired by and reveres our ancestors, but we have to adapt to and live in today's world. We use our history and lore as guides to modern life.

What sorts of beliefs *vis-à-vis* the Gods and their relationships with mankind are imparted to the clergy, and what manner of theological authority do trained clergymen hold?

Our view is that our gods and goddesses are our earliest ancestors; they are "folk." Our folk community derives from them. We revere and honor all of our ancestors but we give the most respect to the elders of our community.

---

8 UPG stands for "unverified (or sometimes unverifiable) personal gnosis," which is a term used by Heathens and other Neopagans to refer to non-exegetically derived theological dogma.

What is the long-term goal of the clergy program? Is it, perhaps, envisioned as a stepping stone towards the establishment of an accredited, degree granting seminary?

I would say that our current goal is "to grow and better serve the folk community by providing trained and capable *goðar* and *gyðjur* to enhance the practice and promotion of Ásatrú." We would certainly like to expand the program as and when this is possible. As said earlier, it is currently a trade school or associate's degree level program. It would be good if it expanded to provide greater academic depth without losing the practicality of helping train people who lead our community rituals. I think it would be excellent if we had a range of degrees from kindred *goðar* up through a doctoral or esoteric knowledge program. But we have a responsibility to be effective; we will do what we think we're able to do with the resources available to us. We would certainly hope that the AFA *goði* and *gyðja* program becomes an inherent institution in our community, providing religious and community leadership and working for its good.

Stefn: Thanks for giving us the opportunity to speak about our program.

Ed: Yes, thank you very much, Chris.

Sal und Sig!

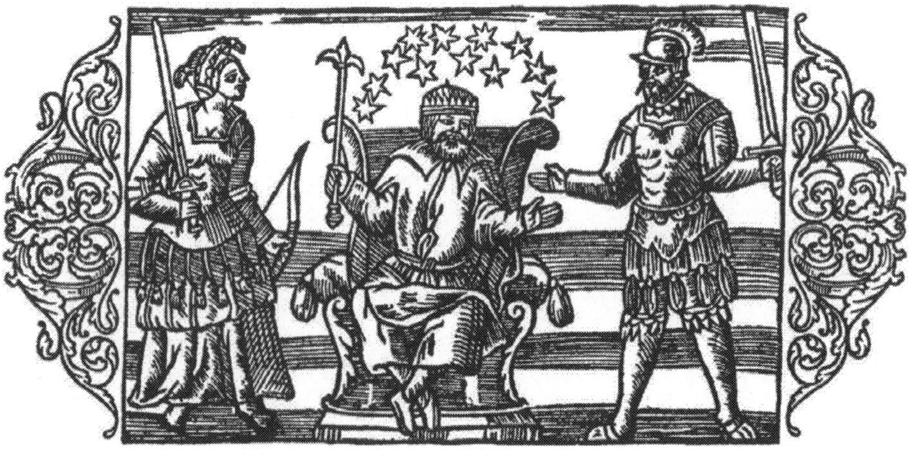

Green Heathenry:
An Interview With Bron Taylor[1]

Bron Taylor is presently a Professor of Religion and Nature at the University of Florida and an Affiliated Scholar with Oslo University's Center for Environment and Development.[2] His work has been published in numerous journal articles, books and the multi-volume *Encyclopedia of Religion and Nature*. His most recent book, *Dark Green Religion: Nature Spirituality and the Planetary Future* (hereafter DGR), represents Taylor's position as an interdisciplinary scholar whose research interests span the fields of environmentalism, religious studies, ethics and sociology. As such, his work primarily addresses the questions revolving around the "conservation of the Earth's biological diversity and how human culture might evolve rapidly enough to arrest and reverse today's intensifying environmental and social crises, and all the suffering, that flows from these trends."[3] This interview is an attempt to bridge the gap between modern Heathenry and Taylor's work—to uncover what connections exist between the two's differing understandings of the sacrality of nature.

In your book *Dark Green Religion: Nature Spirituality and the Planetary Future*, you go to great lengths to establish Henry David Thoreau's corpus of work in its rightful place as the earliest of American expressions of Dark Green Religion (hereafter DGR). In your summary you even offer readers a provocative question to ponder: "To which social groups would Thoreau have been drawn had he been living and writing around and after the first Earth Day in 1970?"[4] Given that Thoreau is very much a philosopher and naturalist that is highly regarded in most (if not all) corners of the Heathen community, given your deep knowledge of this author and his works, in your estimation would he have been keen in identifying himself as a Pagan, perhaps even of the Heathen persuasion? Were he not interested in linking his admiration for nature directly with a religion *per se*, is there a particular group, off the top of your head, that you think he would have relished to have been part of, say the Sierra Club or Earth First! or some such? Do you

---

1 This interview was conducted by Jennifer Roberge-Toll via email between March and June of 2011.
2 Biographical details in the introduction are taken from Taylor's official biography on his website: http://www.brontaylor.com/about/index.html (accessed 1 November, 2011).
3 Ibid.
4 Bron Taylor, *Dark Green Religion: Nature Spirituality and the Planetary Future*, (Berkeley, CA: University of California Press, 2009), 56.

think he would have followed a more John Burroughs bioregional impulse or a more John Muir activist impulse had he had the opportunity to do so?

There were points where Thoreau explicitly expressed a certain affinity with Paganism, sometimes quoting literary exemplars of what he took it to mean. It was not really possible, it seems to me, for Thoreau declare himself to be a Heathen or Pagan when he was writing because there was no obvious above-ground social group identifying itself as such in mid-19th century America. Similarly, only the first hints of environmentalism had emerged by this time, so it's speculative to be sure to think about which religious, environmentalist, or other social groups he would identify with today. But, here are a few pertinent thoughts: As I consider Thoreau's life-direction, I see him as leaving behind Transcendentalism, namely, ancient Platonic metaphysics where this world supposedly reflects some deeper, ultimate, invisible, but real spiritual realm. He had become a naturalist with a worldview unconcerned with such metaphysical speculation, happy to live in this worldly world, which he was entranced by and became sufficient for him. That he immediately saw the explanatory power of Darwin's theory suggests that he would only have moved further in this direction had he more time to assimilate and write about it. So, I think the answer to whether he would identify as some sort of Pagan would depend on whether that Paganism was avowedly supernaturalistic. Those who know Pagan subcultures well, know that some in them are polytheists who we might call religious in a traditional religious sense: they believe that there are non-human spirits or divinities with whom human beings can and should be in some sort of "proper" relation. But, there are also Pagans who value the idea that the natural world is full of spiritual intelligences, but who view such ideas as metaphors for creativity and intelligence in nature, and do not take the gods or goddesses or spirits literally. As you know, contemporary Paganism provides a big umbrella covering many beliefs, experiences and practices…and I would not be surprised were Thoreau alive today that he would spend some time under it, engaged with those who in their various ways consider nature to be sacred and enchanting.

As for what environmental groups Thoreau might be engaged with, I would imagine certainly he would have be involved in the bioregional movement (indeed, he inspired much of it), and would also take up environmentalist causes through mainstream environmental organizations such as the Sierra Club. But, he was also someone who stood up against what he perceived to be great injustices, such as slavery and America's imperial wars, even writing one of the most important essays defending civil disobedience in American letters. If you take the way he felt and thought about things, and add to his data set the escalating extinction crisis and the closely related problems of overpopulation, overconsumption and increasing violence in the struggle for existence among human beings, I would

Figure 1: Bron Taylor

expect he would be a trenchant critic of environmental destruction and social injustice, and would find appropriate modes of resistance to them, including through strategic civil disobedience.

When you refer to certain figures as being "Pagan," for instance on page 62,

you refer to Muir as "more pagan than theistic" or on page 57 of Thoreau, "I would not be surprised to hear Thoreau call himself a pagan," what do you understand by the term "Pagan" exactly? Other than cursorily being non-Abrahamic and non-salvationist in focus to mention but a couple of notions, what are some of Paganism's distinguishing features which meet at the nexus of religion, politics and culture which mark it as a *viable expression of spirituality of some import* in today's Western world? Do you believe that Paganism might one day achieve enough of a critical mass in order to render it no longer a fringe religious element but a force to be reckoned with on the world stage?

I think we can think about Paganism in at least two major ways: either as a broad term for what I call "spiritualities of belonging and connection to nature," wherein nature is considered sacred in some way, and all other forms of life are viewed as our kin; or, it can be seen as a polytheistic religion involving deities of one sort or another, which are usually understood in supernaturalistic or otherworldly ways. With both types, there are ethical responsibilities to be in right relation with these divinities or beings, whether in nature or beyond it or both in and beyond it. I think that for some small but rapidly multiplying segment of the population, Paganism (understood in these ways) is already a viable expression of spirituality. A major point in *Dark Green Religion* is that Paganism can be understood to be a much broader and diverse phenomenon then it typically is understood to be, and that when we understand this breadth, we will apprehend that it is already much more influential than is commonly recognized. This is especially obvious when we consider its naturalistic forms, and the way it is expressed and promoted in the arts, popular culture, museums, academic institutions, and so forth. Because what I was trying to write about was broader than what would come into view if we only look at people who already consider themselves to be Pagan, I did not include Paganism in the title of my book, and only wrestled with whether Paganism is a good trope for the diversity of social phenomena that I discussed the book in a short afterword. Paganism might prove to be the trope that becomes associated with what I have called "dark green religion," but I think it is too early to tell, and other terms may supersede it, such as "nature religion." There is still a lot of antipathy toward what people understand Paganism to be in Western culture that would have to be overcome for the diverse expressions of connection to nature I discussed in my book to congeal under this term. But, as you know, the term is being rehabilitated, and it will be interesting to see how much the more so this occurs in the coming decades.

Somewhat related to the above, in your work, you bring together issues not only of religion and environmentalism and politics but you situate these squarely in a milieu which highlights the importance of an element which

seems often forgotten and shamefully so—culture. Are enough actors on the world stage taking culture's importance seriously in the debate about our planetary future? More specifically it appears that indigenous culture is key in getting heard on the world stage. Do you believe that indigenous European nature religions and therefore their cultures could one day have as powerful a voice with respect to issues affecting our planetary future as other non-European indigenous cultures seem to have now? I'm thinking specifically of future world summits on sustainable development here and more specifically future refinements to the Earth Charter.

I'm not sure, to be honest. I think it will depend on how successful European nature religions are at developing their nature-revering themes. It will also take hard work and political astuteness for folks representing such religions to develop relationships with the gatekeepers in these venues, and thus a place at the table. This is not easy, and moreover, many obstacles to collaborative inter-faith engagement remain (not the least of which is the historical antipathy between monotheistic traditions and religious traditions that are not). But, I think the effort is important, especially if the possibility of what I write in the book is to unfold, namely, a global civil Earth religion.

One of the many striking concepts in your work is that of the *bricolage:* as defined, "an amalgamation of bits and pieces of a wide array of ideas and practices, drawn from diverse cultural systems, religious traditions, and political ideologies."[5] In effect, I believe that this concept in and of itself offers a brilliant manner in which to methodoligize the more creative process of lateral thinking and making the necessary connections between certain elements that heretofore might not have been considered pertinent to a study of religious trends or religious studies as a whole. To wit, in the sections dealing with the "messy impulse to connect with nature," your pleasantly surprising description of rituals of inclusion in your Disney Park examples[6] very much reinforced the notion that religion can indeed be found, but more so, practiced anywhere. I think that many Heathens would very much be in agreement with such a notion of being able to cull expressions of religion or even religiosity, especially rituals of inclusion, from the wider experience of every day life. Can you provide our readers with a bit of background as to how you came to develop this idea of the bricolage; that is to say, what mostly inspired you to make that kind of meta-connection of utilising the bricolage to elucidate new religious currents in the field of religious studies?

---

5 Ibid., 14.
6 Ibid., 134.

I'm glad to hear you think the term opens up explanatory and political possibilities. I've done a lot of fieldwork within radical environmental subcultures and early on I was struck with the creative ways in which people drew on all sorts of things while constructing their understandings of the world and ways to relate to it. I expect that many of your readers, a certain age, for example, were moved by J.R.R. Tokien's *Lord of the Rings* novels, and no small number radical environmentalists identified with its characters and their efforts to thwart the destruction of their world. These works, written by a devout Christian, were being appropriated it for an entirely different purpose, including by those who understood themselves to be Pagan environmentalists. I wrote about these dynamics beginning in 1990, thinking about them as forms of syncretism, which was the commonly used expression at the time. But syncretism evokes in the mind the idea of blending two things and what I was seeing was far more eclectic, so when I first heard of the anthropologist Claude Levi-Strauss using the term bricolage, I appropriated it for my own analytic purposes. I do hear, quite often, that people find the notion good to think.

On a more substantive note with respect to the above example of rituals of inclusion as found in the Disney Park example. Do you feel that such rituals of inclusion are effective in bringing home the point that we, as humans, need to better recognize our animality? If you could act as a freelance adviser for a year at Disney, what are some other rituals of inclusion you would like to see developed by this corporation?

I do think that artistic productions to important cultural work, including rituals of inclusion—working against the typical attitude of human exceptionalism, which makes us think that we are somehow exempt from nature's laws—and by talking with people widely, from those who understand themselves to be involved in nature religion as well as those who do not but are avid environmentalists, that these sorts of cultural works are very evocative for some people, both spiritually and ethically. As you know, in the book I mention the television show Captain Planet, which was developed by cable television mogul Ted Turner. No small number of young people today trace at least some of their environmental awakening to that cartoon. As for what I would recommend to Disney, well, at least at the Wild Animal Kingdom they are doing a number of things very well. The environmental messages are consistent and strong, and I think most of us can recognize the value of some anthropomorphism in kindling felt empathy for other organisms. But, I think that if those working for Disney were more self-conscious about the relationship between spirituality and practice, they could develop ways of involving people more directly in the protection of non-human organisms and their habitats, some of whom they introduce at their theme parks and in their cinematic productions. Imagine if, after a child goes to the Pocahontas site at the Wild Animal Kingdom, instead of just being asked—"will you be a friend of the forest?"—they were given an opportunity to join Jane Goodall's "roots & shoots" program, or take home and plant a tree or shrub selected for being native to their own home, and designed to be easily planted in one's yard. There are all sorts of things that could be done if the vision for it did not run afoul of the overarching profit-maximization agenda that dominates corporations such as Disney. As I have written, Disney worlds are at war. By this I mean there's a struggle under the Disney umbrella between those who hope they can foster social and environmental progress through their artistic and entertaining works and the nationalistic and capitalistic impulses that arguably have been much stronger than Disney's nature-revering ones.

In the conclusion of your book, more specifically on page 213, you, in good company with Worster, Callicott and Cronon, indicate without hesitation or question that all signs point to a phenomenon that can be called Dark Green Religion. You further assert, however: "Like them, I will not predict how this phenomenon will spread. I would be surprised to see it break out like some new ecotopian contagion, however, in part because *I think there are countertrends that may prevent such a development*," [interviewer's italics]. Although countertrends can be gleaned from reading your work, one such being the unabating debate between Creationists and Darwinians, from the micro level in American schools to the macro in ironing out the final draft of the Earth Charter, could you list and describe some other countertrend levels that you have noticed thus far? How might we best be able to counter these?

Let me give you a flippant but perfectly serious answer: I think it's critical that we teach evolution. For if we do not, then we will never evolve in a healthy direction. To embellish: We need to teach an ecological and evolutionary worldview, because it compellingly demonstrates interdependence, and thus mutual dependence, as well as deep kinship, for all species share a common ancestor and are therefore, quite literally, related.

And until we understand ourselves as creatures who came to be who we are though evolution, which for us and at least some other creatures, is a process influenced by our social and cultural relations, we will not understand ourselves to be agents involved in a complex, long-term process of biocultural evolution. And until we understand ourselves in this way, it is unlikely that we will figure out how to participate creatively and humanely, in a way that values all life forms, in this beautiful (and sometimes tragic) process.

This means as well, of course, that people with such a worldview must stand up for it and challenge, amiably and with the strong available evidence, those who resist it.

As a final statement, in your personal coda, you make the following statement: "What I have been long looking for is a sensible religion, one that is rationally defensible as well as socially powerful enough to save us from our least-sensible selves. If there is a *sensible* post-Darwinian religion, then, there must be a *sensory* post-Darwinian religion. For this, dark green religion is a reasonable candidate." Again, from what you know of Heathenry, does it as well make for a reasonable candidate?

Well, I mean no disrespect to those who represent supernaturalistic forms of Paganism, but I think the naturalistic forms are the ones that will have the greatest long-term cultural traction, for they are based on ordinary, everyday senses (as enhanced sometimes by our clever gadgets) and they do not depend on experiences that not everyone has or will have. My hunch is that our species is at the beginning of a long transition toward such naturalistic, sensory, sensual and sensitive (as in empathic) spiritualities. Indeed, I think this is inevitable if we are ever to well adapt to and flourish within the environmental systems we belong to and depend on.

As a final and lighter question, has Mr. Dawkins read your book yet and if so, has he offered you a response?

To my knowledge, he has not, but I hope he will!

Polytheism in the Modern World:
A Conversation With John Michael Greer[1]

Please give us some general background on yourself.

I was born and raised in a very typical suburban American family, not so much atheist or irreligious as simply apathetic toward religious questions; my father's family were lapsed Presbyterians, my mother went through a Southern Baptist phase in her teens and then washed her hands of the whole subject. When the family went through a typical suburban messy divorce, my father remarried a Japanese woman who'd been raised Buddhist but didn't have a great deal of interest in religion either.

So, I grew up curious about religion but pretty much entirely outside of it. The Seventies revival of Christian fundamentalism that hit during my teen years didn't exactly do anything to interest me in the religious mainstream, as I was much more interested in experiencing spiritual realities for myself than in listening to somebody pounding a pulpit. So, I dabbled in Asian mysticism for a while, then took up the occult practices of the Hermetic Order of the Golden Dawn. I spent some twenty years working through the complete Golden Dawn system, mostly on my own, and then got involved in the modern Druid movement, as that tradition's focus on nature as a manifestation of divinity made, and makes, a great deal of sense to me. One thing led to another; in 2003 the elderly members of a mostly defunct Druid order, the Ancient Order of Druids in America (AODA), pretty much handed it to me, hoping I could brush the dust off it and do something with it, and that order and its teachings have been central to my work since then.

What was the impetus behind your conceiving and writing *A World Full of Gods*?[2]

One of the Druid organizations I sampled in the years before AODA monopolized most of my time was very forthright about being polytheist—not pantheist, not panentheist, not any of the other options, but polytheist as in believing in many real and separately existing gods and goddesses. I found that intriguing; of course I'd encountered polytheism before, all the way back to D'Aulaire's *Norse*

---

[1] This interview was conducted by Christopher A. Plaisance via email between September and October 2010.
[2] John Michael Greer, *A World Full of Gods: An Inquiry Into Polytheism*, (Tuscon, AZ: ADF Publishing, 2005).

Gods and Giants, which I read in childhood along with everyone else, but I'd never taken the time to look into it as a live option. So, I went to the local university library and started thumbing through books on philosophy of religion, expecting to find a detailed discussion—and I didn't.

It was quite embarrassing, really. Every book I found behaved as though monotheism and atheism were the only two options, with maybe a bit of room for pantheism in the middle, and brushed polytheism aside as an embarrassment without ever discussing it as an option. Even the staunchest atheists did so; it's as though they all agreed that there was no such thing as a god, but if there was, he had to be the Christian one. I had to go back to Proclus' *Elements of Theology* in the fourth century CE to find a discussion of polytheism that took it seriously. That intrigued me, and I started working out the logic of polytheism, using the intellectual tools developed by the mainstream philosophers of religion, but applying them to the concept of many gods who were powerful without being omnipotent, wise without being omniscient, and good without being omnibenevolent.

The original seed from which the book grew was the cat analogy in chapter six,[3]

---

3 The cat analogy puts forth a simply designed scenario to illustrate how the diversity of religious experience implies polytheism. Greer entreats us to "imagine a village with five houses, the inhabitants of which have singular beliefs about cats—or rather, in four of the five cases, about a single entity called Cat," (81-82). The story's gist is that there are five distinct cats, each of which exclusively visits a single house. When asked about their "belief in feline entities" the householders report their personal experiences of and opinions about the nature of Cat (82). The first explains that there is but one Cat, and that his description of Cat is the only correct one in the village. He explains that the other four householders are describing cats that simply do not exist and that offerings left out by them are "eaten by wandering hobos," (82). The second man similarly believes that there is one Cat, and that *his* Cat is the only Cat. He purports that neighbors' offerings are eaten by sewer rats and that one day "Cat will kill the rats," (83). The third householder once saw Cat sitting atop a fence dividing two houses, and hence believes that there is one Cat, but that Cat moves from house to house, eating offerings from all. The fourth neighbor has never seen a cat and ridicules all of his neighbors' beliefs in Cat. So far, Greer explains, all four homeowners are making the same mistake of extrapolating their individual experiences outward in a way that is *exclusive* and that the others' experiences must be judged differently than his (83). This is largely an analogy for how different monotheistic religions and atheists deal with question at hand. The first real point of difference that we see is in the fifth homeowner, who is a "polyfelist"—believing that each neighbor's differing descriptions point more to the existence of multiple cats rather than a single Cat. This is, of course, representative of the polytheistic position espoused by Greer which permits pluralistic inclusivity of differing experiences of the divine by means of polytheism. The fifth householder, as a polyfelist, is free from the exclusivity of her four

which I wrote up originally for an email discussion about polytheism, then began to expand and develop for what I originally thought was going to be an article for some Pagan publication. From there, like Topsy, it just grew; by the time I'd covered everything I felt needed to be covered, I had a book-length manuscript.

The cat analogy is, indeed, one of the most striking arguments in the book and does seem to do better justice to the issue of the disparity of religious experience than does the more commonly seen elephant analogy of the Hindus —which shows an unmistakable bias towards monotheism/monism.

It's not so much biased, as a specific argument via metaphor for a pluralism of perceptions of a monistic reality. Of course a metaphor proves nothing; it's simply a way to show how something *could* work—in this case, how widely differing perceptions can relate to a single thing. What, though, if the blind men were actually handling a rope, a pillar, a wall, and so on, not different parts of an elephant?

Why do you suppose that philosophers of religion, even when specifically analyzing the very diversity of theophanies,[4] have been so hesitant to follow Occam's Razor and conclude that a likely explanation for a plurality of experience is a plurality of phenomena? Even William James, a self proclaimed pluralist, seemed unable or unwilling to acknowledge this. What is your opinion?

In cultures where Christianity is the normative religious option, a monotheist understanding of religion is hardwired into the culture, and thus into the imaginations of nearly everyone raised in that culture. Even those who think they're breaking out of it simply reiterate the same thing under different guises, like the Goddess monotheists whose deity has been likened, and not inappropriately, to Jehovah in drag. It takes a real leap of imagination to think of gods who are different not merely in name, but in kind, from the one most of us were raised to worship.

Atheism and its various lightweight equivalents, such as agnosticism, involve no such leap of the imagination. The god that atheists disbelieve in is the standard single, omnipotent, omniscient, omnibenevolent deity of conventional monotheism; I'm reminded of the comment in William James' *Varieties of Religious Ex-*

---

neighbors and is able to "assess the other householders' reports using the same standards as she uses for her own, since there is no need for her to doubt anyone else's report in order to defend her own," (86-87).
4   Theophany, from the Greek *theophaneia* (θεοφάνεια), meaning "appearance or manifestation of a God."

perience about the atheist who "believes in No God and worships him daily." Thus, you get a very cozy relationship between Christians and atheists, like the one between Christians and Muslims, or Christians and Jews: in all cases, the disagreements are in matters of detail—existence vs. nonexistence is a question of detail—and reinforce the convictions of all sides that they're the ones in the right.

Throw open the field to polytheism, though, and all of a sudden you have to deal with questions that have been outside the field of discussion for centuries—and what looks like the difference between A and Z is revealed as the difference between F and G, with an entire alphabet of additional possibilities that nobody's been talking about. That process began in the Western world in the late 19th century, when Hinduism became a subject of popular interest, and people had to grapple with the fact that not every faith has a god of the standard Middle Eastern prophetic monotheist brand, and it's gradually ripening as the generations pass.

Going along with the discussion of theophanies and their place in polytheistic thought, we would like to ask you about the "unverified personal *gnōsis*" (UPG) concept that seems to be unique to Neopaganism. Why do you suppose that it has gained such a prominent position in the thought of so many Western polytheists? Do you see it as being a benefit or detriment to the development of philosophical and theological interpretations of polytheism?

Well, to begin with, it's anything but unique to Neopaganism. Every living religion is in a constant state of tension between the personal experiences of its visionaries and ordinary worshippers, on the one hand, and the traditional lore accumulated over the course of its history, on the other. The younger the religion, the greater the tension, because you have only a limited body of approved experience —possibly only that of the founder or founders—and the usual diversity among the experiences of the worshippers. The more mature the faith, the wider the accumulated body of experience, and the more likely there is to be some equivalent of even the weirdest personal revelation.

Now, of course, modern Neopaganism has been handed down from one high priestess to another since the dawn of time, but in this case, the dawn of time was right around 1947 for Wicca and the mid-70s for most of its offshoots. That doesn't give them a lot of time to build up a body of tradition to resolve the tension, so you get it at full intensity and polarization, with hardcore traditionalists on the one hand who basically say "Gerald Gardner plagiarized it, I believe it, that settles it," pitted against people for whom their own personal experience, no matter how whimsical or meretricious, is all that matters. Give them a couple of centuries—if they're still around in a couple of centuries—and they'll have worked it out.

I can say this with some confidence because some of the older traditions from which Wicca and its offshoots emerged have already gone through that. Druidry is one of those. The earliest Druid revivals that anybody's been able to document were in the middle decades of the 18th century—there are traditional claims about a 1717 founding date for one order, but the documentation hasn't surfaced—and it went through its period of epic weirdness in the late 18th and early 19th centuries. By the early 20th century there was a pretty well established set of traditions, practices, and lore in place. This gave 1970s-era Celtic Neopagans such as the late Isaac Bonewits something to rebel against, of course, which is one of the important roles that tradition plays in any religious movement; still, the old Druidry is still very much around, and it's fairly tolerant of its eccentric visionaries.

Contemporary Western polytheisms such as Heathenry, which have a substantial legacy of tradition from the past to draw on, can use that to jumpstart the relation between tradition and individual experience. The risk they run is a bit different; there's always the danger of assuming that the gods have to get permission from a historian before choosing how they will appear to a worshipper. That way lies death by fossilization. A healthy religious tradition values its visionaries, even though it usually has to ride hard on them as well.

The phrase "unverified personal *gnōsis*," by the way, is a massive misnomer. The Greek word *gnōsis* might best be translated "acquaintance," as, in fact, some of the better scholars of Gnosticism do translate it; it's not discursive knowledge, *epistēmē*, or opinion, *doxa*, but the kind of knowledge you have of a person with whom you've spent time. You might not know a single piece of true discursive knowledge about the woman with whom you had a passionate yearlong affair; she might have been in a witness protection program, say, and every detail she ever told you about herself was untrue; but at the end of that affair, you are very, very well acquainted with her.

That's *gnōsis*. The gnostic doesn't want to know facts, even true facts, about the spiritual world; he wants to know it very nearly in the Biblical sense, to be thoroughly acquainted with it, to have the kind of wordless, incommunicable, but unmistakable knowledge you have of a lover, or a family member, or Joe who you used to work with at the auto shop, and whose sister you dated for a while, and whose grandmother is a good friend of your grandmother, and so on. That kind of knowledge is by definition unverifiable, and personal, but it's very real. Of course, it doesn't convert into discursive knowledge except now and again by accident; the fact that you're well acquainted with Joe means that you can guess that his favorite football team lost the Super Bowl the moment you see him the next morning, but it doesn't mean that the yarns he tells about his exploits in the

Navy can be taken at face value.

That's just as true for the religious visionary; his or her experiences are true on their own terms, but not usually a valid source of factual knowledge. When somebody says, "I had a vision of Athena in the form of a great white owl," that's a useful data point; when the same person says, "Athena's owl has therefore always been a great white owl, and this means that the ancient Greeks must have traveled to Lappland to worship her," you've crossed the line from *gnōsis* to *doxa*, and also in this case from valid visionary experience to crackpot fantasy. Still, it's nearly as great a mistake to tell the visionary, "If you saw a great white owl, it can't have been Athena." Athena makes that choice, not you, and she might just decide that she looks good in white this time around.

You touch on a very interesting point (one seldom addressed in Heathenry) in making a distinction between *gnōsis*, *epistēmē* and *doxa* regarding religious knowledge. Do you have any thoughts on how the fundamentally incommunicable and noetic[5] nature of a hierophany relates to the sacred literature that forms the core of so many theologies?

Well, here again, it's important not to draw hard lines across a realm of experience that has few rigid boundaries of its own. Hierophany is a good word here, by the way; a lot of writers use theophany instead, presupposing that a god (*theos*) is always involved, when the range of human spiritual experience extends well beyond experiences of gods or goddesses, or even personalized beings. Countless Daoist mystics, for example, have had experiences of the Dao, which is a process rather than a being and is as impersonal as anything can get. Thus hierophany, an apparition (*phaneia*) of something sacred (*hieros*), is about the only word general enough to fill the bill.

Hierophanies are of many kinds, and the differences among them are not limited to their objects. The kind of knowledge communicated to the person who experiences them can also vary up and down the scale. There is always an element of *gnōsis*, of the incommunicable quality of recognition I talked about earlier, simply because the person who's experienced a hierophany is left with some sense of the flavor of the experience and the personality of the personalized being or beings involved, if there were any; there is also the distinctive sense of the *mysterium tremendum et fascinans*, to use Rudolf Otto's phrase, the fearful and fascinating mystery that's as near a definition of "sacred" as we're likely to get. Still, that may or may not be the core of the experience.

---

5   Noetic, from the Greek *nous* (νοῦς—"intellect"), meaning "of, or relating to, the intellect or mind."

Consider the example of a young Lakota man who goes up into the Black Hills in a sacred manner to find the guardian spirit who will shape his life. He fasts, makes offerings, and waits, and finally his vision quest is rewarded by a vision of a buffalo spirit, let's say, who gives him a sacred chant with healing powers. He returns home and, after appropriate practice and training, becomes a medicine person. What he experienced definitely has a component of *gnōsis*, and fairly crackles with the *mysterium tremendum et fascinans*, to the extent that fifty years later he can make the hair stand up on the back of your neck by talking about his experience; but he's also received *epistēmē* of a very specific kind. He knows a chant, and he knows that if he chants it in a sacred manner, in the appropriate context, it will heal.

The mystic pursues spiritual practice for the sake of *gnōsis*, of the noetic and incommunicable knowledge that opens human awareness to something greater, however conceptualized. Not all religious people are mystics, though, and despite the prejudices of mystics, there's no reason why they should be. There are also people who pursue spiritual practice for the sake of the one kind of *epistēmē* you can get reliably from religious experiences, which is a knowledge of how to work at the boundary between the unseen and the world of ordinary experience. In some cultures, this is what priests do for a living; in other cultures, those who do this for a living are persecuted by priests, and are called sorcerers or witches or what have you, but there are always people who do it, and there are always people who relate to the spiritual this way.

There are also people for whom the point of spiritual practice is the attainment of correct *doxa*. They want to know which actions are good and which are not, which stories about the unseen are true and which are false, and that's why they pray, or offer sacrifices, or what have you. They are almost universally condemned by mystics and mages alike as a pack of blockheads, but they are almost universally the vast majority of people in any society, and their quest is as valid as any other. A great many people who have religious experiences have this kind of religious experiences; they pray and fast or whatever, and then the Virgin Mary or Amitābha Buddha or Jibra'il or Djehuti or whoever they're invoking shows up and either affirms some existing doctrine or presents them with a new one.

If it's an existing doctrine, you get one form of classic conversion experience, and off your visionary goes to the church or the saṅgha or the mosque or the temple or whatever to be welcomed into the community of believers. If it's a new doctrine, you have the birth of a new religion, which will attract as many followers or as few as the personal gifts of its founder can inspire. Mystics don't generally start new religions, and neither do mages; it takes the less convoluted mind that simply wants to know the correct *doxa* that does that. One consequence is that many religions are actually founded by somebody other than the putative founder. In the case of Christianity, for example, Paul of Tarsus was the person who turned a set of inchoate folk beliefs about a minor Jewish prophet of the first century CE into a religion powerful enough to seize the imagination of most of the Classical world over the centuries that followed; in the case of Daoism, it was Zhang Daoling, centuries after Laozi's time, who transformed a philosophical school into a religion.

It's the quest for correct *doxa* that generally gives rise to sacred scriptures. Mystics tend to have a contemptuous attitude toward books, or at least toward any books that they don't write. Mages have the same attitude toward books, if they're the right kind of books, that a blacksmith has to hammers and tongs: they're tools, and they may be valuable tools, but that's all. It's when people want to know what to believe that the book that inspires them gets turned into sacred scripture and becomes a magnet for devotion.

Speaking of sacred texts, there is a seemingly universal trend for peoples to produce them *up to a point* in that people's development and to then crystallize this collection into an immutable canon, incapable of change or growth. Why do you suppose this occurs, and what are the ramifications of this type of process for a religion such as Heathenry, which is viewed by many of its adherents as a resurgent atavism?

Actually, the production of sacred scriptures goes on continuously throughout the life of any literate society—the equivalent process, the production of new oral traditions, is just as continuous in illiterate ones. Consider the reams of sacred scripture generated in America in the 19th and 20th centuries: *The Book of Mormon*, *Oahspe*, *The Secret Doctrine*, *The Urantia Book*, *Dianetics*, and the list goes on. What changes is the willingness of different factions and social groupings in a society to accept any given writing as sacred scripture, and that's always a complex, contested and fluid thing.

The capitalists in your readership will be pleased to know that what governs the acceptance of scriptures seems to be simple supply and demand. When most of the people in a given society want something from sacred scripture that the available supply doesn't provide them, new scriptures get manufactured until the need is filled. Once the need is filled, new products entering the market have to compete with the established brands for market share, and rarely do well until the tastes and needs of the scripture-consuming public shift far enough to open a new market niche. It may be a small niche, in which case you get a sect gathered around some new revelation; it may be a large niche, in which case you get a major religious movement that might someday be able to claw its way into the private dining room of the respectable "world religions."

The reemergence of the *Eddas* and sagas as sacred scripture in the contemporary world is a version of the same process. In the second half of the 20th century, a lot of people were in the market for things that the established religions didn't provide, and the old Germanic faiths did. The fact that Old Icelandic literature could be readily retooled into an elegant, colorful and very readable set of sacred scriptures was a major plus; nobody had to write a new set, and then come up with some other basis for claiming sacred status for them. Age and prophetic vision are the two standard justifications for classifying a book as scripture; if it's a new book, you're pretty much stuck claiming to be a divinely inspired prophet, but if it's an old book, you can claim that it's ancient wisdom from some more interesting time and let it go at that. Gerald Gardner is far from the only example of somebody who tried to get out of the burdensome requirements of the prophet's role by claiming an antiquity for his inventions that they didn't have, but that's a risky move; you always run the risk that somebody will prove that you made it up, and then where are you?

So long as Old Icelandic literature functions as Heathen scripture, then, it's probably safe to assume that its canonical role is unlikely to be usurped by any new prophetic effusion. That's part of the balance between tradition and individual vision I mentioned earlier on in this interview. In the spiritual smorgasbord of the contemporary world, anyone who feels unsatisfied with the Eddas and sagas as scripture is unlikely to express that dissatisfaction with the kind of intense spiritual quest that gives rise to an alternative *doxa*, literally a heterodoxy in opposition to the orthodoxy ("correct *doxa*") of the established tradition; such people will simply go off and try something else, just as the people who came to Heathenry generally got there as a result of personal choice based on dissatisfaction with other religious options.

It's a normal part of any religion that sets its scripture apart from other writings on account of age to see itself as a resurgent atavism; fundamentalist Christianity, for example, which was invented out of whole cloth in the late 19th century by chucking most of historic Christianity into the dumpster and redefining the remnant in radically modern terms, constantly tries to define itself as "that old time religion." Heathenry is a modern religion; its actual "hearth culture," if I may use a term I personally dislike, is 21st century Euro-American industrial society. Still, the charisma of an older time and culture is an important part in many other religions as well, and Heathenry is well within its rights to cultivate that charisma and use it as a source of inspiration.

Changing gears a bit, in Chapter 7 of *A World Full of Gods*, you touch on the problem of the *interpretatio graeca*, using Thunder Gods as an example. Admittedly, this is a theological point about which opinions differ vastly even within specific polytheistic religions; however, I would like to probe a bit deeper to see if there are not some ideas that prove themselves to be utile. Would such a semantic unification—identifying the theonyms of the Thunder Gods of various pantheons as referring back to the same deity—be confined to those Gods who genealogically spring from a common source (such as the Norse Þórr and Slavic Perun do from the Proto-Indo-European *perk^{w}unos) or also apply to morphologically similar Gods (such as the Celtic Taranis and Chinese Lei Gong)?

I'm going to start by taking issue with the word "genealogically" in your question, because the descent of Thorr and Perun from *perk^{w}unos is a matter of linguistics, not genealogy. Thorr is the son of Odin, last I checked, not the son or grandson of *perk^{w}unos. This isn't simply a quibble; perhaps the most pervasive mistake in contemporary Reconstructionist religions in the west is the habit of confusing the origins and history of the gods with the origins and history of the words we use to name the gods.

These are emphatically not the same. If they were the same, then gods would be mere words, human constructs, and we would be wasting our time worshipping them. On the other hand, if the gods exist as primary realities, as every religion teaches, they have a history of their own, which is separate from the history of the names, beliefs, and symbolism that human beings assign to them.

Mythology is a human attempt to communicate what little we know or believe we know about the histories of the gods—where they came from, how they relate to other gods, what their deeds are and what their destiny will be. Comparative linguistics and comparative religion are human attempts to communicate what little we know or believe we know about the history of the way people have talked about their gods, the names and symbols they have assigned them and the stories they have told about them. Both are interesting, but again, they are not the same thing.

So, the question you're asking is whether we should use speculative reconstructions of the historical relationships among names used for gods in human languages to determine whether the gods in question should be equated or not. My answer is no, for two reasons.

The first is that we know for a fact that gods can and do cross linguistic boundaries with perfect ease. For one example out of many, consider the Japanese god Bishamon-ten. He's one of the seven gods of good fortune in Japanese folk religion, but he's originally a Hindu deity, a son of Kubera, who was adopted into Mahayana Buddhism and whose worship spread all over East Asia. Vaiśravaṇa, Bishamon-ten, Duo Wen Tian, Thao Kuwen, and Bayan Namsrai are his names in, respectively, Sanskrit, Japanese, Mandarin Chinese, Thai, and Mongolian. According to current linguistic theory, Sanskrit's an Indo-European language, Mandarin is Sino-Tibetan, Thai belongs to the Tai-Kadai family and Japanese and Mongolian might just possibly both be part of an Altaic superfamily, but everyone in the countries in question who's familiar with the god in question will tell you that of course he's the same god—even though his symbolism varies, sometimes drastically, from place to place.

The second is that I'm convinced that comparative linguistics is overdue for drastic change. We could get into a long discussion of the reasons for that, which would probably not be relevant here. The short version is that the genealogical approach used in comparative linguistics was modeled on the method of constructing evolutionary trees that was standard in 19th and early 20th century biology, and this has long since been superseded by cladistics[6]—a far more rigorous method that has produced results sharply different from the old methods of tracing family trees among species. My sense is that we're within a generation of seeing cladistics applied to the history of languages, and when that happens, quite a bit of the conventional wisdom is likely to go out the window. I personally have my doubts that the concept of a Proto-Indo-European language will survive the process; I've long suspected that this is simply an artifact of the way scholars approach languages—assume that similarities are all original and differences are all later accretions, and you've guaranteed that you'll come up with a phantom protolanguage composed solely of the similarities—but we'll see.

The trend seems to be that reconstructionist religions like Heathenry or Romuva, if they accept this proposition at all, are inclined towards the former, while more eclectic paganisms like Wicca tend towards the latter. Why do you suppose this is the case?

It's a complex issue, and in the last analysis it may just be a matter of subcultural style. Reconstructionist religions tend to have a large percentage of members who pride themselves on their scholarship, or who respect those who do; they take their scholarship mostly from the academic mainstream, where comparative

---

6 Cladistics being a taxonomical methodology which groups members by means of lineal descent as opposed to structural similarities.

linguistics still plays a very important role in the study of history of religions, and so they tend to bring a lot of linguistics to bear on their religions.

Wicca and other less tradition-based religions are much less interested in the academic mainstream; when they interest themselves in scholarship at all, it tends to be toward the fringes of academe if not right over the edge into the realm of rejected knowledge, and in all these fields morphology trumps linguistics. Margaret Murray's fringe history played a central part in launching Wicca, just as Marija Gimbutas' equally idiosyncratic rehash of late 19th century matriarchal-prehistory theories did for the pop-feminist Wicca of the Eighties and Nineties; Robert Graves' much-misunderstood *The White Goddess* helped inspire most of contemporary Paganism, including those groups that most angrily denounce it; Jungian psychology is another major influence that tends to stress morphological similarities rather than linguistic barriers, and then there's also the huge though usually unadmitted influence of late 19th and early 20th century occultism. I've heard Dion Fortune's line "All the gods are one god, all the goddesses are one goddess, and there is one initiator" repeated any number of times by people who have no idea who Dion Fortune was.

My take, in other words, is that the division you've drawn between Reconstructionists using linguistic models and Neopagans using morphological models has nothing in particular to do with the relative merits of the models, and everything to do with the intellectual presuppositions of the two subcultures we're discussing. I'd also suggest that the entire point is moot in all but the most abstract sense, because in actual worship, if you're going to invoke Perun, you invoke Perun—not Perun plus Perkunas plus Thorr, whether or not you want to add Taranis and Shango and St. Michael the Archangel to the mix, but Perun pure and simple.

In surviving polytheisms, and in those extinct ones well enough recorded to judge, that was the rule. Go to a Shinto shrine in Japan and you'll find that it doesn't matter one iota whether or not the Inari (the rice god) of that shrine is the same as the Inari of the shrine twenty miles down the road; this Inari is to be worshiped in a specific way, with his own distinctive titles and offerings, and that's what matters. You go to the next shrine and you worship that Inari in a different way. Classical Mediterranean Paganism was exactly the same; read Pausanius, and you're constantly coming across little shrines with their own unique traditions. This is why Greek and Roman intellectuals ended up postulating, for example, that there were five different gods named Pan, with five different sets of parents.

Syncretism is purely a habit of intellectuals, and it's usually a prologue to monotheism. That was the case in ancient Egypt, where attempts to flatten out the glorious confusion of Egyptian religion into a syncretism that would turn all the deities into manifestations of a solar monotheism had its disastrous outcome in the reign of Akhenaten. It's a sign that people are starting to put their theories ahead of the facts of religious experience. If the gods are what religions claim they are, we can no more understand their nature than a flea in Mozart's wig could have understood his music; all we know is that hierophanies happen and that they are very diverse, and so any attempt to claim a single presence behind any large fraction of the total needs to be recognized as unwarranted speculation.

Regarding the last statement about unwarranted speculation, would you say then that it is perhaps more important to adjust our philosophical models to fit the data concerning hierophanies than to alter our interpretations of hierophanies to suit our philosophical models? In other words, to avoid confirmation bias?

It's not just a matter of confirmation bias. Hierophanies provide us with all the data we have concerning gods. Philosophical models are theories built up on the basis of data. When your data conflicts with your theories, you throw out the theories, not the data; that's a fundamental rule of intellectual honesty.

This view *seems* to favor the empiricist side of the epistemological divide between the British empiricists and Continental rationalists of the Enlightenment. Is hierophany the *only* route to an ontophany of the holy, or can fundamental ontological principles be gleaned from other modes of inquiry and applied to theological domains?

It does indeed favor the empiricist side. It's not accidental that the attempts by Descartes and his followers to create a science of nature on the basis of abstract first principles went nowhere, while the efforts of British empirical scientists gave us the scientific method—the first really major advance in intellectual inquiry since the birth of Greek logic—and the extraordinary discoveries that resulted from it, including those that enable us to have this conversation at a distance.

It's always possible to glean insights from other fields, philosophical or otherwise, and apply them to theology—or for that matter any other field of knowledge. Those insights, however, must always be put to the test of experience to determine their validity. The human mind has a remarkable talent for plausible nonsense, and so its creations—however appealing or apparently convincing—need to be checked against some standard of judgment that's resistant to its appeals.

In theology, any theology, the one standard of this kind that seems to work is a living tradition in constant dialogue with personal experiences of the holy. Since tradition itself is ultimately grounded in the sum total of hierophanies within a given religious community, and adapts itself over time to changes in the objects of religious experience as witnessed by members of that community, it provides the touchstone that determines which concepts are appropriate to it and which are not.

Do you think that the emphasis we see with so many Pagans and Heathens on experience over dogma is relational to the lack of emphasis on the former in the mainstream religions from which many of us came? Has their authoritarianism spurned a rebellion resulting in a kind of religious autodidacticism?

I think it's more complex than that. Authoritarianism is a trait of some sects within the Western religious mainstream, but by no means all, and there are plenty of Christian sects in particular—the wilder end of Pentecostalism comes to mind in particular -- where religious experience is just as central a theme as it is in contemporary Paganism and Heathenry. In fact, there's a huge and almost entirely unrecognized overlap between today's Paganism and much of today's Christianity; they share the same quarrels between personal revelation and tradition, the same centrifugal organizational tendencies, the same habit of conflating the religious and the political spheres and even the centrality of direct relationship between worshipper and deity—what is all the talk about "a personal relationship with Christ," after all, but a discussion of having Jesus as one's patron deity?

As I see it, the rebellious side of contemporary Paganism and Heathenry has two main sources, one creditable, the other a good deal less so. The more positive side is simply that Christianity's experiential dimension, like its doctrinal tradition, appeals nowadays to a very narrow range of human experience. That wasn't always the case; the Christianity of the Middle Ages and Renaissance was a robust, deeply human faith that found a place for a much broader range of human experiences and activities than it does today; but since the Reformation and Counterreformation, Western Christianity has shed its magical dimensions, its rich agricultural and biological side, its warrior tradition—almost everything outside of a very pinched and bloodless notion of moral virtue, a stark terror of sexual passion and an attempt to fix the psyche in a narrow range of pleasantly bland emotional states. The medieval Christian who could swear by God's own bowels, and find nothing inappropriate in the utterance, had a faith that reached right down to the fundamentals of human experience; modern Western Christianity has abandoned that, and so a growing number of people in the contemporary

West have turned away from Christianity in favor of other religions that have room for all of life.

The less creditable side is the contemporary fashion for rebellious posturing and a fake originality that amounts to mapping unexamined assumptions out of popular culture onto any subject you care to name. Real originality requires a thorough knowledge of tradition; you can't even rebel against something effectively unless you thoroughly and deeply understand what it is you're rejecting. Those who ignore tradition, to riff off Santayana's dictum, are condemned to rehash whatever notions the chattering classes of their own time happen to consider new and exciting. It's for this reason, for example, that avant-garde art movements for the last hundred years have kept on reinventing such idiocies as public masturbation as performance art, thinking each time that the idea was completely new, and that each generation of would-be innovators in the ceremonial magic scene have simply watered down the legacy of the last generation: Crowley watered down the Golden Dawn, Austin Osman Spare watered down Crowley, the "chaos magicians" (variously spelled) of the late 20th century watered down Spare, and the current wave of avant-garde occultists are busily trying to water down chaos magic, though it's got to be a struggle at this point.

Today's pop Paganism is riddled with the same sort of thinking. The Wicca of Gerald Gardner and Alex Sanders, whatever else you happen to think of it, posed a robust challenge to the popular thinking of its time and ours. That was its strength but also its vulnerability, because as soon as it caught the public eye, people like Starhawk and Scott Cunningham started coming up with new versions that had all the problematically challenging bits neatly filed off. These days, as often as not, if you meet somebody at a Pagan event, that person's ideas about the nature of existence and the religious dimension of human life are as similar as, if not identical to, those of your most nonreligious neighbors. The flirtation with atheism that has caught on recently in the Neopagan scene is simply the next natural step in the process that will return many of today's self-proclaimed Pagans to the same irreligious attitudes most of their parents have.

That's certainly their right, and it's a normal process in human societies, but it can cause a great deal of confusion when people insist that ideas they lifted from online games, say, are maps of spiritual reality just as valid as those that are either defined by direct personal religious experience, on the one hand, or handed down from the great religious visionaries of the past, on the other. In a very specific sense of validity, the people who make this claim are absolutely right, since by validity they mean "valid as an antinomian pose" or something not too far from that. In most other senses, though, they're smoking their shorts.

On the topic of occultism, what do you make of the extensiveness with which it permeates every level of Heathen and Pagan writing? Nearly all religions have both esoteric and exoteric dimensions, but there seems a distinct tendency within Heathenry to intermingle the two to such a degree that even supposedly introductory works contain material on the runes and *seiðr*. Why do you suppose this is the case, and is it to our detriment or benefit?

From my perspective, this question conflates three very distinct phenomena—magic, occultism, and esotericism. It so happens that in late 19th and early 20th century Western culture, those three things tended to run together much more often than not, but they're not at all the same thing.

Let's start with magic. Every human culture contains methods for shaping experienced reality using methods that our contemporary Western science insists can't possibly work—specifically, methods involving the use of symbol, ritual, and alternate states of consciousness to shape the nonphysical patterns on which, by the central hypothesis of magic, all the phenomena of human experience are modeled. Some cultures treat these methods as ordinary parts of life; some reserve them to professionals, who may or may not be part of a given culture's religious institutions; some reject and denounce them, consigning them to the same sort of cultural underground as, say, prostitution and drug dealing in most Western societies. Contemporary industrial culture belongs to this latter group. One consequence of the relegation of magic to the fringes of modern culture is precisely that fringe religions tend to adopt it enthusiastically; it gives them an additional marketing boost.

The word "occultism" was introduced to the English language by H.P. Blavatsky. It refers properly to those religious movements that claim that a secret ("occult") doctrine is concealed behind all other religious teachings, and identify this secret doctrine with their own teachings. Occultism in this sense is very common in cosmopolitan, literate societies—late classical Pagan Neoplatonism, which claimed to offer the "secret doctrine" behind the whole range of Greek, Egyptian, and eastern Mediterranean Pagan faiths, compares very precisely to the occultism of Blavatsky's Theosophy and its rivals.

Esotericism is something else again. Occultists constantly confuse it with occultism, because it shares the sense of a hidden dimension underlying publicly available teachings, but the esoteric sense of a doctrine is not a separate doctrine that can be extracted from exoteric teachings by some sort of special interpretation. The esoteric sense of a spiritual tradition is *gnōsis* in the sense I mentioned earlier in this interview—that is, recognition, the personal and wordless dimension of knowledge that cannot be reduced to formulae or communicated to anyone who hasn't experienced it for themselves.

It's not completely inappropriate that these three things have been tangled together in the alternative spiritual scene for the last century and a quarter or so. Some of the practices included in the craft of magic can be used to help foster the personal encounter with spiritual realities that defines esotericism; some of the ideas that make sense to people who have had those personal encounters differ widely enough from the conventional wisdom that a separate teaching tends to evolve in groups committed to an esoteric approach to spirituality; and of course many varieties of occultism include instruction in the operative techniques of magic. Still, it's quite possible to do any one of these three things and neither of the others, or to do any two and ignore the third.

I'm not too familiar with contemporary Heathenry, but the broader Pagan scene is rife with magic, occultism and esotericism precisely because the mainstream religions of our time have closed themselves so completely against all three. The rich traditions of Christian magic have been rejected by almost all contemporary denominations; efforts to reinterpret Christian theology and teaching to make them less absurdly literalist have run into a rising tide of hostility; and even the sense of an inner dimension to Christianity has been watered down into talk about "a personal relationship with Jesus" that somehow boils down to a guy in a pulpit telling you who to vote for in the next election. People who are naturally dissatisfied with the barren ideology that results from this sort of thinking turn to today's Pagan and Heathen faiths precisely because the latter can offer them something with more depth and richness, including magical practices, teachings on several levels, and an abiding respect for personal experience.

That being the case, it would be a disaster for the Pagan and Heathen revivals if these things were to be jettisoned in a misguided attempt to claim respectability from a culture that won't grant it anyway. The attempt being made by some people nowadays to turn today's Pagan and Heathen faiths into a slightly more colorful equivalent of the current liberal Christian denominations, complete with salaried clergy and an ample population of esbat-go-to-circle Pagans, was probably inevitable, but this doesn't make it any less unhelpful.

The quest for respectability that you touch on is one that seems a common point with nearly all Heathen and Pagan organizations large enough to be noticed by their surrounding societies at large. With the recent official recognition of Druidry as a religion by the United Kingdom still being fresh in our readers' minds, what do you make of this and similar events in terms of our still developing ecclesiological foundations?

The media has spectacularly distorted the British government decision regarding The Druid Network (TDN). What happened was simply that TDN received the equivalent of nonprofit tax-exempt status, a status that several other Druid organizations have had in Britain for some time. Now, of course, it's relevant that this is happening, but it's not the dramatic event the media has imagined it to be.

It's worth noting, mind you, that The Druid Network received their public charity status by the simple process of going through the usual channels, submitting a solid application to the proper authorities, and behaving in a professional and sensible manner. What they have done, quite simply, is to concentrate on earning respect rather than gaining respectability. That's how new religious movements that succeed generally go about it. The alternative approaches—either aping some other tradition that is perceived to be respectable, on the one hand, or insisting on respect that one has done nothing to earn, on the other—are among the ways that new religious traditions fail.

You mentioned earlier the turn towards a kind of pseudo-atheism within many circles; is this an inevitability, or do you see us finding philosophical depth and clarity while maintaining a strong sense of true polytheism?

Oh, it's not pseudo-atheism that concerns me, but the full-blown variety, which has become increasingly popular in the current Neopagan scene. I think it's inevitable that as "pop paganism" wanes, a great many people whose involvement in Neopaganism was essentially an attempt to be avant-garde and vaguely shocking, rather than a response to genuine religious feelings, will drift out of Paganism and into ordinary unbelief. Still, there's no reason for those people whose commitment to polytheist faiths is based on something more solid to follow that same trajectory.

In closing, what do you think the next few decades have in store for our development? What are your ideal hopes, your worst fears and your realistic prognosis for us?

Well, the hopes, the fears, and the best guesses all start with the recognition that the age of pop Neopaganism is drawing to a close, as the age of pop Theosophy, pop Spiritualism, and so on did in their time. That's going to pose some serious challenges to the whole range of Pagan, Heathen, and Druid groups, among others, but it's also going to offer some important opportunities.

The challenges center on the likelihood that many of the social institutions evolved by the current Pagan counterculture will probably fizzle out in the decades immediately ahead. Pagan festivals, publishers, bookstores, and the like have provided a support system that, despite more than occasional grumbling about Wicca-centric attitudes, a wide range of contemporary alternative spiritualities have used freely. As those go away, those traditions that depend on them for publicity, recruitment, and the like will be facing real problems. On a broader scale, groups and traditions that have built their identity around "we're not pop Wicca"—and there are quite a few that have, some less overtly than others—may find that their appeal wanes when pop Wicca isn't a significant presence any more.

The opportunities unfold in turn from the capacity for today's polytheist faiths to redefine themselves on their own terms, rather than being treated as varieties of modern popular Neopaganism. Heathenry has already made important steps in that direction; some of the Druid orders are trying to do the same thing; but there's a long road ahead for both those movements, and others, as the Neopagan wave recedes.

There are ample opportunities to screw that process up on the grand scale. I think of the way that so many Spiritualist groups ignored the prevalence of overt fraud on the part of mediums until Spiritualism became a laughing stock to the rest of society, or the way that the Theosophical Society gambled everything in the 1920s on creating a mass cult around Jiddu Krishnamurti as the next world messiah, and crashed and burned when Krishnamurti had the integrity to disown the role. I don't think we're likely to see either of those specific outcomes, but the Neopagan scene could quite easily wreck itself in some equally colorful way. If things start spinning toward some such outcome, those traditions that survive will be the ones that distance themselves from Neopaganism as forcefully as possible before things get ugly.

It's equally possible that very large sectors of the Neopagan movement will pursue the chimera of respectability by the mistaken path of discarding everything in contemporary Paganism that differs from the Methodists or the Unitarians, and will find out too late that they've simply turned into Methodists or Unitarians. When I watch people launching Pagan seminaries that don't differ in any significant way from liberal Protestant seminaries, or unthinkingly accept a model of priesthood that has been borrowed point for point from liberal Protestant notions of the ministry, I have to shake my head; it does not seem to have occurred to these people that if most Pagans wanted this sort of thing, they'd have become liberal Protestants. Given that the liberal Protestant denominations are losing members so relentlessly that most of them will be extinct in fifty years, this may not be the best strategy!

I think it's also very possible, though, that some of the movements now lumped in with Neopaganism may be able to establish themselves as distinct and broadly accepted religious options within the broader society. I don't think it's at all a stretch, for example, to imagine a future where most people in the western world know what it means when somebody wears the Thor's Hammer symbol around their neck, and a Heathen who works in a hospital, let's say, would be approached by management and asked to cover Christmas and Easter in exchange for getting time off on Heathen holy days, much the way Jews today swap shifts with their Christian co-workers. I don't think it's any more of a stretch to look toward a future where most towns of any size have some Heathen presence, very often with at least a storefront space (like the storefront churches common among the smaller Christian denominations), a lively calendar of activities and some degree of participation in the wider public sphere. Instead of pursuing respectability, they'll have earned respect, and this will give them the freedom to maintain their own traditions and build their own communities and institutions.

Uses of Wodan: The Development of his Cult and of Medieval Literary Responses to It[1]
PhD Dissertation
University of Leeds, 2002
By Philip Andrew Shaw
275 pages

Reviewed by Henry Lauer

Uses of Wodan: The Development of his Cult and of Medieval Literary Responses to It[2] is an object lesson in the advantages and limitations of radically skeptical research into historical Heathenry. It assaults many of the claims that historians have made about the significance, nature and role of Wodan, offering a stern and valuable reality check to we of the neo-Heathenish persuasion in the process.

However, the thesis also betrays some of the flaws inherent in the reductionist current that coils through parts of contemporary academia; in particular that reductionism is just as vulnerable to sloppy analysis and cavalier claims as any other approach. In both its strengths and weaknesses, *Uses of Wodan* evokes themes that are relevant to any attempt to raise the level of sophistication in neo-Heathen thought.

As a general caveat, this discussion of *Uses of Wodan* necessarily cherry-picks certain motifs and ignores others—it would be far too exhaustive an undertaking to summarize every argument presented in the text. Although I will roughly summarize what seem to be *Uses of Wodan*'s most significant arguments and conclusions, I do not believe that my quick sketches can substitute for reading the original document. From my account, some of Shaw's views may seem less or more sound than is the case; his attack is too nuanced to be fully rendered in a concise discussion.

Shaw basically argues that our view of Wodan—and archaic Heathenry more generally—is heavily biased by the agendas and literary conventions of the Christian authors from whom we draw most of our information. This, of course, is not a novel position, but he nonetheless injects this venerable stance with a good deal of fresh life. Let us begin the grand tour.

---

1 The thesis is available in its entirety at:
   http://etheses.whiterose.ac.uk/393/1/uk_bl_ethos_270854.pdf
2 I do wish someone had told Dr. Shaw about the time-honored rule that a sentence should never be written such that it has a preposition at the end of it.

First of all, Shaw considers the history of mythological and archaeological scholarship back to Saxo Grammaticus in the 8th century. His conclusion of this review is that a number of wild and unsupportable claims about Wodan have become self-evident articles of the academic tradition's faith.

For example, Shaw disputes common interpretations of the symbolism on Germanic bracteates. Bracteates were medallions made by Germanic craft workers which normally featured a head/profile or figure on one side and various images, such as beasts or monsters, on the other. For centuries scholars have interpreted bracteate profiles as images of Wodan. Shaw asks the simple question: on what basis? His review of the literature reveals that there is absolutely no primary evidence linking bracteates to Wodan.

He does note, however, that for reasons of convenience, scholars began to refer to certain such medallions as 'Wodan medallions.' This was not because of any evidence that they depict Wodan, but merely to provide a pithy, if arbitrary, handle. Over time it seems this usage continued in academic circles until it gained a high gloss of familiarity…and the idea that these medallions attest to a wide-ranging Wodanic cult from early times became rumored into legitimacy.

But Shaw—and he is not the first to make this point—notes that the designs of the bracteates owe a tremendous amount to the Roman bracteate tradition, which predates that of the Germanic tribes. Even a cursory examination of Roman bracteates suggests that the Germanic forms are very close imitations. The Roman bracteates also feature heads and profiles—mostly of important leaders, but *not* of gods. Given the Roman connection, Shaw concludes that not only is there no evidence *for* interpreting Germanic bracteates as Wodanic representations, but that plausible competing explanations offer themselves readily (I will return to this theme, however, because there is is counter-evidence to Shaw's argument).

And, thus, he proceeds, dismantling much of the supposed archaeological evidence for a Pan-Germanic Wodanic cult. It is galling but compelling reading for anyone who has ever made wild claims about the significance of Wodan (myself included).

If archaeology fails to establish the supposed breadth of Wodan's veneration, what about the claims made by non-Heathen sources (mostly Christian) about the importance of Wodan as a pan-Germanic deity? Shaw has many points to make on this theme.

Firstly, he addresses the Roman equation of Mercury with Wodan. He argues that Roman mentions of a Germanic god called 'Mercury' as Wodan are inconsistent in usage, and that Mercury as a Roman deity does not seem to match well with the blood-soaked war god that Wodan seems to (at least partly) comprise.[3] Personally, I think he verges into abject pedantry as he explores this thread, but the general point seems fair.

Secondly, Shaw notes that among Christian scholars such as Saxo Grammaticus and Paul the Deacon, it was customary to talk of 'Jupiter and Mercury' as the stock pan-Pagan deities, regardless of the specific nature of the Pagan or Heathen cultures involved. Hence, he argues that when these authors present Wodan as a pan-Germanic god of high importance—and in combination with the paucity of solid archaeological evidence that Shaw's analysis proposes—we cannot rely on their claims at all.

This does not mean Wodan *was not* an important pan-Germanic deity; but it does suggest that Christian authors' claims to that effect may relate more to their own literary conventions than to any actual historical knowledge or intellectual conscience that they may have possessed. For Shaw's purpose, the mission is accomplished, however: another major source of information on Wodan has been, it seems, invalidated.

Of course, it does not beggar the imagination to suppose that related Indo-European religions generally prized 'Jupiter and Mercury' in cognate form, and that Wodan was indeed meant by one of the two—and therefore that this possibly lazy Christian identification nevertheless lies rooted in fact. Despite my reservations about his Tripartite Theory, Georges Dumézil's cross-cultural mythological research does rather endorse such a possibility.

It is not unreasonable to suggest that Christian authors could afford to be vague about the principal gods of Indo-European Heathen and Pagan cultures precisely because the parallels and similarities *were* so pervasive (Dumézil raises his hand again here). We rarely spell out what seems obvious; consequently our descendants can find our records and writings confounding, to say the least. Shaw's keenness to discredit these sources seems incautiously hasty, even if we can agree with him that skepticism is required, and yet often not employed, when handling such material.

---

3   Of course, Mercury does seem much more similar (if still imperfectly so) to the Norse Odin. As we will see, Shaw attempts to argue that Odin and Wodan are not the same person. Yet Odin might represent a bridge between the character of Mercury and that of Wodan (albeit an arguably anachronistic one). In any case, Shaw's attempt to separate Wodan and Odin does not appear to be as compelling as he would like to think.

In that vein it is worth considering, of course, that the need for interpretive caution is widely grasped among researchers investigating contradictory and confusing sources such as Saxo. Shaw is *not* entitled to present himself as taking a novel stance in his skepticism, even if he has adopted a new extreme by attempting to discredit Christian accounts of Heathen belief virtually *a priori.*

Shaw's analysis concludes that Wodan's significance was probably limited to veneration among the Lombards and the Alamanni. He argues this to be a major reduction in the scope that can be attributed to Wodan's worship, and that Wodan perhaps was more of a localized tribal deity and not the pan-Germanic figure that scholarship has generally portrayed. Of course, it is worth recalling that the Alamanni were a large tribal confederacy rather than an insular kin group, and that the religious mode of such a group could easily have had widespread resonance across Germanic Heathenry.

To summarize thus far, Shaw's archaeological and textual analyses argue several main points: that the archaeological evidence for Wodan is grossly overstated; that the internal conventions of Christian writings about Heathenry discredit their value as a source for understanding Heathen myth; and that Wodan's worship was too localized to substantiate the traditional claims of his pan-Germanic appeal.

At this point, Shaw goes on to argue a very controversial claim: that there is no reason to identify the god *Wodan* with the god *Odin*. His argument has three main thrusts.

First, he claims that there is no way to derive the names Wodan and Odin from the same etymological root! Unfortunately, Shaw misapplies Verner's Law to make this claim, and consequentially his argument fails miserably. [4]

---

4 I am infinitely indebted to Antonius Block for his analysis of Shaw's etymological arguments. Block comments that "[i]t is correct, as Shaw states, that in Old English 'þ' and 'ð' were interchangeable. However the same cannot be said for Proto-Germanic. The Proto-Germanic 'ð' is a development from Indo-European 'dh'. If you look at the chain of sound shifts incurred by both Grimm's and Verner's Laws you'll notice that Indo-European 'd' became 't' in Proto-Germanic, so 'ð' was the "only" form of 'd' in the proto language. At the beginnings of words and after 'n' the 'ð' "hardened" to 'd' (which Shaw also points out). It is true that Verner's Law created a voiced 'þ' becoming 'ð' in specific cases, but the reverse is not true. By Shaw's logic, the Old English word *fæder* 'father' couldn't possibly be related to Proto-Germanic *faðer because, as he states with Woden/Woðen, we should have had an OE **fæðer, not the attested *fæder*. Old English 'ð' arises in most cases from the voicing of 'þ' between vowels, not from a Proto-Germanic 'ð' which as I pointed out had already become 'd.'" This

Uses of Wodan

Second, Shaw notes that there is no Heathen source which explicitly equates Wodan and Odin—we only have Christian sources with their own complex biases, assumptions and conventions (some of which I have touched on above).

Third, he considers the various Christian sources indicating the descent of Anglo-Saxon kings from Woden. He notes that across Europe it was not unusual for Christian kings to claim ancestry from euhemerized Heathen gods, and, indeed, that this was a subtle tactic employed to bolster standing in the post-Heathen political landscape.

Shaw believes that the phenomenon of Christian kings claiming a euhemerized Woden as ancestor says a lot more about Christian politics than it does about Heathen belief. Indeed, having excluded this evidence of Anglo-Saxon Woden worship, he goes on to question the significance and presence of Woden in actual Anglo-Saxon Heathenry at all!

Naturally, he does not pause to consider *why* continuity with a Pagan past might have been significant across Christendom (other than to propose that among the Anglo-Saxons a Wodenic forebear might have implied a prestigious Scandinavian origin for one's lineage, were one laboring under the "myth" of Woden and Odin being the same). Of course, the fact that the Sutton Hoo helmet seems to include a depiction of a one-eyed war God (and how many of them can there be?) in its designs seems something of a problem for Shaw (but not, sadly, one that he addresses).[5]

Subversive stuff. As a more or less reconstructed path, neo-Heathenry is vulnerable to having the rug pulled out from all kinds of cherished notions as research into the past carries on its merry way. It is important for us to resist knee-jerk rejection of uncomfortable new claims, however, just as it is important for us to not accept them without critically reflecting on their soundness (even when they employ what amounts to obscurantism to ram home radical claims). *Uses of Wodan* certainly seems to demonstrate that the newest is not always the most rigorous, and science is unfortunately vulnerable to fashions and fads, particularly in fields like archaeology or ancient history where evidence is sparse and ambiguous.

The final arc of Shaw's thesis looks at Snorri Sturluson's writings and their significance for our understanding of Odin. Snorri bashing seems to be a popular pas-

---

 error on Shaw's part goes on to undermine the entirety of his argument. (personal communication, August 13, 2011).
5 John Wills, "Animal Imagery in Anglian Heathenry," *Óðrærir* 1 (2011), 27.

time among contemporary academics ("he made it all up!" they cry) and there is at least some validity to these criticisms of Snorri's work as a reliable source for understanding Heathen mythology.

Yet not all such criticisms are on the mark, and some seem more driven by ivory tower fashion than by sound analysis. The heart of *Uses of Wodan*'s anti-Snorri assault lies in a flimsy jab at the authenticity of the Bolverkr story featured in Snorri's *Skaldskaparmal*. Shaw's analysis seems like an afterthought included to keep in step with the prevailing mode, at least compared with his far more intensive research into the nature of continental Wodanic beliefs.

Shaw (despite some of the problems discussed in this review) therefore claims to have dismantled many cherished Wodan truisms: he was not pan-Germanic, he was not the most important deity, we cannot rely on just about anything the available sources say about him and he and Odin are thoroughly separate entities.

It is unfortunate that so many reservations must be drawn about Shaw's work. His arguments in some cases flat out fail (for example, the etymological separation of Wodan and Odin, which seems possibly inconclusive even if Shaw *had* been right in his controversial division of their root meanings). He focuses on atomization, regionalism and fragmentation, and although I welcome his bid to slay a range of false notions that have accrued around Wodan, his skepticism also represents what has become a somnambulant trend in mainstream academia.

In addition to some of my earlier comments, here are two more examples that illustrate how this atomistic, radically critical approach to myth and history fails.

Firstly, let us consider his claims about the limited archaeological evidence for Wodan, and the subsequent suggestion that Wodan was not widely worshiped. It must be recalled that only a tiny proportion of the pool of original objects that existed in Heathen times remains. Although new finds are constantly being made, we will only ever have a very fragmentary grasp on the archaeological puzzles that history has bequeathed. It follows that archaeologically-based claims about the generality or specificity of any aspect of Heathen culture are a cagey and uncertain business.

Shaw rightly points to the proliferation of matron cult statuettes as compelling evidence for the widespread matriarchal beliefs of the early Germanic Heathens (they are a kind of archaeological "gold standard" as far as variety and abundance go). Then again, they may have survived in abundance because of their durable materials or because of their Romano-Germanic provenance, while other widespread remnants of Germanic culture, made from wood or bone, perished in

Figure 1: A bracteate from the National Museum of Denmark (DR BR42) exhibiting the term "alu."

the intervening years. In any case, absence of evidence is not evidence of absence: there is middle ground between pan-Germanic Wodan and tribe-specific Wodan.

We also need to revisit the notion that the Germanic tribes held bracteates in identical significance to the Romans. For example, runic magical formulae such as *alu* have been found carved on bracteates, suggesting that the Germanic groups adapted them to mystical purposes. A Migration Age bracteate from Fünen, Denmark includes the runic inscription *alu* and also, arguably, the term *houaz* —High One, which happens to be one of Odin's epithets.[6]

---

6 Tineke Looijenga, *Runes Around the North Sea and on the Continent AD 150-700;*

Indeed, it appears that only recently a 4th century Gothic amulet dedicated to "Odin," (we can assume this is not the exact text on the amulet) was unearthed at a site in Bulgaria.[7] If this find has been correctly interpreted then it hurts many of the claims in Shaw's thesis rather badly. Given the gulf of historical uncertainty that assails us, Shaw is right to be critical. Yet ironically, his own position settles on a different kind of certainty, one that is in principle just as vulnerable to collapse in the face of new archaeological finds.

Secondly, regarding Shaw's claim that there are no directly Heathen primary sources which explicitly liken Wodan to Odin. Shaw does not pause to consider the following question: Why would, for argument's sake, a 9th century Odinist compose a poem offering helpful information like "oh, by the way, my 9th century Norse Odin is/is not the same as the figure Wodan worshiped by continental Germans in a different language three hundred years ago?"

After all, we can be confident of the parity of, say, Thunor, Donner, and Thor across their respective cultures, yet we would not expect to find a Heathen text explicitly identifying the three names as referring to the one being. That sort of cross-cultural reflexivity is simply out of character for organic folk religion and Shaw's complaint of its lack in the case of Odin/Wodan is a distinctly anachronistic piece of thinking.[8]

If there is no sound reason for us to expect the existence of a Heathen primary source likening Wodan to Odin then consequently the absence of such a source seems rather insignificant. If such evidence appeared it would destroy Shaw's argument, certainly, but in the meantime Shaw's complaint about the absence of such an anachronism is in poor intellectual form.

Does it seem likely that, even if the same entity, Odin and Wodan would have differences? Certainly, just as we would expect with the kinds of regional, linguistic and cultural variations involved. But, surely most of us are thoughtful enough to recognize this. In a slightly different vein, it does not seem implausible that it would take an outsider—perhaps a Christian observer—to directly make the comparison between individual Germanic groups and their deities.

Texts and Contexts (PhD thesis, Rijksuniversiteit, 1997), 177.

7 "Discovery of Gothic amulet at Bulgaria's Perperikon," *The Sofia Echo*, http://www.sofiaecho.com/2011/07/14/1123260_archaeology-discovery-of-gothic-amulet-at-bulgarias-perperikon (accessed July 17, 2011).

8 Given Shaw's Mercury—Wodan skepticism I can image he would resist accepting such evidence in the implausible case that it did turn up.

Not all Christian texts conform with Shaw's skepticism about their worth as sources on Heathen mythologies or worldviews. For example, Bil Linzie has argued that the *Heliand*, an Old Saxon adaptation of the Bible that clads the story of Christ's life in the costume of Heathen cultural norms, shows that Christian evangelists must have had a strong understanding of their target audience; all the better to frame the argument for conversion.[9] If Christian evangelists had this level of familiarity with Heathen culture then perhaps *Uses of Wodan* is over--eager to dismiss the veracity of Saxo or Paul the Deacon.

Despite my reservations about a number of Shaw's more extreme claims, I am somewhat partial to his down-playing of the significance of Wodan (and for the record I claim a very strong subjective feeling of connection to the deity). I believe that the image we see in some Old Norse sources of Wodan as a Zeus-analogue rings false. I wonder whether for some modern Heathens 'Odin-enthroned-on-a-cloud' reflects a failure to extricate themselves from a prior Christian mentality, namely that of subservience to 'Our Father who art in heaven.'

To me Wodan/Odin/etc. is a force of fury and ecstasy, which are the same thing. The image of his quest as the snake-god Bolverkr, for example, captures something far more essential about him in my personal view than the image of him as a cloud-king. Speaking phenomenologically, he seems to me more a subterranean river of fire bursting up from the earth's crust (or from Mimameith's depths) than he does a sky-hopping 'big daddy' looking down over creation. I cannot help but feel the Old Norse depictions of Odin as such an airy figure betray either Christian influence, an attempt to compete with Christianity's sometime 'God-above' grandiosity, or possibly even relate to the internal politics of Old Norse nobility at the time (I happily admit to the speculative nature of these comments, although on the other hand they are hardly novel).[10]

One benefit of Shaw encouraging us to take a reality check on the status of Wodan is that he implicitly invites us to revisit the significance of Thor and Frey to the original Heathens. Frey in particular seems to have been an important god of sovereignty, war and magic, but in the clutches of Dumézil-inspired confirmation bias he is sometimes relegated to being little more than the earth's manwhore. In other words, if we reconsider our estimation of Wodan's significance to historical Heathenry we also *gain* the opportunity to experience other aspects of our Heathen heritage more richly. This is underscored by Wills' observation

---

9   Bil Linzie, *Drinking at the Well of Mimir* (self-published, 2000), 196. Available at: http://www.angelfire.com/nm/seidhman/book.pdf

10 I also find it hard to accept that so sinister and eerie a god as Wodan/Odin would really have garnered the popularity and ubiquity of a more accessible and unambiguous deity such as Thor.

that designs on Anglo-Saxon trappings of war seem to emphasize Ingvi-Frey, with Woden coming in a poor second.[11]

And, of course, Shaw's approach implies the need for a more nuanced attitude towards 'unsubstantiated personal gnosis' (UPG) in contemporary Heathenry. I argued in the first issue of this journal that there is nothing wrong with innovation and invention within Heathenry so long as we are honest with ourselves about it.[12] Shaw shows some ways that even supposedly critically-minded academics can diverge wildly from what can be historically attested (and even demonstrates that divergence himself at some points). The rest of us can benefit from this reminder about the ease with which confirmation bias ('the prover proves what the thinker thinks') and wishful thinking can lead us astray. Just because an academic said it *does not* necessarily make it less "fluffy." The sometime tendency of "reconstructionist" Heathens to swallow academic opinion wholesale is a dangerous habit.

In other words, Shaw's attempted execution of various sacred Wodanic cows need not discourage our attempts to cobble together a contemporary Heathen spirituality. It simply reminds us that we have to admit to ourselves that we can be less certain than we would like when it comes to being true to the historical example. We must hope that in spirit at least we have appropriately expressed and honored the archaic impulse that brings joy and solace to our lives. And we must fight dogmatism and self-righteousness whenever we find it within ourselves, else make of ourselves unwitting buffoons.

Aside from disputing some of his more radical claims, I have one other significant reservation about *Uses of Wodan,* specifically regarding some of its concluding remarks. In Shaw's view, much of what we think we know about Wodan turns out to be a jumble of convention and hearsay from Christian authors and bears little or no relevance to actual Heathenry at all. Yet he then suggests that textual analysis of these, the Christian authors, is *more interesting* than the Heathen cultures they purport to document anyway! Coming at the end of his thesis, this statement seems like an unconscious betrayal of an ulterior (possibly unconscious) purpose: to denigrate contemporary interest—however quixotic it may be—in pre-Christian mythology.

This lack of interest in, and empathy for, the old Heathens seems not uncommon among contemporary academics. Perhaps this is just part of the lazy post-

---

11 John Wills, 27.
12 Henry Lauer "Cognitive Bias and Contemporary Heathenism," *The Journal of Contemporary Heathen Thought* 1: (2010), 43-62.

everything superficiality that haunts all the trendier parts of Humanities research in modern times. Contrast Shaw's casual disregard with the bracing enthusiasm that animates, say, H. R. Ellis Davidson's seminal works on Heathen myth and religion (regardless of the latter authors flaws)! It is tempting to wonder whether Shaw's apparent contempt for Heathenry might be a partial motivator for the tone and thrust of his whole thesis.

Uses of Wodan: The Development of his Cult and of Medieval Literary Responses to It is thought-provoking and challenging. It needs to be read with the same critical spirit that it attempts to espouse (to wit: it seems belabored with exactly the kind of double dealing that Shaw takes others to task over). It is a little ironic that Shaw's critique of Heathen historiography itself reflects a set of internal conventions and literary mores—those of the academic audience for which he writes. If this subtle contradiction does not disqualify Shaw from contributing to our understanding of Wodan, then it follows that the Christian sources he disparages might also be more reliable than he would have us think.

Staðagaldr: A Primer of Physical Runework
By Paul Waggener
Photography by Diana Saunders
Self Published, 2010
41 pages

Reviewed by Christopher A. Plaisance

This short book is, at the time of this review, the latest offering in the field of English language *staða* literature. *Staða*, defined by Waggener as the "physical positions of the rune staves,"[1] is the direct continuation of the *Runengymnastik* and *Runenyoga* developed in the 1930s by Friedrich Bernhard Marby and Siegfried Adolf Kummer respectively—a practice which was only introduced to the Anglosphere with the 1984 publication of Edred Thorsson's *Futhark*.[2] Waggener acknowledges that there is an argument against the inclusion of *staða* within Heathenry praxis on the grounds that it is not an historically authentic practice, and he addresses this with the usual counterview that such techniques were at one time ubiquitous throughout the Indo-European world, and that their presence in Germanic antiquity is attested by works of art depicting figures adopting rune-like postures such as the Golden Horns of Gallehus.[3] Waggener spends precious little time delving into this issue, only mentioning it in the introduction. As such, the remaining five chapters are explorations of *staða* as taught and practiced today by esoteric schools such as the Rune-Gild and Galdragildi.

The first chapter is largely an examination of the idea common in contemporary runic circles of the cosmic Yggdrasil having an anthropic reflection which constitutes the internal psychic structure of man—an idea which cannot but call to mind the Hermetic maxim of the microcosm being patterned after the macrocosm. The second chapter deals with several techniques of meditation and breath-control. Unsurprisingly, both the methodology delineated and the pneumatological theories connecting the breath with a kind of vital energy which can be consciously channeled throughout the body parallel those found in Haṭhayoga, a fact previously acknowledged by the author.[4] Chapter three further develops these parallels by likening the Germanic practice of *galdr*, a term Waggener notes has come to designate a variety of techniques for vocalizing runes and magical formulæ, with the Indian *mantra*.[5] The fourth and final chapter consists of

---

1 Waggener, ii.
2 Edred Thorsson, *Futhark: A Handbook of Rune Magic*, (York Beach: Samuel Weiser, Inc., 1984), 20.
3 Waggener, ii.
4 Waggener, 3.
5 Waggener, 14-15.

Staðagaldr

a sequence of twenty-four photographs of Waggener demonstrating the *staða* of each rune of the Elder Futhark, with each photo being accompanied with a paragraph explaining that particular *staða* performance.

While the book provides neither a scholarly exploration of the origins of *staða* nor the metaphysical hermeneutic of the Germanic myths that are implicit in the system used, it succeeds admirably in being the *first* work dealing with *staða* to do so with the aid of photographic aids as opposed to crudely drawn representations of the same. Waggener also provides *staða* which are different from those found in Thorsson's works, most notably Þ (*þurisaz*), R (*raiðō*), < (*kēnaz*), ᚹ (*wunjō*), I (*isa*), ᛉ (*jera*), ᛈ (*perþ*), S (*sōwulō*), B (*berkana*), M (*ehwaz*), and ᛚ (*laguz*). The final chapter, a single page, proves to be one of the most interesting in the whole book, being a sketch of constructing *staða* for bindrunes, something rarely, if ever, even mentioned in print. Waggener not only muses over the organic method through which such postures are to be developed, but also leaves the reader with a photographic example of such a *staða*. For the average Heathen reader, this will not likely be high up on the reading list (no more so than a text on bibliomantic methodology would be for Christians), but students of Germanic magic will likely want to add this interesting little book to their queues.

Wyrd Words: A Collection of Essays on Germanic Heathenry
By Swain Wodening [Berry Canote]
Huntsville, MO: Wednesbury Shire, 2010
140 pages

Reviewed by Christopher A. Plaisance

Wyrd Words is a collection of essays culled from the author's blog, covering a broad spectrum of topics—including everything from ethical advice in "Living the Twelve Aetheling Thews," to gender roles in "Women in Asatru and Germanic Heathenry," to musings on the place of the hierophantic experience in modern Heathen discourse in "The Role of Unsubstantiated Personal Gnosis." The essays are all rather short, ranging from one to eight pages a piece, and are written in a mixture of styles, with some consisting of the author's opinions on the topic in question and others being small research papers. The author's affiliation with the Þéodisc Geléafa in particular and with reconstructionist Anglo-Saxon Heathenry in general being well known in the American Heathen community, it comes as no surprise that many of the book's papers are centered around the Anglo-Saxon experience: "Reconstructing Anglo-Saxon Heathenism," "Why Theodish Belief?" "Anglo-Saxon Witchcraft," etc. What the sum total results in is a mixed bag of interesting essays that, by the author's admission in the foreword is "not organized in any particular way."[1]

While the disorganization of the essays does not, in and of itself, make for unpleasant reading—indeed, as this is the type of book which one is inclined to read discontinuously, the organization matters little—the form of the book does. To say that the editing is bad would be wrong, for that would imply *that* some form of editing and/or proofreading actually took place. The text is presented with a non-justified, ragged right hand margin. There are obvious hyperlinks randomly interspersed in paragraph bodies that the author failed to convert into normal text when he copy/pasted the essays from his blog into the text document. There are repeated instances of question marks showing up where apostrophes ought to be (e.g. "Lord?s," and "heaven?s" in the first essay). The text changes colors, from black to gray, mid-paragraph throughout the book. Typographic styles are not consistent, with the author shifting between smart quotes (" ") and dumb quotes (" ") repeatedly. Citations are often completely absent from block quotations, and at other times are incomplete, disabling the reader from referring to the quotation's source. And the list goes on.

---

[1] Wodening, 1.

What is so concerning about this complete removal of the editorial phase of the publishing process is that Wodening is not alone in his dismissal of it. This is becoming an endemic problem with self-published Heathen books and is one that is bound to prevent the books in question from being taken seriously by academically minded audiences. Such shoddy presentations of ideas give the impression that the books in question are the works of amateurs and are not to be taken seriously, which is likely the exact opposite intention of the authors. This is unfortunate for *Wyrd Words* because the ideas expressed are *not* bad. There is much contained therein from which Heathens can gain and will appreciate. Wodening is certainly a well read author who is capable of synthesizing a great amount of historical and literary data into a viable text. Yet, a good author is often times a terrible editor, and it is a shame to see what *could* be an excellent addition to the sparse field of contemporary Heathen literature marred by the exclusion of such a necessary part of the publishing cycle.

The Folk **(DVD)**
Directed by Shawn Owens
Hermetic Productions, 2009
Running Time: 45 Minutes (not including extras)

Reviewed by Helsson

The oft-maligned and chronically misunderstood Germanic Heathen movement has, in terms of being able to visually "see" the fruition of such a reconstructive movement, very little in the way of modern-day media to take advantage of.

The Folk chronicles Runehof Kindred, based out of Minnesota, and the various activities that they participate in. There is no real indication of the time frame this documentary covers, but it is somewhat understood that decent amount of time was spent with the kindred in order to fully try and understand just what this particular way of living entails.

Included within the main body of the documentary are the various perspectives of the kindred members on matters of faith, socio-political implications of traditional Germanic themes and even reminiscences on how their upbringings led them to the path they travel today. One gets a very good impression of the diversity that Heathenry brings to the table, as each person interviewed has very different, subjective views about how they view their Gods and faith.

The "folkish" issue is indirectly dealt with during the course of the documentary, and one really finds little indication that any of the kindred members nor any of the other contacts interviewed really hold strict adherence to such a paradigm, save for one particular interview with a young lady in the extras section of the DVD. This sort of oversight of the folkish train of thought within the Germanic Heathen tradition might offend some purists, however this author found it handled very tactfully, and important subject matter, such as ancestral and cultural reverence is explained with great care so that the average (uninitiated) viewer can easily get a better understanding of these matters without coming to racist-based conclusions about the Heathen movement at large.

Another positive point about the documentary is emphasis on family, whether kindred-based family or blood relations. Heathendom requires interaction of the in-person variety, especially in this hollow age of "virtual" friendships aided via the Internet, to be a living and dynamic way of existence. This sort of philosophy is not implicitly stated within the confines of the exposé, however one can merely witness the positive emotion displayed between the individual kindred members during the scene involving *symbel* and understand at that very moment why it is essential these ties be cultivated in the flesh.

The main two issues with the documentary as a whole are length and editing. The length of the main feature is only forty-five minutes, and it is painfully obvious that such a non-mainstream "Pagan" religion deserves much more focus than can be portrayed in under an hour. Other Heathen persons are also interviewed during the course of the film that have no direct relation to the kindred in question, and no explanation is given as to who these individuals truly are.

In summation, *The Folk* is an excellent start, but hopefully not the end, of documenting the modern-day Heathen movement on such a modern medium as digital film. The film truly accomplishes a tearing down of the stereotype of the "drunken Viking warrior religion" premise that many critics of Heathenry espouse. More of these sorts of works will be needed in the future for the Germanic Heathen movement to ever be considered a viable, realistic alternative to the more visible mainstream religions out there.

Included on the DVD are extras, including additional (short) interviews with those included on the main feature and an entire Twelfth Night *blót*. Inquisitive and open-minded viewers may also enjoy the inclusion of two of the director's self-made films, which are chock-full of (non-Heathen) occult themes.

Deep Ancestors: Practicing the Religion of the Proto-Indo-Europeans
By Ceisiwr Serith
Tucson, AZ: ADF Publishing, 2009
293 pages

Reviewed by Christopher A. Plaisance

The religion of the Proto-Indo-Europeans (PIE) is a continuing point of interest for those participating in the Heathen revival. As the only real written codifications occurred after the conversions, a great deal of information was lost. That being the case, practitioners of Germanic polytheism have come to rely on common Indo-European (IE) sources to reconstruct those beliefs that were extinguished before the written word came to Northern Europe. Needless to say, it is a risky business looking to IE sources which emerged after the PIE peoples broke ranks and became the Germanics, Celts, Balts, etc., as the culturally specific idiosyncrasies that differentiate one branch of the IE tree from another make it extremely difficult to reconstruct missing material from one branch by drawing on material from another. A far safer course is to go directly to the source and rebuild the particular Germanic expression from the original religion of the PIE people. Compounded with this is the interest that individuals whose ancestries draw from several branches of the IE tree would have in researching and possibly practicing the religion that was common to *all* of their ancestors.

Given this overriding interest in PIE religion by Heathen reconstructionists, it would seem to follow that a book such as Serith's would be a boon, yet the result is a text that is more frustrating than utile. Serith prefaces the book with the assertion that it "is not written for...scholars," so he has "dispensed with most of the scholarly apparatus."[1] What this means is that, while the book *does* contain a large bibliography, it contains no more than a handful of citations and no index whatsoever. Now in *some* kinds of texts, a thoroughgoing non-scholarly approach would be perfectly acceptable. In this instance, however, it becomes unacceptable. Serith is quick to admit that the present work, like all reconstructions of pre-conversion European religions strikes a delicate balance between tradition and innovation. He claims to have "tried to make it clear when...[he has] recreated and when...[he has] innovated," however the near complete lack of internal citations makes it impossible for a non-specialist to discern what material is authentically reconstructed and what is Serith's innovation.

The haphazard scattering of citations throughout the volume makes it rather unclear what kind of reader this text is intended for. For scholars in the field, a

---

[1] Serith, 3.

book bereft of supporting references is obviously unsuitable as a reference itself. Yet, it seems somewhat strange to suppose that a book which is composed of nearly three hundred pages of linguistic exegesis would be of interest to the general reader uninterested in scholastic technicalities. For the would-be practitioner of PIE religion, the book's problem is particularly obvious in that it is impossible for a reader who has not previously memorized all of Serith's sources to discern what is authentically PIE and what is strictly Serith. And, to incorporate *any* of the book's material, it is essential to know what is authentic and what is speculation. For, in the absence of verification, the only praxis which can be derived from the book is Ceisiwr-Serith-ism.

What is so *frustrating* about this book is that it *is* a fascinating work. The very notion of a reconstruction of PIE religion that is practicable in today's world is tantalizing. And, to Serith's credit, the book is literally chock-full of what *appears* to be amazing material. Yet without any sources to back up his assertions, the book is all but useless both to Heathens looking to draw on it as reference *and* for those individuals interested in practicing PIE religion. What this reviewer hopes for is a second edition that corrects these defects. Such a volume would be immensely interesting and useful.

Summoning the Gods: Essays on Paganism in a God-Forsaken World
By Collin Cleary
Edited by Greg Johnson
San Francisco, CA: Counter-Current Publishing Ltd., 2011
Limited Hardcover Edition
294 pages

Reviewed by Christopher A. Plaisance

Collin Cleary's first book, *Summoning the Gods*, is a collection of essays dealing with a wide range of topics pertinent to modern Heathenry. Although all but two of the essays contained therein were previously published in either *TYR: Myth—Culture—Tradition* or *Rûna*, the presentation of these works as a single collection results in the emergence of a more coherent presentation of Cleary's philosophy than was previously demonstrated by a single paper in isolation. The essays—some being extended book reviews and other straight-forward papers—challenge the reader's preconceptions both of what Heathenry *was* in the past and how it might be revived *today*. He makes the case that so far "pagans have shied away from the philosophical and theological questions their project raises," and that "what neo-paganism seems desperately to need is a theology."[1] The book's contents are divided into three thematic sections: "Neo-Paganism," "Nordic Paganism," and "Among the Ruins."

The first section is composed of three papers: "Knowing the Gods," "Summoning the Gods: The Phenomenology of Divine Presence" and "Paganism Without Gods: Alain de Benoist's *On Being a Pagan*." The first two papers form a sequential pair which deal principally with the epistemology of religious experience. Beginning with the assumptions that there are Gods, Cleary's central proposition in these papers is that our ancestors—by virtue of an "openness" which is presented as the natural epistemological mode of ancient man—experienced the world not as lifeless material forms, as does modern man, but as a plenum of divine forms. Resting on the Traditionalism[2] of Julius Evola, Cleary proposes that polytheism was the natural consequence of Traditional man's experience of nature as numinous. These ideas are carried forward into the section's final essay, which is a lengthy critical review of de Benoist's hugely influential book.

---

1 Cleary, 62.
2 The Evolian brand of Traditionalism which Cleary appeals to throughout the book is far less concerned with the recovery of historical traditions than it is in uncovering the gnostic truth that is akin to a Platonic Form of Tradition. As such, Traditionalism adheres to an understanding of man's spiritual history in which we are currently living in the last and most degenerate of a cycle of ages (e.g. Hinduism's *Kali Yuga*, Hesiod's Iron Age).

As with the previous essays, Cleary thoroughly condemns modernity, concurring with de Benoist's characterization of Christianity as fundamentally breaking with Pagan Tradition by bifurcating the world into ontologically distinct worldly and divine spheres, and atheistic humanism as continuing in this vein by replacing God with man. Cleary, however, questions de Benoist's use of Nietzschean relativism as the guiding philosophy of the Pagan revival, arguing that he should have looked to the Aristotelian and Heideggerian streams of philosophy instead. Tying together all three papers is Cleary's proposed solution to the central problem he sees with the Pagan revival: how can we know the Gods? He concludes that in order for Paganism to succeed in today's world, what must be reconstructed is not the particular rites and beliefs of our ancestors, but rather the mode in which they approached the Gods.

The second section contains a selection of essays that break from the previous section's approach of dealing with issues pertaining to Paganism in general, focusing on the particularly Heathen expression. The first, "What God Did Odin Worship," is an exploration of the meaning of Odin's self-sacrifice as found in the "Rúnatals þáttr" section of the *Hávamál*. It is a highly speculative paper that, through the method of comparative religion, analyzes Odin's act in tandem with Hindu Shaivism. Cleary's thesis is that, like Shiva, Odin is a God with multiple hypostases, or faces. One side parallels the Hindu Rudra; this is Odin in his guise as the wild God of war and fury. The second side mirrors Shiva as the transcendent fountain of becoming. From this, Cleary concludes that it is the latter Odin to whom the former sacrifices himself; in other words, the outer identity is given over to the inner. The section's second paper, "Philosophical Notes on the Runes," is an attempt to treat the runes as a system of philosophical principles that describe something similar to the metaphysical scheme of Hegel. As with the last essay, this is an extremely speculative piece which breaks dramatically from historical and conventional explanations of the individual meanings of and relationships between the runes. It is certainly a *tour de force*, but the reader's response will likely depend on how inclined towards accepting Hegel's notoriously idiosyncratic metaphysics they are. Third up is "The Missing Man in Norse Cosmogony," which, like this section's first paper, attempts to solve a problem in Norse mythology by means of an appeal to comparative religion. In this case, the problem is that in the Proto-Indo-European cosmogenic myth, the world is created by two brothers: *Yemo and *Manu. Yet, in the Norse tale, Ymir (cognate to *Yemo) is devoid of a brother. Cleary finds this "missing man" in the fraternal triad of Odin-Vili-Ve. The final paper in this section, "Karl Maria Wiligut's Commandments of Gôt," is a critical review of Michael Moynihan and Stephen Flowers' presentation of Wiligut's writings in *The Secret King: Karl Maria Wiligut, Himmler's Lord of the Runes*. This paper's thesis is that Wiligut's writings present a coherent, albeit deeply flawed, mystical philosophy.

Throughout the section, the overriding theme is that of Odianism[3]—that Odin is less a God to be worshiped as a supernatural other and more a God to be imitated. Cleary is, however keen to avoid the humanist mistake of equating man with God, by maintaining that Odin "is an entity ontologically distinct from man, but which constitutes the characteristics which make us human," turning him into something not *too* far off from the Platonic Form of Man—a universal which the Odian strives towards actualizing in his particular experience.[4]

The final section breaks from the explicit treatment of Pagan religiosity and delves into the territory of Radical Traditionalism. Both essays, "Patrick McGoohan's *The Prisoner*" and "The Spiritual Journey of Alejandro Jodorowsky," continue Cleary's criticism of modernity by means of analyses of the television series *The Prisoner* and Jodorowsky's spiritual autobiography. While these papers veer quite far from the aforementioned two sections, they may yet be of interest to readers who sympathize with Cleary's anti-modernism. However, as he sees Traditionalism and Paganism as intrinsically tied, the rejection of materialism and individualism that we see in these papers *does* lead us towards an understanding of the Pagan *Weltanschauung*. For, Cleary tells us that "modernity is essentially a war against finitude or limitation of any kind, and that the return of the Gods will be affected by a "return to our ancestors' acceptance of finitude."[5] Traditionalism posits that the Gods "show themselves precisely in that which resists us" and "are the mysterious facticities of life which stop us in our tracks because they are bigger than we are, and we are powerless against them."[6] And, it is through a return to the *openness* of our ancestors that we are able to encounter the Gods as they are—as metaphysical Titans who delimit the very boundaries of the world.

Cleary's *Summoning the Gods* is a landmark publication in the intellectual wing of the Heathen revival. While all readers will certainly not agree entirely with the conclusions he reaches in his analysis, his application of the intellectual tools of the Western philosophical tradition is precisely what Heathenry *needs* to un-

---

3   Odianism is the philosophy developed by Stephen E. Flowers (aka Edred Thorsson). In this school of thought the "Odian does not so much seek to worship an external god-form of Ódhinn as he does him-*Self* to embody and to develop the Self-concept and consciousness given by *the god*. Whereas other religious cults turn outward to the objective manifestation of the particular god, the cult of Ódhinn turns inward and seeks a deification of the Self. The Odian does not worship his god—he becomes his god," (*Runelore: A Handbook of Esoteric Runology*, [York Beach, ME: Weiser/Red Wheel, LLC., 1987], 179).
4   Cleary, 126.
5   Ibid., 190-191.
6   Ibid., 191.

derstand itself as a phenomenon existing in today's world. Cleary manages to penetrate, by means of these analyses, deep into the core of polytheistic religiosity, and such penetrating insight is something that simply cannot go unnoticed by those who would see Heathenry succeed in addressing fundamental questions about its own nature. The presence of a thinker of Cleary's stature within Heathenry is a testament to the vibrancy and health of modern Heathen thought. This book should, accordingly, be a welcome addition to *any* thinking Heathen's book shelf.

Editorial Staff

CHRISTOPHER A. PLAISANCE, *Editor in Chief*, is a graduate student at the University of Exeter's Center for the Study of Esotericism. He holds a BA in philosophy from the American Military University and an AA in Mandarin Chinese from the Defense Language Institute. His current research interests include Neoplatonic theories of sacrifice as applied to contemporary polytheistic praxis, the dual current of the psychologization of religion and the sacralization of psychology, and the history of the development of the ideas of tutelary Gods in Western Esotericism. He is presently a member of the Ásatrú Folk Assembly, the Troth, and the Center for Process Studies.

VINCENT REX SODEN, *Editor*, studied European History, Philosophy and the German language at Temple University in Philadelphia. His interests in history and philosophy led him to the study of the pre-Christian beliefs of Northern Europe. The works of J.R.R. Tolkien, in which he sought to envision the myth and lore of the Anglo-Saxons prior to the Norman conquest of England, have also resonated deeply with him. Vince now learns as much as he can about the pre-Christian faith of his forefathers through reading and conversations with like-minded individuals such as those involved with the production of this journal. He was born and raised in Pennsylvania.

BEN MCGARR, *Editor*, is a writer on local history for whom the landscape of his native North West England is his chief inspiration. He read Anthropology and Archaeology at Durham University, after which Wanderlust led him to spend the next seven years working and traveling in Russia. Translation of Russian works on Eurasian history and ancient Slavonic Paganism takes pride of place among his ongoing projects, for its own intrinsic interest as well as the benefit that might accrue to the Heathen movement from the greater accessibility of such a rich resource of cognates and comparisons. He divides his time between Devon, Manchester and Granada.

Contributors

STEPHEN M. BORTHWICK received his Masters Degree in social science from the University of Chicago and Baccalaureate Degree in history from the Catholic University of America in Washington, DC. His primary research interests are the interaction of religion and identity politics and the interaction of spirituality and civilization; his theological foci include the philosophy of religion, the nature of divinity, teleology and scriptural exegesis. His primary influences include Heraclitus, Plato, Plotinus, Augustine of Hippo and Meister Eckhart.

ARROWYN CRABAN-LAUER started drawing when she was three years old. She fancies that perhaps through the path of eye to mind…to hand…to pencil…to paper…to eye, she is in essence trying to get a grip on the crazy flux of earthly existence. Trying to interpret, and understand, and then influence the flow of life. And her reasons still have not changed since she was three—she just has more words now. Arrowyn also lends her creative skills to her freelance graphic and web design business, Verdandi Design as well as her very expensive hobby, *Hex Magazine* which she reigns over as Administrator, Editor and Art Director.

ZACREY MONTE HANSEN studied Integrated Studies at Utah Valley University. A Utah native, his research interests include the mythographical implications of the political and martial maneuvering by the Æsir and Hrímþursar.

HELSSON is an aspiring poet and dark ambient artist who is dedicated to reviving an organic form of Germanic Heathen-based witchcraft. He is currently working on a chapbook of poetry that explores themes of necromancy, death worship and Germanic sorcery.

HENRY LAUER informally studies Germanic history and mythology, as well as being one of the editors of the contemporary Heathen publication *Hex Magazine*. He has a somewhat quixotic interest in inviting academia to reflect upon itself in the spirit (if not the letter) of Edmund Husserl's phenomenological challenge.

ÞORBERT LÍNLEÁH, a lifetime native of the Virginian Commonwealth, has been involved in Ésatréow (Ásatrú) and Þéodisc Geléafa since 1999. As an ordained and licensed Heathen minister, Þorbert serves as the *weófodþegn* (priest) of the Ealdríce Hæðengyld, a budding Anglo-Saxon Heathen fellowship in Richmond. Þorbert holds a BA in Philosophy and Religious Studies from Christopher Newport University and is presently working on his MLA at the University of Richmond. In addition to writing for *JOCHT*, Þorbert has become a regular contribut-

Contributors

or to *Hex Magazine*.

JENNIFER ROBERGE-TOLL studied at the University of Ottawa, McGill University and Queen's University. She obtained an honors BA in religious studies and psychology (cum laude), and a further Bachelor's degree in social work. She also studied urban and regional planning at the Master's level. Her research interests include the following: dark green religion's relationship with Heathenry; cosmology and Heathenry, specifically the rapprochement of science and religion; and lore as a psychological healing tool.

STEPHEN POLLINGTON has been writing books on Anglo-Saxon England for more than two decades. His many published titles include works on Old English language, military culture, healing, herblore, runes and feasting in the "meadhall." He has recorded a double CD of readings in Old English and has lectured widely on aspects of Anglo-Saxon culture since 1991. He has also contributed to a number of television and radio programs, and was the script adviser to the groundbreaking *1000 AD*, in which dramatic dialogue was spoken entirely in Old English and Old Norse. Since 2001, Stephen has been researching pre-Christian material culture with special regard to the religious and social meaning of art styles and motifs.

KRIS STEVENSON graduated from Leicester University in 2002 with a BA in Archaeology. His research interests within Germanic mythology currently include the study of Heathen concepts within the writings of Nietzsche, Tolkien's "spirit of courage" within Old English literature and an analysis of Vedic and Eddic creation myths.

Printed in Great Britain
by Amazon.co.uk, Ltd.,
Marston Gate.